Shelley Gaskin • Robert L. Ferre

GO!
with Microsoft®
Word 2010 Brief

Custom Edition for Baker College
INF 112 Word Processing

Taken from:
GO! with Microsoft® Word 2010, Brief Edition
by Shelley Gaskin and Robert L. Ferrett

Cover Art: Courtesy of PhotoDisc/Getty Images.

Taken from:

GO! with Microsoft® Word 2010, Brief Edition
by Shelley Gaskin and Robert L. Ferrett
Copyright © 2011 by Pearson Education, Inc.
Published by Prentice Hall
Upper Saddle River, New Jersey 07458

This special edition published in cooperation with Pearson Learning Solutions.

All trademarks, service marks, registered trademarks, and registered service marks are the property of their respective owners and are used herein for identification purposes only.

Pearson Learning Solutions, 501 Boylston Street, Suite 900, Boston, MA 02116
A Pearson Education Company
www.pearsoned.com

Printed in the United States of America

4 5 6 7 8 9 10 V303 16 15 14 13 12

000200010270751829

CB

ISBN 10: 1-256-29985-5
ISBN 13: 978-1-256-29985-1

Brief Contents

GO! **Walkthrough** .... **xvi**

Common Features

Chapter 1 **Using the Common Features of Microsoft Office 2010** **1**

Word

Chapter 1 **Creating Documents with Microsoft Word 2010** **49**

Chapter 2 **Using Tables and Templates to Create Resumes and Cover Letters** **105**

Chapter 3 **Creating Research Papers, Newsletters, and Merged Mailing Labels** **163**

Business Running Case 1: Word Chapters 1–3 .... **219**

Glossary **G-1**

Index **I-1**

Contents

GO! Walkthrough xvi

Common Features

Chapter 1 Using the Common Features of Microsoft Office 2010 1

PROJECT 1A PowerPoint File 2

Objective 1 Use Windows Explorer to Locate Files and Folders   **3**
   Activity 1.01 Using Windows Explorer to Locate Files and Folders   3

Objective 2 Locate and Start a Microsoft Office 2010 Program   **6**
   Activity 1.02 Locating and Starting a Microsoft Office 2010 Program   6

Objective 3 Enter and Edit Text in an Office 2010 Program   **9**
   Activity 1.03 Entering and Editing Text in an Office 2010 Program   9

Objective 4 Perform Commands from a Dialog Box   **11**
   Activity 1.04 Performing Commands from a Dialog Box   11

Objective 5 Create a Folder, Save a File, and Close a Program   **13**
   Activity 1.05 Creating a Folder, Saving a File, and Closing a Program   13

Objective 6 Add Document Properties and Print a File   **18**
   Activity 1.06 Adding Document Properties and Printing a File   18

PROJECT 1B Word File 21

Objective 7 Open an Existing File and Save it with a New Name   **22**
   Activity 1.07 Opening an Existing File and Saving it with a New Name   22

Objective 8 Explore Options for an Application   **25**
   Activity 1.08 Viewing Application Options   25

Objective 9 Perform Commands from the Ribbon   **26**
   Activity 1.09 Performing Commands from the Ribbon   26
   Activity 1.10 Minimizing and Using the Keyboard to Control the Ribbon   31

Objective 10 Apply Formatting in Office Programs   **32**
   Activity 1.11 Formatting and Viewing Pages   32
   Activity 1.12 Formatting Text   34
   Activity 1.13 Using the Office Clipboard to Cut, Copy, and Paste   38
   Activity 1.14 Viewing Print Preview and Printing a Word Document   41

Objective 11 Use the Microsoft Office 2010 Help System   **43**
   Activity 1.15 Using the Microsoft Office 2010 Help System in Excel   43

Objective 12 Compress Files   **44**
   Activity 1.16 Compressing Files   44
   Summary, Key Terms, Matching, and Multiple Choice   46-48

Word

Chapter 1 Creating Documents with Microsoft Word 2010

Chapter 1 Creating Documents with Microsoft Word 2010 49

PROJECT 1A   Flyer 50

Objective 1 Create a New Document and Insert Text   51
Activity 1.01 Starting a New Word Document and Inserting Text   51

Objective 2 Insert and Format Graphics   53
Activity 1.02 Formatting Text Using Text Effects   53
Activity 1.03 Inserting and Resizing Pictures   54
Activity 1.04 Wrapping Text Around a Picture   55
Activity 1.05 Moving a Picture   56
Activity 1.06 Applying Picture Styles and Artistic Effects   57
Activity 1.07 Adding a Page Border   57

Objective 3 Insert and Modify Text Boxes and Shapes   58
Activity 1.08 Inserting a Shape   58
Activity 1.09 Inserting a Text Box   60
Activity 1.10 Moving, Resizing, and Formatting Shapes and Text Boxes   60

Objective 4 Preview and Print a Document   62
Activity 1.11 Adding a File Name to the Footer   62
Activity 1.12 Previewing and Printing a Document   64

PROJECT 1B   Information Handout 66

Objective 5 Change Document and Paragraph Layout   67
Activity 1.13 Setting Margins   67
Activity 1.14 Aligning Text   68
Activity 1.15 Changing Line Spacing   70
Activity 1.16 Indenting Text and Adding Space After Paragraphs   71

Objective 6 Create and Modify Lists   73
Activity 1.17 Creating a Bulleted List   73
Activity 1.18 Creating a Numbered List   74
Activity 1.19 Customizing Bullets   77

Objective 7 Set and Modify Tab Stops   78
Activity 1.20 Setting Tab Stops   78
Activity 1.21 Modifying Tab Stops   79

Objective 8 Insert a SmartArt Graphic   80
Activity 1.22 Inserting a SmartArt Graphic   80
Activity 1.23 Modifying a SmartArt Graphic   81
Summary, Key Terms, Matching, and Multiple Choice   84-85
Skills Review   86
Mastering Word   92
GO! Fix It   98
GO! Make It   99
GO! Solve It   100
Rubric   102
GO! Think   103
You and GO!   104

Chapter 2 Using Tables and Templates to Create Resumes and Cover Letters 105

PROJECT 2A Resume 106

Objective 1 Create a Table 107
    Activity 2.01 Creating a Table 107

Objective 2 Add Text to a Table 108
    Activity 2.02 Adding Text to a Table 108
    Activity 2.03 Inserting Existing Text into a Table Cell 109
    Activity 2.04 Creating Bulleted Lists in a Table 110

Objective 3 Format a Table 111
    Activity 2.05 Changing the Width of Table Columns 111
    Activity 2.06 Adding Rows to a Table 112
    Activity 2.07 Merging Cells 113
    Activity 2.08 Formatting Text in Cells 114
    Activity 2.09 Changing the Table Borders 116

PROJECT 2B Cover Letter and Resume 119

Objective 4 Create a New Document from an Existing Document 120
    Activity 2.10 Creating a Letterhead 120
    Activity 2.11 Creating a Document from an Existing Document 121

Objective 5 Change and Reorganize Text 123
    Activity 2.12 Recording AutoCorrect Entries 123
    Activity 2.13 Creating a Cover Letter 124
    Activity 2.14 Finding and Replacing Text 126
    Activity 2.15 Selecting and Moving Text to a New Location 128
    Activity 2.16 Inserting and Formatting a Table in a Document 130

Objective 6 Use the Proofing Options 130
    Activity 2.17 Checking Spelling and Grammar Errors 131
    Activity 2.18 Using the Thesaurus 133

Objective 7 Create a Document Using a Template 134
    Activity 2.19 Locating and Opening a Template 134
    Activity 2.20 Replacing Template Placeholder Text 135
    Activity 2.21 Removing Template Controls and Formatting the Resume 138
    Activity 2.22 Saving a Resume as a Web Page 139

Summary, Key Terms, Matching, and Multiple Choice 140-141

Skills Review 142

Mastering Word 149

GO! Fix It 156

GO! Make It 157

GO! Solve It 158

Rubric 160

GO! Think 161

You and GO! 162

Chapter 3   Creating Research Papers, Newsletters, and Merged Mailing Labels **163**

PROJECT 3A   Research Paper **164**

Objective 1 Create a Research Paper   **165**
  Activity 3.01 Formatting Text and Page Numbers in a Research Paper   165

Objective 2 Insert Footnotes in a Research Paper   **167**
  Activity 3.02 Inserting Footnotes   168
  Activity 3.03 Modifying a Footnote Style   169

Objective 3 Create Citations and a Bibliography in a Research Paper   **172**
  Activity 3.04 Adding Citations   172
  Activity 3.05 Inserting Page Breaks   175
  Activity 3.06 Creating a Reference Page   176
  Activity 3.07 Managing Document Properties   177

PROJECT 3B   Newsletter with Mailing Labels **180**

Objective 4 Format a Multiple-Column Newsletter   **181**
  Activity 3.08 Changing One Column of Text to Two Columns   181
  Activity 3.09 Formatting Multiple Columns   182
  Activity 3.10 Inserting a Column Break   183
  Activity 3.11 Inserting a ClipArt Image   184
  Activity 3.12 Inserting a Screenshot   186

Objective 5 Use Special Character and Paragraph Formatting   **186**
  Activity 3.13 Applying the Small Caps Font Effect   186
  Activity 3.14 Adding a Border and Shading to a Paragraph   188

Objective 6 Create Mailing Labels Using Mail Merge   **189**
  Activity 3.15 Opening the Mail Merge Wizard Template   189
  Activity 3.16 Completing the Mail Merge Wizard   192
  Activity 3.17 Previewing and Printing the Mail Merge Document   194

Summary, Key Terms, Matching, and Multiple Choice   196-197

Skills Review   198

Mastering Word   205

GO! Fix It   212

GO! Make It   213

GO! Solve It   214

Rubric   216

GO! Think   217

You and GO!   218

Business Running Case 1: Word Chapters 1–3 .... **219**

Glossary **G-1**

Index **I-1**

GO! System Contributors

We thank the following people for their hard work and support in making the *GO!* System all that it is!

Instructor Resource Authors

Adickes, Erich	Parkland College	Holland, Susan	Southeast Community College-Nebraska
Baray, Carrie	Ivy Tech Community College		
Clausen, Jane	Western Iowa Tech Community College	Landenberger, Toni	Southeast Community College-Nebraska
Crossley, Connie	Cincinnati State Technical and Community College	McMahon, Richard	University of Houston—Downtown
		Miller, Sandra	Wenatchee Valley College
Emrich, Stefanie	Metropolitan Community College of Omaha, Nebraska	Niebur, Katherine	Dakota County Technical College
		Nowakowski, Anthony	Buffalo State
Faix, Dennis	Harrisburg Area Community College	Pierce, Tonya	Ivy Tech Community College
Hadden, Karen	Western Iowa Tech Community College	Roselli, Diane	Harrisburg Area Community College
		St. John, Steve	Tulsa Community College
Hammerle, Patricia	Indiana University/Purdue University at Indianapolis	Sterr, Jody	Blackhawk Technical College
		Thompson, Joyce	Lehigh Carbon Community College
Hines, James	Tidewater Community College	Tucker, William	Austin Community College

Technical Editors

Matthew Bisi	Barbara Edington	Joyce Nielsen	Jan Snyder
Mary Corcoran	Sarah Evans	Janet Pickard	Mara Zebest
Lori Damanti	Adam Layne	Sean Portnoy	

Student Reviewers

Albinda, Sarah Evangeline	Phoenix College	Innis, Tim	Tulsa Community College
Allen, John	Asheville-Buncombe Tech Community College	Jarboe, Aaron	Central Washington University
		Key, Penny	Greenville Technical College
Alexander, Steven	St. Johns River Community College	Klein, Colleen	Northern Michigan University
Alexander, Melissa	Tulsa Community College	Lloyd, Kasey	Ivy Tech Bloomington
Bolz, Stephanie	Northern Michigan University	Moeller, Jeffrey	Northern Michigan University
Berner, Ashley	Central Washington University	Mullen, Sharita	Tidewater Community College
Boomer, Michelle	Northern Michigan University	Nelson, Cody	Texas Tech University
Busse, Brennan	Northern Michigan University	Nicholson, Regina	Athens Tech College
Butkey, Maura	Central Washington University	Niehaus, Kristina	Northern Michigan University
Cates, Concita	Phoenix College	Nisa, Zaibun	Santa Rosa Community College
Charles, Marvin	Harrisburg Area Community College	Nunez, Nohelia	Santa Rosa Community College
		Oak, Samantha	Central Washington University
Christensen, Kaylie	Northern Michigan University	Oberly, Sara	Harrisburg Area Community College Lancaster
Clark, Glen D. III	Harrisburg Area Community College		
		Oertii, Monica	Central Washington University
Cobble, Jan N.	Greenville Technical College	Palenshus, Juliet	Central Washington University
Connally, Brianna	Central Washington University	Pohl, Amanda	Northern Michigan University
Davis, Brandon	Northern Michigan University	Presnell, Randy	Central Washington University
Davis, Christen	Central Washington University	Reed, Kailee	Texas Tech University
De Jesus Garcia, Maria	Phoenix College	Ritner, April	Northern Michigan University
Den Boer, Lance	Central Washington University	Roberts, Corey	Tulsa Community College
Dix, Jessica	Central Washington University	Rodgers, Spencer	Texas Tech University
Moeller, Jeffrey	Northern Michigan University	Rodriguez, Flavia	Northwestern State University
Downs, Elizabeth	Central Washington University	Rogers, A.	Tidewater Community College
Elser, Julie	Harrisburg Area Community College	Rossi, Jessica Ann	Central Washington University
		Rothbauer, Taylor	Trident Technical College
Erickson, Mike	Ball State University	Rozelle, Lauren	Texas Tech University
Frye, Alicia	Phoenix College	Schmadeke, Kimberly	Kirkwood Community College
Gadomski, Amanda	Northern Michigan University	Shafapay, Natasha	Central Washington University
Gassert, Jennifer	Harrisburg Area Community College	Shanahan, Megan	Northern Michigan University
		Sullivan, Alexandra Nicole	Greenville Technical College
Gross, Mary Jo	Kirkwood Community College	Teska, Erika	Hawaii Pacific University
Gyselinck, Craig	Central Washington University	Torrenti, Natalie	Harrisburg Area Community College
Harrison, Margo	Central Washington University		
Hatt, Patrick	Harrisburg Area Community College	Traub, Amy	Northern Michigan University
Heacox, Kate	Central Washington University	Underwood, Katie	Central Washington University
Hedgman, Shaina	Tidewater College	Walters, Kim	Central Washington University
Hill, Cheretta	Northwestern State University	Warren, Jennifer L.	Greenville Technical College
Hochstedler, Bethany	Harrisburg Area Community College Lancaster	Wilson, Kelsie	Central Washington University
		Wilson, Amanda	Green River Community College
Homer, Jean	Greenville Technical College	Wylie, Jimmy	Texas Tech University

Series Reviewers

Abraham, Reni	Houston Community College	Cannon, Kim	Greenville Technical College
Addison, Paul	Ivy Tech Community College	Carreon, Cleda	Indiana University—Purdue University, Indianapolis
Agatston, Ann	Agatston Consulting Technical College	Carriker, Sandra	North Shore Community College
Akuna, Valeria, Ph.D.	Estrella Mountain Community College	Casey, Patricia	Trident Technical College
		Cates, Wally	Central New Mexico Community College
Alexander, Melody	Ball Sate University	Chaffin, Catherine	Shawnee State University
Alejandro, Manuel	Southwest Texas Junior College	Chauvin, Marg	Palm Beach Community College, Boca Raton
Alger, David	Tidewater Community College Chesapeake Campus	Challa, Chandrashekar	Virginia State University
Allen, Jackie	Rowan-Cabarrus Community College	Chamlou, Afsaneh	NOVA Alexandria
Ali, Farha	Lander University	Chapman, Pam	Wabaunsee Community College
Amici, Penny	Harrisburg Area Community College	Christensen, Dan	Iowa Western Community College
Anderson, Patty A.	Lake City Community College	Clay, Betty	Southeastern Oklahoma State University
Andrews, Wilma	Virginia Commonwealth College, Nebraska University	Collins, Linda D.	Mesa Community College
Anik, Mazhar	Tiffin University	Cone, Bill	Northern Arizona University
Armstrong, Gary	Shippensburg University	Conroy-Link, Janet	Holy Family College
Arnold, Linda L.	Harrisburg Area Community College	Conway, Ronald	Bowling Green State University
		Cornforth, Carol G.	WVNCC
Ashby, Tom	Oklahoma City Community College	Cosgrove, Janet	Northwestern CT Community
		Courtney, Kevin	Hillsborough Community College
Atkins, Bonnie	Delaware Technical Community College	Coverdale, John	Riverside Community College
		Cox, Rollie	Madison Area Technical College
Aukland, Cherie	Thomas Nelson Community College	Crawford, Hiram	Olive Harvey College
		Crawford, Sonia	Central New Mexico Community College
Bachand, LaDonna	Santa Rosa Community College		
Bagui, Sikha	University of West Florida	Crawford, Thomasina	Miami-Dade College, Kendall Campus
Beecroft, Anita	Kwantlen University College		
Bell, Paula	Lock Haven College	Credico, Grace	Lethbridge Community College
Belton, Linda	Springfield Tech. Community College	Crenshaw, Richard	Miami Dade Community College, North
Bennett, Judith	Sam Houston State University	Crespo, Beverly	Mt. San Antonio College
Bhatia, Sai	Riverside Community College	Crooks, Steven	Texas Tech University
Bishop, Frances	DeVry Institute—Alpharetta (ATL)	Crossley, Connie	Cincinnati State Technical Community College
Blaszkiewicz, Holly	Ivy Tech Community College/Region 1	Curik, Mary	Central New Mexico Community College
Boito, Nancy	HACC Central Pennsylvania's Community College	De Arazoza, Ralph	Miami Dade Community College
		Danno, John	DeVry University/Keller Graduate School
Borger-Boglin, Grietje L.	San Antonio College/Northeast Lakeview College		
Branigan, Dave	DeVry University	Davis, Phillip	Del Mar College
Bray, Patricia	Allegany College of Maryland	Davis, Richard	Trinity Valley Community College
Britt, Brenda K.	Fayetteville Technical Community College	Davis, Sandra	Baker College of Allen Park
		Dees, Stephanie D.	Wharton County Junior College
Brotherton, Cathy	Riverside Community College	DeHerrera, Laurie	Pikes Peak Community College
Brown, Judy	Western Illinois University	Delk, Dr. K. Kay	Seminole Community College
Buehler, Lesley	Ohlone College	Denton, Bree	Texas Tech University
Buell, C	Central Oregon Community College	Dix, Jeanette	Ivy Tech Community College
		Dooly, Veronica P.	Asheville-Buncombe Technical Community College
Burns, Christine	Central New Mexico Community College		
		Doroshow, Mike	Eastfield College
Byars, Pat	Brookhaven College	Douglas, Gretchen	SUNYCortland
Byrd, Julie	Ivy Tech Community College	Dove, Carol	Community College of Allegheny
Byrd, Lynn	Delta State University, Cleveland, Mississippi	Dozier, Susan	Tidewater Community College, Virginia Beach Campus
Cacace, Richard N.	Pensacola Junior College	Driskel, Loretta	Niagara Community College
Cadenhead, Charles	Brookhaven College	Duckwiler, Carol	Wabaunsee Community College
Calhoun, Ric	Gordon College	Duhon, David	Baker College
Cameron, Eric	Passaic Community College	Duncan, Mimi	University of Missouri-St. Louis
Canine, Jill	Ivy Tech Community College of Indiana	Duthie, Judy	Green River Community College
		Duvall, Annette	Central New Mexico Community College
Cannamore, Madie	Kennedy King		

Ecklund, Paula — Duke University

Eilers, Albert — Cincinnati State Technical and Community College

Eng, Bernice — Brookdale Community College

Epperson, Arlin — Columbia College

Evans, Billie — Vance-Granville Community College

Evans, Jean — Brevard Community College

Feuerbach, Lisa — Ivy Tech East Chicago

Finley, Jean — ABTCC

Fisher, Fred — Florida State University

Foster, Nancy — Baker College

Foster-Shriver, Penny L. — Anne Arundel Community College

Foster-Turpen, Linda — CNM

Foszcz, Russ — McHenry County College

Fry, Susan — Boise State University

Fustos, Janos — Metro State

Gallup, Jeanette — Blinn College

Gelb, Janet — Grossmont College

Gentry, Barb — Parkland College

Gerace, Karin — St. Angela Merici School

Gerace, Tom — Tulane University

Ghajar, Homa — Oklahoma State University

Gifford, Steve — Northwest Iowa Community College

Glazer, Ellen — Broward Community College

Gordon, Robert — Hofstra University

Gramlich, Steven — Pasco-Hernando Community College

Graviett, Nancy M. — St. Charles Community College, St. Peters, Missouri

Greene, Rich — Community College of Allegheny County

Gregoryk, Kerry — Virginia Commonwealth State

Griggs, Debra — Bellevue Community College

Grimm, Carol — Palm Beach Community College

Guthrie, Rose — Fox Valley Technical College

Hahn, Norm — Thomas Nelson Community College

Haley-Hunter, Deb — Bluefield State College

Hall, Linnea — Northwest Mississippi Community College

Hammerschlag, Dr. Bill — Brookhaven College

Hansen, Michelle — Davenport University

Hayden, Nancy — Indiana University—Purdue University, Indianapolis

Hayes, Theresa — Broward Community College

Headrick, Betsy — Chattanooga State

Helfand, Terri — Chaffey College

Helms, Liz — Columbus State Community College

Hernandez, Leticia — TCI College of Technology

Hibbert, Marilyn — Salt Lake Community College

Hinds, Cheryl — Norfolk State University

Hines, James — Tidewater Community College

Hoffman, Joan — Milwaukee Area Technical College

Hogan, Pat — Cape Fear Community College

Holland, Susan — Southeast Community College

Holliday, Mardi — Community College of Philadelphia

Hollingsworth, Mary Carole — Georgia Perimeter College

Hopson, Bonnie — Athens Technical College

Horvath, Carrie — Albertus Magnus College

Horwitz, Steve — Community College of Philadelphia

Hotta, Barbara — Leeward Community College

Howard, Bunny — St. Johns River Community

Howard, Chris — DeVry University

Huckabay, Jamie — Austin Community College

Hudgins, Susan — East Central University

Hulett, Michelle J. — Missouri State University

Humphrey, John — Asheville Buncombe Technical Community College

Hunt, Darla A. — Morehead State University, Morehead, Kentucky

Hunt, Laura — Tulsa Community College

Ivey, Joan M. — Lanier Technical College

Jacob, Sherry — Jefferson Community College

Jacobs, Duane — Salt Lake Community College

Jauken, Barb — Southeastern Community

Jerry, Gina — Santa Monica College

Johnson, Deborah S. — Edison State College

Johnson, Kathy — Wright College

Johnson, Mary — Kingwood College

Johnson, Mary — Mt. San Antonio College

Jones, Stacey — Benedict College

Jones, Warren — University of Alabama, Birmingham

Jordan, Cheryl — San Juan College

Kapoor, Bhushan — California State University, Fullerton

Kasai, Susumu — Salt Lake Community College

Kates, Hazel — Miami Dade Community College, Kendall

Keen, Debby — University of Kentucky

Keeter, Sandy — Seminole Community College

Kern-Blystone, Dorothy Jean — Bowling Green State

Kerwin, Annette — College of DuPage

Keskin, Ilknur — The University of South Dakota

Kinney, Mark B. — Baker College

Kirk, Colleen — Mercy College

Kisling, Eric — East Carolina University

Kleckner, Michelle — Elon University

Kliston, Linda — Broward Community College, North Campus

Knuth, Toni — Baker College of Auburn Hills

Kochis, Dennis — Suffolk County Community College

Kominek, Kurt — Northeast State Technical Community College

Kramer, Ed — Northern Virginia Community College

Kretz, Daniel — Fox Valley Technical College

Laird, Jeff — Northeast State Community College

Lamoureaux, Jackie — Central New Mexico Community College

Lange, David — Grand Valley State

LaPointe, Deb — Central New Mexico Community College

Larsen, Jacqueline Anne — A-B Tech

Larson, Donna — Louisville Technical Institute

Laspina, Kathy — Vance-Granville Community College

Le Grand, Dr. Kate — Broward Community College

Lenhart, Sheryl — Terra Community College

Leonard, Yvonne — Coastal Carolina Community College

Letavec, Chris — University of Cincinnati

Lewis, Daphne L, Ed.D. — Wayland Baptist University

Lewis, Julie — Baker College-Allen Park

Liefert, Jane — Everett Community College

Lindaman, Linda	Black Hawk Community College
Lindberg, Martha	Minnesota State University
Lightner, Renee	Broward Community College
Lindberg, Martha	Minnesota State University
Linge, Richard	Arizona Western College
Logan, Mary G.	Delgado Community College
Loizeaux, Barbara	Westchester Community College
Lombardi, John	South University
Lopez, Don	Clovis-State Center Community College District
Lopez, Lisa	Spartanburg Community College
Lord, Alexandria	Asheville Buncombe Tech
Lovering, LeAnne	Augusta Technical College
Lowe, Rita	Harold Washington College
Low, Willy Hui	Joliet Junior College
Lucas, Vickie	Broward Community College
Luna, Debbie	El Paso Community College
Luoma, Jean	Davenport University
Luse, Steven P.	Horry Georgetown Technical College
Lynam, Linda	Central Missouri State University
Lyon, Lynne	Durham College
Lyon, Pat Rajski	Tomball College
Macarty, Matthew	University of New Hampshire
MacKinnon, Ruth	Georgia Southern University
Macon, Lisa	Valencia Community College, West Campus
Machuca, Wayne	College of the Sequoias
Mack, Sherri	Butler County Community College
Madison, Dana	Clarion University
Maguire, Trish	Eastern New Mexico University
Malkan, Rajiv	Montgomery College
Manning, David	Northern Kentucky University
Marcus, Jacquie	Niagara Community College
Marghitu, Daniela	Auburn University
Marks, Suzanne	Bellevue Community College
Marquez, Juanita	El Centro College
Marquez, Juan	Mesa Community College
Martin, Carol	Harrisburg Area Community College
Martin, Paul C.	Harrisburg Area Community College
Martyn, Margie	Baldwin-Wallace College
Marucco, Toni	Lincoln Land Community College
Mason, Lynn	Lubbock Christian University
Matutis, Audrone	Houston Community College
Matkin, Marie	University of Lethbridge
Maurel, Trina	Odessa College
May, Karen	Blinn College
McCain, Evelynn	Boise State University
McCannon, Melinda	Gordon College
McCarthy, Marguerite	Northwestern Business College
McCaskill, Matt L.	Brevard Community College
McClellan, Carolyn	Tidewater Community College
McClure, Darlean	College of Sequoias
McCrory, Sue A.	Missouri State University
McCue, Stacy	Harrisburg Area Community College
McEntire-Orbach, Teresa	Middlesex County College
McKinley, Lee	Georgia Perimeter College
McLeod, Todd	Fresno City College
McManus, Illyana	Grossmont College
McPherson, Dori	Schoolcraft College
Meck, Kari	HACC
Meiklejohn, Nancy	Pikes Peak Community College
Menking, Rick	Hardin-Simmons University

Meredith, Mary	University of Louisiana at Lafayette
Mermelstein, Lisa	Baruch College
Metos, Linda	Salt Lake Community College
Meurer, Daniel	University of Cincinnati
Meyer, Colleen	Cincinnati State Technical and Community College
Meyer, Marian	Central New Mexico Community College
Miller, Cindy	Ivy Tech Community College, Lafayette, Indiana
Mills, Robert E.	Tidewater Community College, Portsmouth Campus
Mitchell, Susan	Davenport University
Mohle, Dennis	Fresno Community College
Molki, Saeed	South Texas College
Monk, Ellen	University of Delaware
Moore, Rodney	Holland College
Morris, Mike	Southeastern Oklahoma State University
Morris, Nancy	Hudson Valley Community College
Moseler, Dan	Harrisburg Area Community College
Nabors, Brent	Reedley College, Clovis Center
Nadas, Erika	Wright College
Nadelman, Cindi	New England College
Nademlynsky, Lisa	Johnson & Wales University
Nagengast, Joseph	Florida Career College
Nason, Scott	Rowan Cabarrus Community College
Ncube, Cathy	University of West Florida
Newsome, Eloise	Northern Virginia Community College Woodbridge
Nicholls, Doreen	Mohawk Valley Community College
Nicholson, John R.	Johnson County Community College
Nielson, Phil	Salt Lake Community College
Nunan, Karen L.	Northeast State Technical Community College
O'Neal, Lois Ann	Rogers State University
Odegard, Teri	Edmonds Community College
Ogle, Gregory	North Community College
Orr, Dr. Claudia	Northern Michigan University South
Orsburn, Glen	Fox Valley Technical College
Otieno, Derek	DeVry University
Otton, Diana Hill	Chesapeake College
Oxendale, Lucia	West Virginia Institute of Technology
Paiano, Frank	Southwestern College
Pannell, Dr. Elizabeth	Collin College
Patrick, Tanya	Clackamas Community College
Paul, Anindya	Daytona State College
Peairs, Deb	Clark State Community College
Perez, Kimberly	Tidewater Community College
Porter, Joyce	Weber State University
Prince, Lisa	Missouri State University-Springfield Campus
Proietti, Kathleen	Northern Essex Community College
Puopolo, Mike	Bunker Hill Community College
Pusins, Delores	HCCC
Putnam, Darlene	Thomas Nelson Community College

Raghuraman, Ram	Joliet Junior College	Sullivan, Denise	Westchester Community College
Rani, Chigurupati	BMCC/CUNY	Sullivan, Joseph	Joliet Junior College
Reasoner, Ted Allen	Indiana University—Purdue	Swart, John	Louisiana Tech University
Reeves, Karen	High Point University	Szurek, Joseph	University of Pittsburgh at Greensburg
Remillard, Debbie	New Hampshire Technical Institute	Taff, Ann	Tulsa Community College
Rhue, Shelly	DeVry University	Taggart, James	Atlantic Cape Community College
Richards, Karen	Maplewoods Community College	Tarver, Mary Beth	Northwestern State University
Richardson, Mary	Albany Technical College	Taylor, Michael	Seattle Central Community College
Rodgers, Gwen	Southern Nazarene University	Terrell, Robert L.	Carson-Newman College
Rodie, Karla	Pikes Peak Community College	Terry, Dariel	Northern Virginia Community College
Roselli, Diane Maie	Harrisburg Area Community College	Thangiah, Sam	Slippery Rock University
Ross, Dianne	University of Louisiana in Lafayette	Thayer, Paul	Austin Community College
Rousseau, Mary	Broward Community College, South	Thompson, Joyce	Lehigh Carbon Community College
Rovetto, Ann	Horry-Georgetown Technical College	Thompson-Sellers, Ingrid	Georgia Perimeter College
Rusin, Iwona	Baker College	Tomasi, Erik	Baruch College
Sahabi, Ahmad	Baker College of Clinton Township	Toreson, Karen	Shoreline Community College
Samson, Dolly	Hawaii Pacific University	Townsend, Cynthia	Baker College
Sams, Todd	University of Cincinnati	Trifiletti, John J.	Florida Community College at Jacksonville
Sandoval, Everett	Reedley College	Trivedi, Charulata	Quinsigamond Community College, Woodbridge
Santiago, Diana	Central New Mexico Community College	Tucker, William	Austin Community College
Sardone, Nancy	Seton Hall University	Turgeon, Cheryl	Asnuntuck Community College
Scafide, Jean	Mississippi Gulf Coast Community College	Turpen, Linda	Central New Mexico Community College
Scheeren, Judy	Westmoreland County Community College	Upshaw, Susan	Del Mar College
Scheiwe, Adolph	Joliet Junior College	Unruh, Angela	Central Washington University
Schneider, Sol	Sam Houston State University	Vanderhoof, Dr. Glenna	Missouri State University-Springfield Campus
Schweitzer, John	Central New Mexico Community College	Vargas, Tony	El Paso Community College
Scroggins, Michael	Southwest Missouri State University	Vicars, Mitzi	Hampton University
Sedlacek, Brenda	Tidewater Community College	Villarreal, Kathleen	Fresno
Sell, Kelly	Anne Arundel Community College	Vitrano, Mary Ellen	Palm Beach Community College
Sever, Suzanne	Northwest Arkansas Community College	Vlaich-Lee, Michelle	Greenville Technical College
Sewell, John	Florida Career College	Volker, Bonita	Tidewater Community College
Sheridan, Rick	California State University-Chico	Waddell, Karen	Butler Community College
Silvers, Pamela	Asheville Buncombe Tech	Wahila, Lori (Mindy)	Tompkins Cortland Community College
Sindt, Robert G.	Johnson County Community College	Wallace, Melissa	Lanier Technical College
Singer, Noah	Tulsa Community College	Walters, Gary B.	Central New Mexico Community College
Singer, Steven A.	University of Hawai'i, Kapi'olani Community College	Waswick, Kim	Southeast Community College, Nebraska
Sinha, Atin	Albany State University	Wavle, Sharon M.	Tompkins Cortland Community College
Skolnick, Martin	Florida Atlantic University	Webb, Nancy	City College of San Francisco
Smith, Kristi	Allegany College of Maryland	Webb, Rebecca	Northwest Arkansas Community College
Smith, Patrick	Marshall Community and Technical College	Weber, Sandy	Gateway Technical College
Smith, Stella A.	Georgia Gwinnett College	Weissman, Jonathan	Finger Lakes Community College
Smith, T. Michael	Austin Community College	Wells, Barbara E.	Central Carolina Technical College
Smith, Tammy	Tompkins Cortland Community Collge	Wells, Lorna	Salt Lake Community College
Smolenski, Bob	Delaware County Community College	Welsh, Jean	Lansing Community College Nebraska
Smolenski, Robert	Delaware Community College	White, Bruce	Quinnipiac University
Southwell, Donald	Delta College	Willer, Ann	Solano Community College
Spangler, Candice	Columbus State	Williams, Mark	Lane Community College
Spangler, Candice	Columbus State Community College	Williams, Ronald D.	Central Piedmont Community College
Stark, Diane	Phoenix College	Wilms, Dr. G. Jan	Union University
Stedham, Vicki	St. Petersburg College, Clearwater	Wilson, Kit	Red River College
Stefanelli, Greg	Carroll Community College	Wilson, MaryLou	Piedmont Technical College
Steiner, Ester	New Mexico State University	Wilson, Roger	Fairmont State University
Stenlund, Neal	Northern Virginia Community College, Alexandria	Wimberly, Leanne	International Academy of Design and Technology
St. John, Steve	Tulsa Community College		
Sterling, Janet	Houston Community College		
Stoughton, Catherine	Laramie County Community College		
Sullivan, Angela	Joliet Junior College		

Contributors continued

Winters, Floyd	Manatee Community College
Worthington, Paula	Northern Virginia Community College
Wright, Darrell	Shelton State Community College
Wright, Julie	Baker College
Yauney, Annette	Herkimer County Community College

Yip, Thomas	Passaic Community College
Zavala, Ben	Webster Tech
Zaboski, Maureen	University of Scranton
Zlotow, Mary Ann	College of DuPage
Zudeck, Steve	Broward Community College, North
Zullo, Matthew D.	Wake Technical Community College

About the Authors

Shelley Gaskin, Series Editor, is a professor in the Business and Computer Technology Division at Pasadena City College in Pasadena, California. She holds a bachelor's degree in Business Administration from Robert Morris College (Pennsylvania), a master's degree in Business from Northern Illinois University, and a doctorate in Adult and Community Education from Ball State University. Before joining Pasadena City College, she spent 12 years in the computer industry where she was a systems analyst, sales representative, and Director of Customer Education with Unisys Corporation. She also worked for Ernst & Young on the development of large systems applications for their clients. She has written and developed training materials for custom systems applications in both the public and private sector, and has written and edited numerous computer application textbooks.

This book is dedicated to my students, who inspire me every day.

Robert L. Ferrett recently retired as the Director of the Center for Instructional Computing at Eastern Michigan University, where he provided computer training and support to faculty. He has authored or co-authored more than 70 books on Access, PowerPoint, Excel, Publisher, WordPerfect, Windows, Word, OpenOffice, and Computer Fundamentals. He has been designing, developing, and delivering computer workshops for more than three decades. Before writing for the *GO! Series*, Bob was a series editor for the Learn Series. He has a bachelor's degree in Psychology, a master's degree in Geography, and a master's degree in Interdisciplinary Technology from Eastern Michigan University. His doctoral studies were in Instructional Technology at Wayne State University.

I'd like to dedicate this book to my wife Mary Jane,
whose constant support has been so important all these years.

A Microsoft® Office textbook designed for student success!

- **Project-Based** – Students learn by creating projects that they will use in the real world.

- **Microsoft Procedural Syntax** – Steps are written to put students in the right place at the right time.

- **Teachable Moment** – Expository text is woven into the steps—at the moment students need to know it—not chunked together in a block of text that will go unread.

- **Sequential Pagination** – Students have actual page numbers instead of confusing letters and abbreviations.

Student Outcomes and Learning Objectives – Objectives are clustered around projects that result in student outcomes.

Project Activities – A project summary stated clearly and quickly.

Project Files – Clearly shows students which files are needed for the project and the names they will use to save their documents.

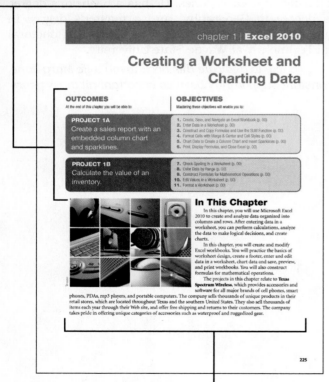

Scenario – Each chapter opens with a story that sets the stage for the projects the student will create.

Project Results – Shows students how their final outcome will appear.

Key Feature

Microsoft Procedural Syntax – Steps are written to put the student in the right place at the right time.

Color Coding – Color variations between the two projects in each chapter make it easy to identify which project students are working on.

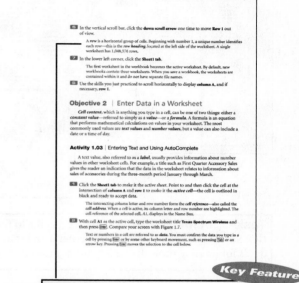

Key Feature

Sequential Pagination – Students are given actual page numbers to navigate through the textbook instead of confusing letters and abbreviations.

Key Feature

Teachable Moment – Expository text is woven into the steps—at the moment students need to know it—not chunked together in a block of text that will go unread.

End-of-Chapter

Content-Based Assessments – Assessments with defined solutions.

Objective List - Every project includes a listing of covered objectives from Projects A and B.

End-of-Chapter

Outcomes-Based Assessments – Assessments with open-ended solutions.

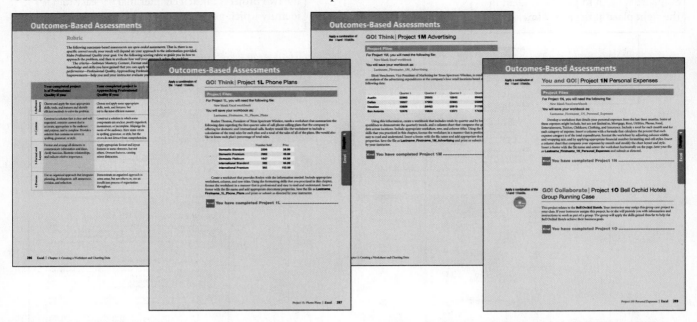

Task-Specific Rubric – A matrix specific to the **GO! Solve It** projects that states the criteria and standards for grading these defined-solution projects.

Outcomes Rubric – A matrix specific to the **GO! Think** projects that states the criteria and standards for grading these open-ended assessments.

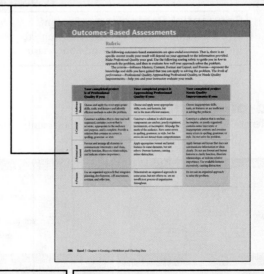

Student CD – All student data files readily available on a CD that comes with the book.

Podcasts – Videos that teach some of the more difficult topics when working with Microsoft applications.

Student Videos – A visual and audio walk-through of every A and B project in the book (see sample images on following page).

Student Videos! –
Each chapter comes with two videos that include audio, demonstrating the objectives and activities taught in the chapter.

All Instructor materials available on the IRCD

Instructor Materials

Annotated Instructor Edition - An instructor tool includes a full copy of the student textbook annotated with teaching tips, discussion topics, and other useful pieces for teaching each chapter.

Assignment Sheets – Lists all the assignments for the chapter. Just add in the course information, due dates, and points. Providing these to students ensures they will know what is due and when.

Scripted Lectures – Classroom lectures prepared for you.

Annotated Solution Files – Coupled with the assignment tags, these create a grading and scoring system that makes grading so much easier for you.

PowerPoint Lectures – PowerPoint presentations for each chapter.

Scoring Rubrics – Can be used either by students to check their work or by you as a quick check-off for the items that need to be corrected.

Syllabus Templates - For 8-week, 12-week, and 16-week courses.

Test Bank – Includes a variety of test questions for each chapter.

Companion Website – Online content such as the Online Study Guide, Glossary, and Student Data Files are all at www.pearsonhighered.com/go.

Using the Common Features of Microsoft Office 2010

OUTCOMES
At the end of this chapter you will be able to:

OBJECTIVES
Mastering these objectives will enable you to:

PROJECT 1A
Create, save, and print a Microsoft Office 2010 file.

1. Use Windows Explorer to Locate Files and Folders (p. 3)
2. Locate and Start a Microsoft Office 2010 Program (p. 6)
3. Enter and Edit Text in an Office 2010 Program (p. 9)
4. Perform Commands from a Dialog Box (p. 11)
5. Create a Folder, Save a File, and Close a Program (p. 13)
6. Add Document Properties and Print a File (p. 18)

PROJECT 1B
Use the Ribbon and dialog boxes to perform common commands in a Microsoft Office 2010 file.

7. Open an Existing File and Save It with a New Name (p. 22)
8. Explore Options for an Application (p. 25)
9. Perform Commands from the Ribbon (p. 26)
10. Apply Formatting in Office Programs (p. 32)
11. Use the Microsoft Office 2010 Help System (p. 43)
12. Compress Files (p. 44)

olly/Shutterstock

In This Chapter

In this chapter, you will use Windows Explorer to navigate the Windows folder structure, create a folder, and save files in Microsoft Office 2010 programs. You will also practice using the features of Microsoft Office 2010 that are common across the major programs that comprise the Microsoft Office 2010 suite. These common features include creating, saving, and printing files.

Common features also include the new Paste Preview and Microsoft Office Backstage view. You will apply formatting, perform commands, and compress files. You will see that creating professional-quality documents is easy and quick in Microsoft Office 2010, and that finding your way around is fast and efficient.

The projects in this chapter relate to **Oceana Palm Grill**, which is a chain of 25 casual, full-service restaurants based in Austin, Texas. The Oceana Palm Grill owners plan an aggressive expansion program. To expand by 15 additional restaurants in North Carolina and Florida by 2018, the company must attract new investors, develop new menus, and recruit new employees, all while adhering to the company's quality guidelines and maintaining its reputation for excellent service. To succeed, the company plans to build on its past success and maintain its quality elements.

Project 1A PowerPoint File

myitlab
Project 1A Training

In Activities 1.01 through 1.06, you will create a PowerPoint file, save it in a folder that you create by using Windows Explorer, and then print the file or submit it electronically as directed by your instructor. Your completed PowerPoint slide will look similar to Figure 1.1.

Project Files

For Project 1A, you will need the following file:

New blank PowerPoint presentation

You will save your file as:

Lastname_Firstname_1A_Menu_Plan

Project Results

Oceana Palm Grill Menu Plan

Prepared by Firstname Lastname
For Laura Hernandez

Figure 1.1
Project 1A Menu Plan

Objective 1 | Use Windows Explorer to Locate Files and Folders

A *file* is a collection of information stored on a computer under a single name, for example, a Word document or a PowerPoint presentation. Every file is stored in a *folder*—a container in which you store files—or a *subfolder*, which is a folder within a folder. Your Windows operating system stores and organizes your files and folders, which is a primary task of an operating system.

You *navigate*—explore within the organizing structure of Windows—to create, save, and find your files and folders by using the *Windows Explorer* program. Windows Explorer displays the files and folders on your computer, and is at work anytime you are viewing the contents of files and folders in a *window*. A window is a rectangular area on a computer screen in which programs and content appear; a window can be moved, resized, minimized, or closed.

Activity 1.01 | Using Windows Explorer to Locate Files and Folders

1 Turn on your computer and display the Windows *desktop*—the opening screen in Windows that simulates your work area.

> **Note | Comparing Your Screen with the Figures in This Textbook**
>
> Your screen will match the figures shown in this textbook if you set your screen resolution to 1024 × 768. At other resolutions, your screen will closely resemble, but not match, the figures shown. To view your screen's resolution, on the Windows 7 desktop, right-click in a blank area, and then click Screen resolution. In Windows Vista, right-click a blank area, click Personalize, and then click Display Settings. In Windows XP, right-click the desktop, click Properties, and then click the Settings tab.

2 In your CD/DVD tray, insert the **Student CD** that accompanies this textbook. Wait a few moments for an **AutoPlay** window to display. Compare your screen with Figure 1.2.

> *AutoPlay* is a Windows feature that lets you choose which program to use to start different kinds of media, such as music CDs, or CDs and DVDs containing photos; it displays when you plug in or insert media or storage devices.

> **Note | If You Do Not Have the Student CD**
>
> If you do not have the Student CD, consult the inside back flap of this textbook for instructions on how to download the files from the Pearson Web site.

Figure 1.2

AutoPlay window

Close button

Windows desktop (yours may vary in color and arrangement)

3 In the upper right corner of the **AutoPlay** window, move your mouse over—*point* to—the **Close** button ![Close button], and then *click*—press the left button on your mouse pointing device one time.

4 On the left side of the **Windows taskbar**, click the **Start** button 🌐 to display the **Start menu**. Compare your screen with Figure 1.3.

The *Windows taskbar* is the area along the lower edge of the desktop that contains the *Start button* and an area to display buttons for open programs. The Start button displays the *Start menu*, which provides a list of choices and is the main gateway to your computer's programs, folders, and settings.

Figure 1.3

Computer on Start menu

Start menu (your array of programs may vary)

Windows 7 taskbar

Start button

5 On the right side of the **Start menu**, click **Computer** to see the disk drives and other hardware connected to your computer. Compare your screen with Figure 1.4, and then take a moment to study the table in Figure 1.5.

The *folder window* for *Computer* displays. A folder window displays the contents of the current folder, *library*, or device, and contains helpful parts so that you can navigate within Windows.

In Windows 7, a library is a collection of items, such as files and folders, assembled from *various locations*; the locations might be on your computer, an external hard drive, removable media, or someone else's computer.

The difference between a folder and a library is that a library can include files stored in *different locations*—any disk drive, folder, or other place that you can store files and folders.

Figure 1.4

Back and Forward

Address bar

File list

Navigation pane

Folder window toolbar

Views button

Search box

Preview pane button

Details pane

Window Part	Use to:
Address bar	Navigate to a different folder or library, or go back to a previous one.
Back and Forward buttons	Navigate to other folders or libraries you have already opened without closing the current window. These buttons work in conjunction with the address bar; that is, after you use the address bar to change folders, you can use the Back button to return to the previous folder.
Details pane	Display the most common file properties—information about a file, such as the author, the date you last changed the file, and any descriptive *tags*, which are custom file properties that you create to help find and organize your files.
File list	Display the contents of the current folder or library. In Computer, the file list displays the disk drives.
Folder window for *Computer*	Display the contents of the current folder, library, or device. The Folder window contains helpful features so that you can navigate within Windows.
Folder window toolbar	Perform common tasks, such as changing the view of your files and folders or burning files to a CD. The buttons available change to display only relevant tasks.
Navigation pane	Navigate to, open, and display favorites, libraries, folders, saved searches, and an expandable list of drives.
Preview pane button	Display (if you have chosen to open this pane) the contents of most files without opening them in a program. To open the preview pane, click the Preview pane button on the toolbar to turn it on and off.
Search box	Look for an item in the current folder or library by typing a word or phrase in the search box.
Views button	Choose how to view the contents of the current location.

Figure 1.5

6 On the toolbar of the **Computer** folder window, click the **Views button arrow** 📇 ▾ — the small arrow to the right of the Views button—to display a list of views that you can apply to the file list. If necessary, on the list, click **Tiles**.

The Views button is a *split button*; clicking the main part of the button performs a *command* and clicking the arrow opens a menu or list. A command is an instruction to a computer program that causes an action to be carried out.

When you open a folder or a library, you can change how the files display in the file list. For example, you might prefer to see large or small *icons*—pictures that represent a program, a file, a folder, or some other object—or an arrangement that lets you see various types of information about each file. Each time you click the Views button, the window changes, cycling through several views—additional view options are available by clicking the Views button arrow.

Another Way

Point to the CD/DVD drive, right-click, and then click Open.

7 In the **file list**, under **Devices with Removable Storage**, point to your **CD/DVD Drive**, and then *double-click*—click the left mouse button two times in rapid succession— to display the list of folders on the CD. Compare your screen with Figure 1.6.

When double-clicking, keep your hand steady between clicks; this is more important than the speed of the two clicks.

Figure 1.6

Views button indicates Details view

List of folders on the CD in Details view

Views button arrow

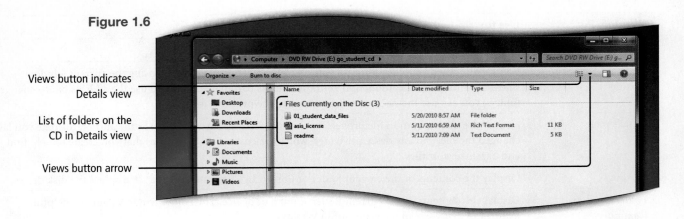

8 In the **file list**, point to the folder **01_student_data_files** and double-click to display the list of subfolders in the folder. Double-click to open the folder **01_common_features**. Compare your screen with Figure 1.7.

The Student Resource CD includes files that you will use to complete the projects in this textbook. If you prefer, you can also copy the **01_student_data_files** folder to a location on your computer's hard drive or to a removable device such as a *USB flash drive*, which is a small storage device that plugs into a computer USB port. Your instructor might direct you to other locations where these files are located; for example, on your learning management system.

Figure 1.7

Address bar displays sequence of folders

One folder in the *01_common_features* folder

9 In the upper right corner of the **Computer** window, click the **Close** button to redisplay your desktop.

Objective 2 | Locate and Start a Microsoft Office 2010 Program

Microsoft Office 2010 includes programs, servers, and services for individuals, small organizations, and large enterprises. A *program*, also referred to as an *application*, is a set of instructions used by a computer to perform a task, such as word processing or accounting.

Activity 1.02 | Locating and Starting a Microsoft Office 2010 Program

1 On the **Windows taskbar**, click the **Start** button to display the **Start** menu.

2 From the displayed **Start** menu, locate the group of **Microsoft Office 2010** programs on your computer—the Office program icons from which you can start the program may be located on your Start menu, in a Microsoft Office folder on the **All Programs** list, on your desktop, or any combination of these locations; the location will vary depending on how your computer is configured.

All Programs is an area of the Start menu that displays all the available programs on your computer system.

3 Examine Figure 1.8, and notice the programs that are included in the Microsoft Office Professional Plus 2010 group of programs. (Your group of programs may vary.)

Microsoft Word is a word processing program, with which you create and share documents by using its writing tools.

Microsoft Excel is a spreadsheet program, with which you calculate and analyze numbers and create charts.

Microsoft Access is a database program, with which you can collect, track, and report data.

Microsoft PowerPoint is a presentation program, with which you can communicate information with high-impact graphics and video.

Additional popular Office programs include *Microsoft Outlook* to manage e-mail and organizational activities, *Microsoft Publisher* to create desktop publishing documents such as brochures, and *Microsoft OneNote* to manage notes that you make at meetings or in classes and to share notes with others on the Web.

The Professional Plus version of Office 2010 also includes *Microsoft SharePoint Workspace* to share information with others in a team environment and *Microsoft InfoPath Designer and Filler* to create forms and gather data.

Figure 1.8

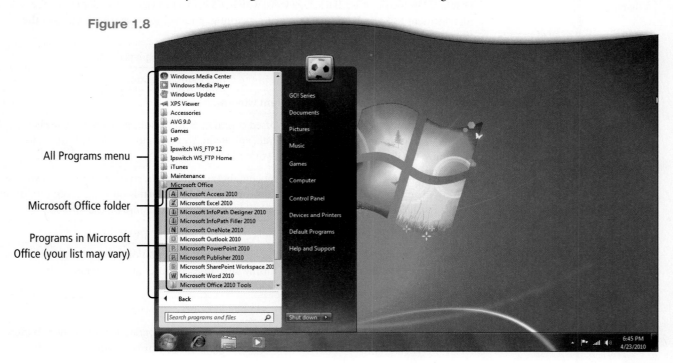

All Programs menu

Microsoft Office folder

Programs in Microsoft Office (your list may vary)

4 Click to open the program **Microsoft PowerPoint 2010**. Compare your screen with Figure 1.9, and then take a moment to study the description of these screen elements in the table in Figure 1.10.

Figure 1.9

Screen Element	Description
File tab	Displays Microsoft Office Backstage view, which is a centralized space for all of your file management tasks such as opening, saving, printing, publishing, or sharing a file—all the things you can do *with* a file.
Group names	Indicate the name of the groups of related commands on the displayed tab.
PowerPoint Slide pane	Displays a large image of the active slide in the PowerPoint program.
Program-level control buttons	Minimizes, restores, or closes the program window.
Quick Access Toolbar	Displays buttons to perform frequently used commands and resources with a single click. The default commands include Save, Undo, and Redo. You can add and delete buttons to customize the Quick Access Toolbar for your convenience.
Ribbon	Displays a group of task-oriented tabs that contain the commands, styles, and resources you need to work in an Office 2010 program. The look of your Ribbon depends on your screen resolution. A high resolution will display more individual items and button names on the Ribbon.
Ribbon tabs	Display the names of the task-oriented tabs relevant to the open program.
Slides/Outline pane	Displays either thumbnails of the slides in a PowerPoint presentation (Slides tab) or the outline of the presentation's content (Outline tab). In each Office 2010 program, different panes display in different ways to assist you.
Status bar	Displays file information on the left and View and Zoom on the right.
Title bar	Displays the name of the file and the name of the program. The program window control buttons—Minimize, Maximize/Restore Down, and Close—are grouped on the right side of the title bar.

Figure 1.10

Objective 3 | Enter and Edit Text in an Office 2010 Program

All of the programs in Office 2010 require some typed text. Your keyboard is still the primary method of entering information into your computer. Techniques to *edit*—make changes to—text are similar among all of the Office 2010 programs.

Activity 1.03 | Entering and Editing Text in an Office 2010 Program

1 In the middle of the PowerPoint Slide pane, point to the text *Click to add title* to display the I pointer, and then click one time.

The *insertion point*—a blinking vertical line that indicates where text or graphics will be inserted—displays.

In Office 2010 programs, the mouse *pointer*—any symbol that displays on your screen in response to moving your mouse device—displays in different shapes depending on the task you are performing and the area of the screen to which you are pointing.

2 Type **Oceana Grille Info** and notice how the insertion point moves to the right as you type. Point slightly to the right of the letter *e* in *Grille* and click to place the insertion point there. Compare your screen with Figure 1.11.

Figure 1.11

Insertion point

3 On your keyboard, locate and press the Backspace key to delete the letter *e*.

Pressing Backspace removes a character to the left of the insertion point.

4 Point slightly to the left of the *I* in *Info* and click one time to place the insertion point there. Type **Menu** and then press Spacebar one time. Compare your screen with Figure 1.12.

By *default*, when you type text in an Office program, existing text moves to the right to make space for new typing. Default refers to the current selection or setting that is automatically used by a program unless you specify otherwise.

Figure 1.12

Menu inserted

5 Press ⌈Del⌉ four times to delete *Info* and then type **Plan**

> Pressing ⌈Del⌉ removes—deletes—a character to the right of the insertion point.

6 With your insertion point blinking after the word *Plan*, on your keyboard, hold down the ⌈Ctrl⌉ key. While holding down ⌈Ctrl⌉, press ⌈←⌉ three times to move the insertion point to the beginning of the word *Grill*.

> This is a **keyboard shortcut**—a key or combination of keys that performs a task that would otherwise require a mouse. This keyboard shortcut moves the insertion point to the beginning of the previous word.
>
> A keyboard shortcut is commonly indicated as ⌈Ctrl⌉ + ⌈←⌉ (or some other combination of keys) to indicate that you hold down the first key while pressing the second key. A keyboard shortcut can also include three keys, in which case you hold down the first two and then press the third. For example, ⌈Ctrl⌉ + ⌈Shift⌉ + ⌈←⌉ selects one word to the left.

7 With the insertion point blinking at the beginning of the word *Grill*, type **Palm** and press ⌈Spacebar⌉.

8 Click anywhere in the text *Click to add subtitle*. With the insertion point blinking, type the following and include the spelling error: **Prepered by Annabel Dunham**

9 With your mouse, point slightly to the left of the *A* in *Annabel*, hold down the left mouse button, and then **drag**—hold down the left mouse button while moving your mouse—to the right to select the text *Annabel Dunham*, and then release the mouse button. Compare your screen with Figure 1.13.

> The **Mini toolbar** displays commands that are commonly used with the selected object, which places common commands close to your pointer. When you move the pointer away from the Mini toolbar, it fades from view.
>
> To **select** refers to highlighting, by dragging with your mouse, areas of text or data or graphics so that the selection can be edited, formatted, copied, or moved. The action of dragging includes releasing the left mouse button at the end of the area you want to select. The Office programs recognize a selected area as one unit, to which you can make changes. Selecting text may require some practice. If you are not satisfied with your result, click anywhere outside of the selection, and then begin again.

Figure 1.13

Mini toolbar displays ——

Annabel Dunham selected ——

10 With the text *Annabel Dunham* selected, type your own firstname and lastname.

In any Windows-based program, such as the Microsoft Office 2010 programs, selected text is deleted and then replaced when you begin to type new text. You will save time by developing good techniques to select and then edit or replace selected text, which is easier than pressing the [Del] key numerous times to delete text that you do not want.

11 Notice that the misspelled word *Prepered* displays with a wavy red underline; additionally, all or part of your name might display with a wavy red underline.

Office 2010 has a dictionary of words against which all entered text is checked. In Word and PowerPoint, words that are *not* in the dictionary display a wavy red line, indicating a possible misspelled word or a proper name or an unusual word—none of which are in the Office 2010 dictionary.

In Excel and Access, you can initiate a check of the spelling, but wavy red underlines do not display.

12 Point to *Prepered* and then ***right-click***—click your right mouse button one time.

The Mini toolbar and a ***shortcut menu*** display. A shortcut menu displays commands and options relevant to the selected text or object—known as ***context-sensitive commands*** because they relate to the item you right-clicked.

Here, the shortcut menu displays commands related to the misspelled word. You can click the suggested correct spelling *Prepared*, click Ignore All to ignore the misspelling, add the word to the Office dictionary, or click Spelling to display a ***dialog box***. A dialog box is a small window that contains options for completing a task. Whenever you see a command followed by an ***ellipsis*** (…), which is a set of three dots indicating incompleteness, clicking the command will always display a dialog box.

13 On the displayed shortcut menu, click **Prepared** to correct the misspelled word. If necessary, point to any parts of your name that display a wavy red underline, right-click, and then on the shortcut menu, click Ignore All so that Office will no longer mark your name with a wavy underline in this file.

More Knowledge | Adding to the Office Dictionary

The main dictionary contains the most common words, but does not include all proper names, technical terms, or acronyms. You can add words, acronyms, and proper names to the Office dictionary by clicking Add to Dictionary when they are flagged, and you might want to do so for your own name and other proper names and terms that you type often.

Objective 4 | Perform Commands from a Dialog Box

In a dialog box, you make decisions about an individual object or topic. A dialog box also offers a way to adjust a number of settings at one time.

Activity 1.04 | Performing Commands from a Dialog Box

1 Point anywhere in the blank area above the title *Oceana Palm Grill Menu Plan* to display the ⬆ pointer.

2 Right-click to display a shortcut menu. Notice the command *Format Background* followed by an ellipsis (…). Compare your screen with Figure 1.14.

Recall that a command followed by an ellipsis indicates that a dialog box will display if you click the command.

Figure 1.14

Shortcut menu ——————

Ellipsis following command ——————

3 Click **Format Background** to display the **Format Background** dialog box, and then compare your screen with Figure 1.15.

Figure 1.15

Fill selected ——————

Format Background dialog box ——————

Options related to the background fill ——————

4 On the left, if necessary, click **Fill** to display the **Fill** options.

Fill is the inside color of an object. Here, the dialog box displays the option group names on the left; some dialog boxes provide a set of tabs across the top from which you can display different sets of options.

5 On the right, under **Fill**, click the **Gradient fill** option button.

The dialog box displays additional settings related to the gradient fill option. An *option button* is a round button that enables you to make one choice among two or more options. In a gradient fill, one color fades into another.

6 Click the **Preset colors arrow**—the arrow in the box to the right of the text *Preset colors*—and then in the gallery, in the second row, point to the fifth fill color to display the ScreenTip *Fog*.

A *gallery* is an Office feature that displays a list of potential results. A *ScreenTip* displays useful information about mouse actions, such as pointing to screen elements or dragging.

7 Click **Fog**, and then notice that the fill color is applied to your slide. Click the **Type arrow**, and then click **Rectangular** to change the pattern of the fill color. Compare your screen with Figure 1.16.

Figure 1.16

Gradient fill option
button selected

Rectangular displays

Close button

8 At the bottom of the dialog box, click **Close**.

As you progress in your study of Microsoft Office, you will practice using many dialog boxes and applying dramatic effects such as this to your Word documents, Excel spreadsheets, Access databases, and PowerPoint slides.

Objective 5 | Create a Folder, Save a File, and Close a Program

A *location* is any disk drive, folder, or other place in which you can store files and folders. Where you store your files depends on how and where you use your data. For example, for your classes, you might decide to store primarily on a removable USB flash drive so that you can carry your files to different locations and access your files on different computers.

If you do most of your work on a single computer, for example your home desktop system or your laptop computer that you take with you to school or work, store your files in one of the Libraries—Documents, Music, Pictures, or Videos—provided by your Windows operating system.

Although the Windows operating system helps you to create and maintain a logical folder structure, take the time to name your files and folders in a consistent manner.

Activity 1.05 | Creating a Folder, Saving a File, and Closing a Program

A PowerPoint presentation is an example of a file. Office 2010 programs use a common dialog box provided by the Windows operating system to assist you in saving files. In this activity, you will create a folder on a USB flash drive in which to store files. If you prefer to store on your hard drive, you can use similar steps to store files in your My Documents folder in your Documents library.

1 Insert a USB flash drive into your computer, and if necessary, **Close** ▣ the **AutoPlay** dialog box. If you are not using a USB flash drive, go to Step 2.

> As the first step in saving a file, determine where you want to save the file, and if necessary, insert a storage device.

2 At the top of your screen, in the title bar, notice that *Presentation1 – Microsoft PowerPoint* displays.

> Most Office 2010 programs open with a new unsaved file with a default name—*Presentation1*, *Document1*, and so on. As you create your file, your work is temporarily stored in the computer's memory until you initiate a Save command, at which time you must choose a file name and location in which to save your file.

3 In the upper left corner of your screen, click the **File tab** to display **Microsoft Office Backstage** view. Compare your screen with Figure 1.17.

> Microsoft Office *Backstage view* is a centralized space for tasks related to *file* management; that is why the tab is labeled *File*. File management tasks include, for example, opening, saving, printing, publishing, or sharing a file. The *Backstage tabs*—*Info*, *Recent*, *New*, *Print*, *Save & Send*, and *Help*—display along the left side. The tabs group file-related tasks together.

> Above the Backstage tabs, *Quick Commands*—*Save*, *Save As*, *Open*, and *Close*—display for quick access to these commands. When you click any of these commands, Backstage view closes and either a dialog box displays or the active file closes.

> Here, the *Info tab* displays information—*info*—about the current file. In the center panel, various file management tasks are available in groups. For example, if you click the Protect Presentation button, a list of options that you can set for this file that relate to who can open or edit the presentation displays.

> On the Info tab, in the right panel, you can also examine the *document properties*. Document properties, also known as *metadata*, are details about a file that describe or identify it, such as the title, author name, subject, and keywords that identify the document's topic or contents. On the Info page, a thumbnail image of the current file displays in the upper right corner, which you can click to close Backstage view and return to the document.

More Knowledge | Deciding Where to Store Your Files

Where should you store your files? In the libraries created by Windows 7 (Documents, Pictures, and so on)? On a removable device like a flash drive or external hard drive? In Windows 7, it is easy to find your files, especially if you use the libraries. Regardless of where you save a file, Windows 7 will make it easy to find the file again, even if you are not certain where it might be.

In Windows 7, storing all of your files within a library makes sense. If you perform most of your work on your desktop system or your laptop that travels with you, you can store your files in the libraries created by Windows 7 for your user account—Documents, Pictures, Music, and so on. Within these libraries, you can create folders and subfolders to organize your data. These libraries are a good choice for storing your files because:

- From the Windows Explorer button on the taskbar, your libraries are always just one click away.
- The libraries are designed for their contents; for example, the Pictures folder displays small images of your digital photos.
- You can add new locations to a library; for example, an external hard drive, or a network drive. Locations added to a library behave just like they are on your hard drive.
- Other users of your computer cannot access your libraries.
- The libraries are the default location for opening and saving files within an application, so you will find that you can open and save files with fewer navigation clicks.

Figure 1.17

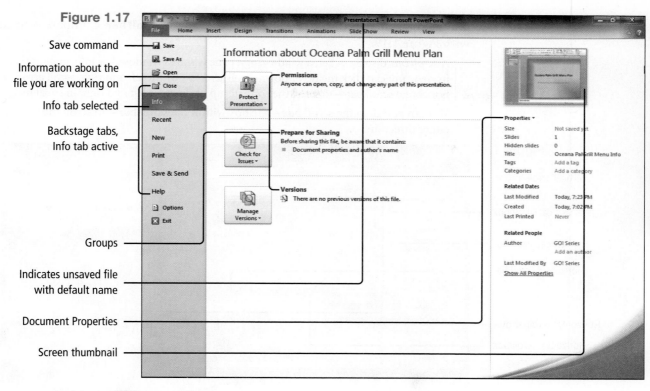

Save command

Information about the file you are working on

Info tab selected

Backstage tabs, Info tab active

Groups

Indicates unsaved file with default name

Document Properties

Screen thumbnail

4 Above the **Backstage tabs**, click **Save** to display the **Save As** dialog box.

Backstage view closes and the Save As dialog box, which includes a folder window and an area at the bottom to name the file and set the file type, displays.

When you are saving something for the first time, for example a new PowerPoint presentation, the Save and Save As commands are identical. That is, the Save As dialog box will display if you click Save or if you click Save As.

Note | Saving Your File

After you have named a file and saved it in your desired location, the Save command saves any changes you make to the file without displaying any dialog box. The Save As command will display the Save As dialog box and let you name and save a new file based on the current one—in a location that you choose. After you name and save the new document, the original document closes, and the new document—based on the original one—displays.

---

5 In the **Save As** dialog box, on the left, locate the **navigation pane**; compare your screen with Figure 1.18.

By default, the Save command opens the Documents library unless your default file location has been changed.

Figure 1.18

Save As dialog box
Address bar

Default save location

Navigation pane

File list (yours will vary)

File name box

Save as type defaults to *PowerPoint Presentation*

6 On the right side of the **navigation pane**, point to the **scroll bar**. Compare your screen with Figure 1.19.

A *scroll bar* displays when a window, or a pane within a window, has information that is not in view. You can click the up or down scroll arrows—or the left and right scroll arrows in a horizontal scroll bar—to scroll the contents up or down or left and right in small increments.

You can also drag the *scroll box*—the box within the scroll bar—to scroll the window in either direction.

Figure 1.19

Vertical scroll arrows

Vertical scroll box

Vertical scroll bar

Horizontal scroll bar

Horizontal scroll arrows

Horizontal scroll box

7 Click the **down scroll arrow** as necessary so that you can view the lower portion of the **navigation pane**, and then click the icon for your USB flash drive. Compare your screen with Figure 1.20. (If you prefer to store on your computer's hard drive instead of a USB flash drive, in the navigation pane, click Documents.)

Figure 1.20

Drive letter of your USB flash drive (yours will vary)

New folder button

File list on USB flash drive (yours may contain files or folders)

USB flash drive selected (yours will vary)

8 On the toolbar, click the **New folder** button.

In the file list, a new folder is created, and the text *New folder* is selected.

9 Type **Common Features Chapter 1** and press Enter. Compare your screen with Figure 1.21.

In Windows-based programs, the Enter key confirms an action.

Figure 1.21

New folder

10 In the **file list**, double-click the name of your new folder to open it and display its name in the **address bar**.

11 In the lower portion of the dialog box, click in the **File name** box to select the existing text. Notice that Office inserts the text at the beginning of the presentation as a suggested file name.

12 On your keyboard, locate the ⌐ key. Notice that the Shift of this key produces the underscore character. With the text still selected, type **Lastname_Firstname_1A_ Menu_Plan** Compare your screen with Figure 1.22.

> You can use spaces in file names, however some individuals prefer not to use spaces. Some programs, especially when transferring files over the Internet, may not work well with spaces in file names. In general, however, unless you encounter a problem, it is OK to use spaces. In this textbook, underscores are used instead of spaces in file names.

Figure 1.22

File name box indicates your file name

Save as type box indicates *PowerPoint Presentation*

Save button

13 In the lower right corner, click **Save**; or press Enter. See Figure 1.23.

> Your new file name displays in the title bar, indicating that the file has been saved to a location that you have specified.

Figure 1.23

File name in title bar

14 In the text that begins *Prepared by*, click to position the insertion point at the end of your name, and then press Enter to move to a new line. Type **For Laura Hernandez**

15 Click the **File tab** to display **Backstage** view. At the top of the center panel, notice that the path where your file is stored displays. Above the Backstage tabs, click **Close** to close the file. In the message box, click **Save** to save the changes you made and close the file. Leave PowerPoint open.

> PowerPoint displays a message asking if you want to save the changes you have made. Because you have made additional changes to the file since your last Save operation, an Office program will always prompt you to save so that you do not lose any new data.

Objective 6 | Add Document Properties and Print a File

The process of printing a file is similar in all of the Office applications. There are differences in the types of options you can select. For example, in PowerPoint, you have the option of printing the full slide, with each slide printing on a full sheet of paper, or of printing handouts with small pictures of slides on a page.

Activity 1.06 | Adding Document Properties and Printing a File

> **Alert! | Are You Printing or Submitting Your Files Electronically?**
>
> If you are submitting your files electronically only, or have no printer attached, you can still complete this activity. Complete Steps 1-9, and then submit your file electronically as directed by your instructor.

1 In the upper left corner, click the **File tab** to display **Backstage** view. Notice that the **Recent tab** displays.

Because no file was open in PowerPoint, Office applies predictive logic to determine that your most likely action will be to open a PowerPoint presentation that you worked on recently. Thus, the Recent tab displays a list of PowerPoint presentations that were recently open on your system.

2 At the top of the **Recent Presentations** list, click your **Lastname_Firstname_1A_Menu_Plan** file to open it.

3 Click the **File tab** to redisplay **Backstage** view. On the right, under the screen thumbnail, click **Properties**, and then click **Show Document Panel**. In the **Author** box, delete the existing text, and then type your firstname and lastname. Notice that in PowerPoint, some variation of the slide title is automatically inserted in the Title box. In the **Subject** box, type your Course name and section number. In the **Keywords** box, type **menu plan** and then in the upper right corner of the **Document Properties** panel, click the **Close the Document Information Panel** button ☒.

Adding properties to your documents will make them easier to search for in systems such as Microsoft SharePoint.

> **Another Way**
>
> Press Ctrl + P or Ctrl + F2 to display the Print tab in Backstage view.

4 Redisplay **Backstage** view, and then click the **Print tab**. Compare your screen with Figure 1.24.

On the Print tab in Backstage view, in the center panel, three groups of printing-related tasks display—Print, Printer, and Settings. In the right panel, the *Print Preview* displays, which is a view of a document as it will appear on the paper when you print it.

At the bottom of the Print Preview area, on the left, the number of pages and arrows with which you can move among the pages in Print Preview display. On the right, *Zoom* settings enable you to shrink or enlarge the Print Preview. Zoom is the action of increasing or decreasing the viewing area of the screen.

Figure 1.24

Your default printer (yours may differ)

Three groups of printing-related tasks: *Print, Printer, Settings*

Print tab selected in Backstage view

Print Preview (yours may display in shades of gray if a non-color printer is attached)

Color (yours may differ if a non-color printer is attached)

Zoom tools

Page navigation arrows

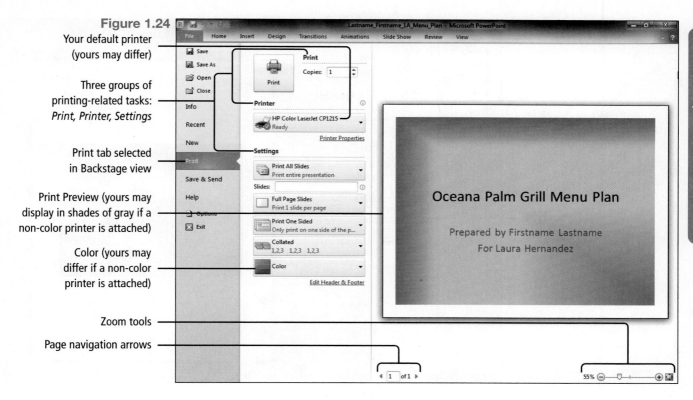

5 Locate the **Settings group**, and notice that the default setting is to **Print All Slides** and to print **Full Page Slides**—each slide on a full sheet of paper.

6 Point to **Full Page Slides**, notice that the button glows orange, and then click the button to display a gallery of print arrangements. Compare your screen with Figure 1.25.

Figure 1.25

Gallery of possible print arrangements

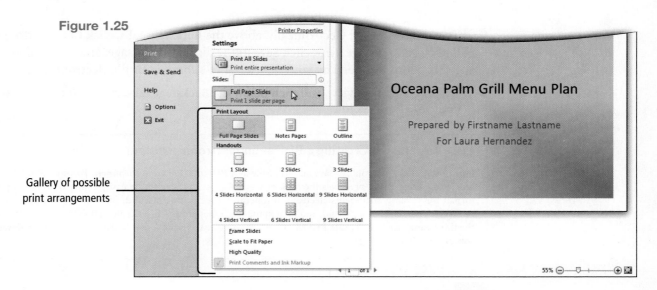

7 In the displayed gallery, under **Handouts**, click **1 Slide**, and then compare your screen with Figure 1.26.

The Print Preview changes to show how your slide will print on the paper in this arrangement.

Figure 1.26

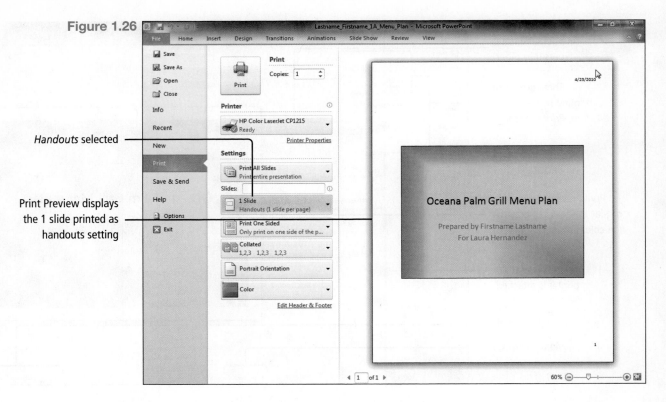

Handouts selected ——

Print Preview displays
the 1 slide printed as
handouts setting

---

8 To submit your file electronically, skip this step and move to Step 9. To print your slide, be sure your system is connected to a printer, and then in the **Print group**, click the **Print** button. On the Quick Access Toolbar, click **Save** 🔲, and then move to Step 10.

> The handout will print on your default printer—on a black and white printer, the colors will print in shades of gray. Backstage view closes and your file redisplays in the PowerPoint window.

9 To submit your file electronically, above the **Backstage tabs**, click **Close** to close the file and close **Backstage** view, click **Save** in the displayed message, and then follow the instructions provided by your instructor to submit your file electronically.

Another Way

In the upper right corner of your PowerPoint window, click the red Close button.

10 Display **Backstage** view, and then below the **Backstage tabs**, click **Exit** to close your file and close PowerPoint.

More Knowledge | Creating a PDF as an Electronic Printout

From Backstage view, you can save an Office file as a **PDF file**. **Portable Document Format** (PDF) creates an image of your file that preserves the look of your file, but that cannot be easily changed. This is a popular format for sending documents electronically, because the document will display on most computers. From Backstage view, click Save & Send, and then in the File Types group, click Create PDF/XPS Document. Then in the third panel, click the Create PDF/XPS button, navigate to your chapter folder, and then in the lower right corner, click Publish.

End You have completed Project 1A ————————————————

Project 1B Word File

myitlab
Project 1B Training

Project Activities

In Activities 1.07 through 1.16, you will open, edit, save, and then compress a Word file. Your completed document will look similar to Figure 1.27.

Project Files

For Project 1B, you will need the following file:

cf01B_Cheese_Promotion

You will save your Word document as:

Lastname_Firstname_1B_Cheese_Promotion

Project Results

Memo

TO:	Laura Mabry Hernandez, General Manager
FROM:	Donna Jackson, Executive Chef
DATE:	December 17, 2014
SUBJECT:	Cheese Specials on Tuesdays

To increase restaurant traffic between 4:00 p.m. and 6:00 p.m., I am proposing a trial cheese event in one of the restaurants, probably Orlando. I would like to try a weekly event on Tuesday evenings where the focus is on a good selection of cheese.

I envision two possibilities: a selection of cheese plates or a cheese bar—or both. The cheeses would have to be matched with compatible fruit and bread or crackers. They could be used as appetizers, or for desserts, as is common in Europe. The cheese plates should be varied and diverse, using a mixture of hard and soft, sharp and mild, unusual and familiar.

I am excited about this new promotion. If done properly, I think it could increase restaurant traffic in the hours when individuals want to relax with a small snack instead of a heavy dinner.

The promotion will require that our employees become familiar with the types and characteristics of both foreign and domestic cheeses. Let's meet to discuss the details and the training requirements, and to create a flyer that begins something like this:

Oceana Palm Grill Tuesday Cheese Tastings

Lastname_Firstname_1B_Cheese_Promotion

Figure 1.27
Project 1B Cheese Promotion

Objective 7 | Open an Existing File and Save It with a New Name

In any Office program, use the Open command to display the **Open dialog box**, from which you can navigate to and then open an existing file that was created in that same program.

The Open dialog box, along with the Save and Save As dialog boxes, are referred to as **common dialog boxes**. These dialog boxes, which are provided by the Windows programming interface, display in all of the Office programs in the same manner. Thus, the Open, Save, and Save As dialog boxes will all look and perform the same in each Office program.

Activity 1.07 | Opening an Existing File and Saving it with a New Name

In this activity, you will display the Open dialog box, open an existing Word document, and then save it in your storage location with a new name.

1 Determine the location of the student data files that accompany this textbook, and be sure you can access these files.

For example:

If you are accessing the files from the Student CD that came with this textbook, insert the CD now.

If you copied the files from the Student CD or from the Pearson Web site to a USB flash drive that you are using for this course, insert the flash drive in your computer now.

If you copied the files to the hard drive of your computer, for example in your Documents library, be sure you can locate the files on the hard drive.

2 Determine the location of your **Common Features Chapter 1** folder you created in Activity 1.05, in which you will store your work from this chapter, and then be sure you can access that folder.

For example:

If you created your chapter folder on a USB flash drive, insert the flash drive in your computer now. This can be the same flash drive where you have stored the student data files; just be sure to use the chapter folder you created.

If you created your chapter folder in the Documents library on your computer, be sure you can locate the folder. Otherwise, create a new folder at the computer at which you are working, or on a USB flash drive.

3 Using the technique you practiced in Activity 1.02, locate and then start the **Microsoft Word 2010** program on your system.

Another Way

In the Word (or other program) window, press Ctrl + F12 to display the Open dialog box.

4 On the Ribbon, click the **File tab** to display **Backstage** view, and then click **Open** to display the **Open** dialog box.

5 In the **navigation pane** on the left, use the scroll bar to scroll as necessary, and then click the location of your student data files to display the location's contents in the **file list**. Compare your screen with Figure 1.28.

For example:

If you are accessing the files from the Student CD that came with your book, under Computer, click the CD/DVD.

If you are accessing the files from a USB flash drive, under Computer, click the flash drive name.

If you are accessing the files from the Documents library of your computer, under Libraries, click Documents.

Figure 1.28

Open dialog box

Scroll bar in
navigation pane

Navigation pane

CD/DVD selected
(or location of your
student files)

Another Way

Point to a folder name,
right-click, and then
from the shortcut
menu, click Open.

6 Point to the folder **01_student_data_files** and double-click to open the folder. Point to the subfolder **01_common_features**, double-click, and then compare your screen with Figure 1.29.

Figure 1.29

File list displays
the contents of the
01_common_features folder

Another Way

Click one time to select
the file, and then press
Enter or click the Open
button in the lower
right corner of the
dialog box.

7 In the **file list**, point to the **chapter_01** subfolder and double-click to open it. In the **file list**, point to Word file **cf01B_Cheese_Promotion** and then double-click to open and display the file in the Word window. On the Ribbon, on the **Home tab**, in the **Paragraph group**, if necessary, click the **Show/Hide** button ¶ so that it is active—glowing orange. Compare your screen with Figure 1.30.

On the title bar at the top of the screen, the file name displays. If you opened the document from the Student CD, (*Read-Only*) will display. If you opened the document from another source to which the files were copied, (*Read-Only*) might not display. ***Read-Only*** is a property assigned to a file that prevents the file from being modified or deleted; it indicates that you cannot save any changes to the displayed document unless you first save it with a new name.

Figure 1.30

File name displays in the
title bar (*Read-only* will
display if opened from
the CD)

Show/Hide button active

Word document displays
in the Word window

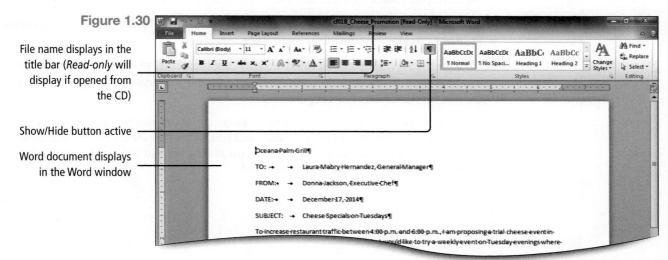

Alert! | Do You See a Message to Enable Editing or Enable Content?

In Office 2010, some files open in *Protected View* if the file appears to be from a potentially risky location, such as the Internet. Protected View is a new security feature in Office 2010 that protects your computer from malicious files by opening them in a restricted environment until you enable them. *Trusted Documents* is another security feature that remembers which files you have already enabled. You might encounter these security features if you open a file from an e-mail or download files from the Internet; for example, from your college's learning management system or from the Pearson Web site. So long as you trust the source of the file, click Enable Editing or Enable Content—depending on the type of file you receive—and then go ahead and work with the file.

Another Way
Press F12 to display the Save As dialog box.

8 Click the **File tab** to display **Backstage** view, and then click the **Save As** command to display the **Save As** dialog box. Compare your screen with Figure 1.31.

The Save As command displays the Save As dialog box where you can name and save a *new* document based on the currently displayed document. After you name and save the new document, the original document closes, and the new document—based on the original one—displays.

Figure 1.31

Save As dialog box

Navigation pane

Current file name selected

Default type is *Word Document*

9 In the **navigation pane**, click the location in which you are storing your projects for this chapter—the location where you created your **Common Features Chapter 1** folder; for example, your USB flash drive or the Documents library.

10 In the **file list**, double-click the necessary folders and subfolders until your **Common Features Chapter 1** folder displays in the **address bar**.

11 Click in the **File name** box to select the existing file name, or drag to select the existing text, and then using your own name, type **Lastname_Firstname_1B_Cheese_Promotion** Compare your screen with Figure 1.32.

As you type, the file name from your 1A project might display briefly. Because your 1A project file is stored in this location and you began the new file name with the same text, Office predicts that you might want the same or similar file name. As you type new characters, the suggestion is removed.

Figure 1.32

Your folder name in
address bar

File name box displays
your new file name

Save button

12 In the lower right corner of the **Save As** dialog box, click **Save**; or press Enter. Compare your screen with Figure 1.33.

The original document closes, and your new document, based on the original, displays with the name in the title bar.

Figure 1.33

New document
name in title bar

Insertion point at
beginning of document

Objective 8 | Explore Options for an Application

Within each Office application, you can open an *Options dialog box* where you can select program settings and other options and preferences. For example, you can set preferences for viewing and editing files.

Activity 1.08 | Viewing Application Options

1 Click the **File tab** to display **Backstage** view. Under the **Help tab**, click **Options**.

2 In the displayed **Word Options** dialog box, on the left, click **Display**, and then on the right, locate the information under **Always show these formatting marks on the screen**.

When you press Enter, Spacebar, or Tab on your keyboard, characters display to represent these keystrokes. These screen characters do not print, and are referred to as *formatting marks* or *nonprinting characters*.

3 Under **Always show these formatting marks on the screen**, be sure the last check box, **Show all formatting marks**, is selected—select it if necessary. Compare your screen with Figure 1.34.

Figure 1.34

Word Options dialog box

Display selected

Information about formatting marks

Check box selected

4 In the lower right corner of the dialog box, click **OK**.

Objective 9 | Perform Commands from the Ribbon

The ***Ribbon***, which displays across the top of the program window, groups commands and features in a manner that you would most logically use them. Each Office program's Ribbon is slightly different, but all contain the same three elements: ***tabs***, ***groups***, and ***commands***.

Tabs display across the top of the Ribbon, and each tab relates to a type of activity; for example, laying out a page. Groups are sets of related commands for specific tasks. Commands—instructions to computer programs—are arranged in groups, and might display as a button, a menu, or a box in which you type information.

You can also minimize the Ribbon so only the tab names display. In the minimized Ribbon view, when you click a tab the Ribbon expands to show the groups and commands, and then when you click a command, the Ribbon returns to its minimized view. Most Office users, however, prefer to leave the complete Ribbon in view at all times.

Activity 1.09 | Performing Commands from the Ribbon

1 Take a moment to examine the document on your screen.

This document is a memo from the Executive Chef to the General Manager regarding a new restaurant promotion.

2 On the Ribbon, click the **View tab**. In the **Show group**, if necessary, click to place a check mark in the **Ruler** check box, and then compare your screen with Figure 1.35.

> When working in Word, display the rulers so that you can see how margin settings affect your document and how text aligns. Additionally, if you set a tab stop or an indent, its location is visible on the ruler.

Figure 1.35

Quick Access Toolbar

Ruler selected

Button to minimize Ribbon

Rulers

3 On the Ribbon, click the **Home tab**. In the **Paragraph group**, if necessary, click the **Show/Hide** button [¶] so that it glows orange and formatting marks display in your document. Point to the button to display information about the button, and then compare your screen with Figure 1.36.

> When the Show/Hide button is active—glowing orange—formatting marks display. Because formatting marks guide your eye in a document—like a map and road signs guide you along a highway—these marks will display throughout this instruction. Many expert Word users keep these marks displayed while creating documents.

Figure 1.36

Show/Hide button glows orange

Paragraph group

ScreenTip for Show/Hide button

Paragraph mark

Tab mark

4 In the upper left corner of your screen, above the Ribbon, locate the **Quick Access Toolbar**.

> The *Quick Access Toolbar* contains commands that you use frequently. By default, only the commands Save, Undo, and Redo display, but you can add and delete commands to suit your needs. Possibly the computer at which you are working already has additional commands added to the Quick Access Toolbar.

5 At the end of the Quick Access Toolbar, click the **Customize Quick Access Toolbar** button [▾].

6 Compare your screen with Figure 1.37.

A list of commands that Office users commonly add to their Quick Access Toolbar displays, including *Open*, *E-mail*, and *Print Preview and Print*. Commands already on the Quick Access Toolbar display a check mark. Commands that you add to the Quick Access Toolbar are always just one click away.

Here you can also display the More Commands dialog box, from which you can select any command from any tab to add to the Quick Access Toolbar.

Figure 1.37

Customize Quick Access Toolbar

Popular commands to add

Existing commands checked

Displays *More Commands* dialog box

Another Way

Right-click any command on the Ribbon, and then on the shortcut menu, click Add to Quick Access Toolbar.

7 On the displayed list, click **Print Preview and Print**, and then notice that the icon is added to the **Quick Access Toolbar**. Compare your screen with Figure 1.38.

The icon that represents the Print Preview command displays on the Quick Access Toolbar. Because this is a command that you will use frequently while building Office documents, you might decide to have this command remain on your Quick Access Toolbar.

Figure 1.38

Icon for Print Preview command added to Quick Access Toolbar

8 In the first line of the document, be sure your insertion point is blinking to the left of the *O* in *Oceana*. Press Enter one time to insert a blank paragraph, and then click to the left of the new paragraph mark (¶) in the new line.

The ***paragraph symbol*** is a formatting mark that displays each time you press Enter.

9 On the Ribbon, click the **Insert tab**. In the **Illustrations group**, point to the **Clip Art** button to display its ScreenTip.

Many buttons on the Ribbon have this type of ***enhanced ScreenTip***, which displays more descriptive text than a normal ScreenTip.

10 Click the **Clip Art** button.

The Clip Art ***task pane*** displays. A task pane is a window within a Microsoft Office application that enables you to enter options for completing a command.

11 In the **Clip Art** task pane, click in the **Search for** box, delete any existing text, and then type **cheese grapes** Under **Results should be:**, click the arrow at the right, if necessary click to *clear* the check mark for **All media types** so that no check boxes are selected, and then click the check box for **Illustrations**. Compare your screen with Figure 1.39.

Figure 1.39

Search term

Blank paragraph

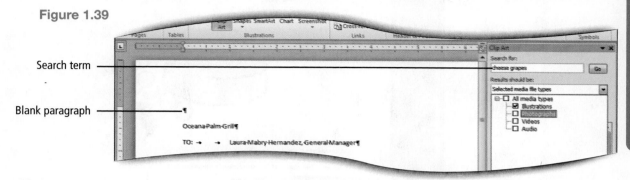

12 Click the **Results should be arrow** again to close the list, and then if necessary, click to place a check mark in the **Include Office.com content** check box.

By selecting this check box, the search for clip art images will include those from Microsoft's online collections of clip art at www.office.com.

13 At the top of the **Clip Art** task pane, click **Go**. Wait a moment for clips to display, and then locate the clip indicated in Figure 1.40.

Figure 1.40

Check box selected

Locate this image

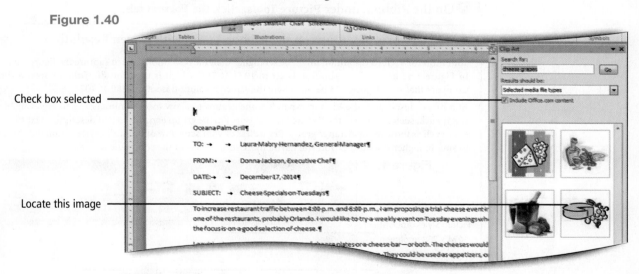

14 Click the image indicated in Figure 1.40 one time to insert it at the insertion point, and then in the upper right corner of the **Clip Art** task pane, click the **Close** ✕ button.

Alert! | If You Cannot Locate the Image

If the image shown in Figure 1.40 is unavailable, select a different cheese image that is appropriate.

---

15 With the image selected—surrounded by a border—on the Ribbon, click the **Home tab**, and then in the **Paragraph group**, click the **Center** button ☰. Click anywhere outside of the bordered picture to *deselect*—cancel the selection. Compare your screen with Figure 1.41.

Figure 1.41

Center button

Image inserted in
document and
centered horizontally

16 Point to the inserted clip art image, and then watch the last tab of the Ribbon as you click the image one time to select it.

> The *Picture Tools* display and an additional tab—the *Format* tab—is added to the Ribbon. The Ribbon adapts to your work and will display additional tabs—referred to as *contextual tabs*—when you need them.

17 On the Ribbon, under **Picture Tools**, click the **Format tab**.

Alert! | The Size of Groups on the Ribbon Varies with Screen Resolution

Your monitor's screen resolution might be set higher than the resolution used to capture the figures in this book. In Figure 1.42 below, the resolution is set to 1024 × 768, which is used for all of the figures in this book. Compare that with Figure 1.43 below, where the screen resolution is set to 1280 × 1024.

At a higher resolution, the Ribbon expands some groups to show more commands than are available with a single click, such as those in the Picture Styles group. Or, the group expands to add descriptive text to some buttons, such as those in the Arrange group. Regardless of your screen resolution, all Office commands are available to you. In higher resolutions, you will have a more robust view of the commands.

Figure 1.42

Picture Styles group at
1024 x 768 resolution

Arrange group at
1024 x 768 resolution

Figure 1.43

More styles show

Picture Styles at
1280 x 1024

Arrange group at
1280 x 1024

Expanded buttons

18 In the **Picture Styles group**, point to the first style to display the ScreenTip *Simple Frame, White*, and notice that the image displays with a white frame.

19 Watch the image as you point to the second picture style, and then to the third, and then to the fourth.

This is ***Live Preview***, a technology that shows the result of applying an editing or formatting change as you point to possible results—*before* you actually apply it.

20 In the **Picture Styles group**, click the fourth style—**Drop Shadow Rectangle**—and then click anywhere outside of the image to deselect it. Notice that the Picture Tools no longer display on the Ribbon. Compare your screen with Figure 1.44.

Contextual tabs display only when you need them.

Figure 1.44

Picture Tools no longer display on the Ribbon

Drop Shadow Rectangle picture style applied to image

21 In the upper left corner of your screen, on the Quick Access Toolbar, click the **Save** button 🖫 to save the changes you have made.

Activity 1.10 | Minimizing and Using the Keyboard to Control the Ribbon

Instead of a mouse, some individuals prefer to navigate the Ribbon by using keys on the keyboard. You can activate keyboard control of the Ribbon by pressing the Alt key. You can also minimize the Ribbon to maximize your available screen space.

1 On your keyboard, press the Alt key, and then on the Ribbon, notice that small labels display. Press N to activate the commands on the **Insert tab**, and then compare your screen with Figure 1.45.

Each label represents a ***KeyTip***—an indication of the key that you can press to activate the command. For example, on the Insert tab, you can press F to activate the Clip Art task pane.

Figure 1.45

KeyTips indicate that
keyboard control
of the Ribbon is active

2 Press [Esc] to redisplay the KeyTips for the tabs. Then, press [Alt] again to turn off keyboard control of the Ribbon.

3 Point to any tab on the Ribbon and right-click to display a shortcut menu.

Here you can choose to display the Quick Access Toolbar below the Ribbon or minimize the Ribbon to maximize screen space. You can also customize the Ribbon by adding, removing, renaming, or reordering tabs, groups, and commands on the Ribbon, although this is not recommended until you become an expert Office user.

Another Way

Double-click the active tab; or, click the Minimize the Ribbon button at the right end of the Ribbon.

4 Click **Minimize the Ribbon**. Notice that only the Ribbon tabs display. Click the **Home tab** to display the commands. Click anywhere in the document, and notice that the Ribbon reverts to its minimized view.

Another Way

Double-click any tab to redisplay the full Ribbon.

5 Right-click any Ribbon tab, and then click **Minimize the Ribbon** again to turn the minimize feature off.

Most expert Office users prefer to have the full Ribbon display at all times.

6 Point to any tab on the Ribbon, and then on your mouse device, roll the mouse wheel. Notice that different tabs become active as your roll the mouse wheel.

You can make a tab active by using this technique, instead of clicking the tab.

Objective 10 | Apply Formatting in Office Programs

Formatting is the process of establishing the overall appearance of text, graphics, and pages in an Office file—for example, in a Word document.

Activity 1.11 | Formatting and Viewing Pages

In this activity, you will practice common formatting techniques used in Office applications.

1 On the Ribbon, click the **Insert tab**, and then in the **Header & Footer group**, click the **Footer** button.

Another Way
On the Design tab, in the Insert group, click Quick Parts, click Field, and then under Field names, click FileName.

2 At the top of the displayed gallery, under **Built-In**, click **Blank**. At the bottom of your document, with *Type text* highlighted in blue, using your own name type the file name of this document **Lastname_Firstname_1B_Cheese_Promotion** and then compare your screen with Figure 1.46.

Header & Footer Tools are added to the Ribbon. A ***footer*** is a reserved area for text or graphics that displays at the bottom of each page in a document. Likewise, a ***header*** is a reserved area for text or graphics that displays at the top of each page in a document. When the footer (or header) area is active, the document area is inactive (dimmed).

Figure 1.46

Design tab added

Header & Footer Tools active

Document area inactive (dimmed) when footer area is active

Close Header and Footer button

Your file name

Footer area displays

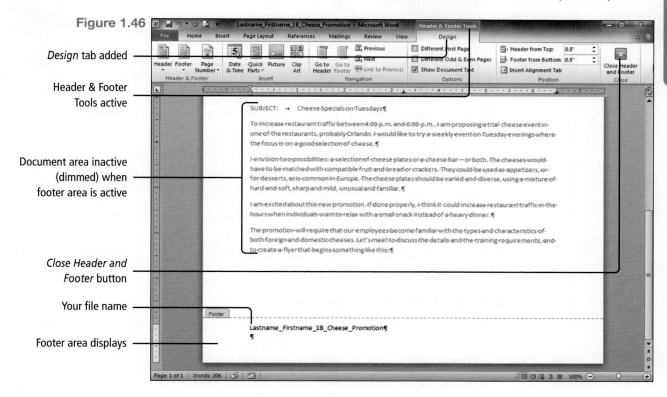

3 On the Ribbon, on the **Design tab**, in the **Close group**, click the **Close Header and Footer** button.

4 On the Ribbon, click the **Page Layout tab**. In the **Page Setup group**, click the **Orientation** button, and notice that two orientations display—*Portrait* and *Landscape*. Click **Landscape**.

In ***portrait orientation***, the paper is taller than it is wide. In ***landscape orientation***, the paper is wider than it is tall.

5 In the lower right corner of the screen, locate the **Zoom control** buttons.

To ***zoom*** means to increase or decrease the viewing area. You can zoom in to look closely at a section of a document, and then zoom out to see an entire page on the screen. You can also zoom to view multiple pages on the screen.

6 Drag the **Zoom slider** to the left until you have zoomed to approximately *60%*. Compare your screen with Figure 1.47.

Figure 1.47

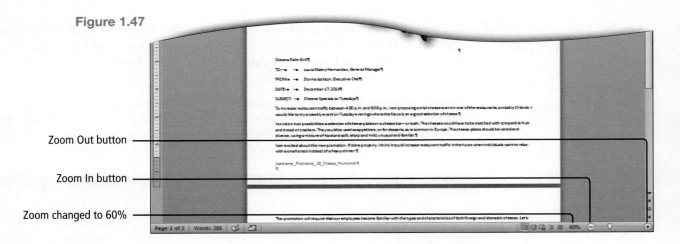

Zoom Out button

Zoom In button

Zoom changed to 60%

7 On the **Page Layout tab**, in the **Page Setup group**, click the **Orientation** button, and then click **Portrait**.

Portrait orientation is commonly used for business documents such as letters and memos.

8 In the lower right corner of your screen, click the **Zoom In** button ⊕ as many times as necessary to return to the **100%** zoom setting.

Use the zoom feature to adjust the view of your document for editing and for your viewing comfort.

9 On the Quick Access Toolbar, click the **Save** button 🖫 to save the changes you have made to your document.

Activity 1.12 | Formatting Text

1 To the left of *Oceana Palm Grill*, point in the margin area to display the 🔏 pointer and click one time to select the entire paragraph. Compare your screen with Figure 1.48.

Use this technique to select complete paragraphs from the margin area. Additionally, with this technique you can drag downward to select multiple-line paragraphs—which is faster and more efficient than dragging through text.

Figure 1.48

Paragraph selected

2 On the Ribbon, click the **Home tab**, and then in the **Paragraph group**, click the **Center** button ▤ to center the paragraph.

Alignment refers to the placement of paragraph text relative to the left and right margins. *Center alignment* refers to text that is centered horizontally between the left and right margins. You can also align text at the left margin, which is the default alignment for text in Word, or at the right margin.

3 On the **Home tab**, in the **Font group**, click the **Font button arrow** [Calibri (Body) ▾]. At the top of the list, point to **Cambria**, and as you do so, notice that the selected text previews in the Cambria font.

> A *font* is a set of characters with the same design and shape. The default font in a Word document is Calibri, which is a *sans serif* font—a font design with no lines or extensions on the ends of characters.
>
> The Cambria font is a *serif* font—a font design that includes small line extensions on the ends of the letters to guide the eye in reading from left to right.
>
> The list of fonts displays as a gallery showing potential results. For example, in the Font gallery, you can see the actual design and format of each font as it would look if applied to text.

4 Point to several other fonts and observe the effect on the selected text. Then, at the top of the **Font** gallery, under **Theme Fonts**, click **Cambria**.

> A *theme* is a predesigned set of colors, fonts, lines, and fill effects that look good together and that can be applied to your entire document or to specific items.
>
> A theme combines two sets of fonts—one for text and one for headings. In the default Office theme, Cambria is the suggested font for headings.

5 With the paragraph *Oceana Palm Grill* still selected, on the **Home tab**, in the **Font group**, click the **Font Size button arrow** [11 ▾], point to **36**, and then notice how Live Preview displays the text in the font size to which you are pointing. Compare your screen with Figure 1.49.

Figure 1.49

Font Size button

Font button

Font Size list

Pointing to 36 pt font size

Oceana Palm Grill centered,
Cambria font applied

6 On the displayed list of font sizes, click **20**.

> Fonts are measured in *points*, with one point equal to 1/72 of an inch. A higher point size indicates a larger font size. Headings and titles are often formatted by using a larger font size. The word *point* is abbreviated as *pt*.

7 With *Oceana Palm Grill* still selected, on the **Home tab**, in the **Font group**, click the **Font Color button arrow** [A ▾]. Under **Theme Colors**, in the seventh column, click the last color—**Olive Green, Accent 3, Darker 50%**. Click anywhere to deselect the text.

8 To the left of *TO:*, point in the left margin area to display the 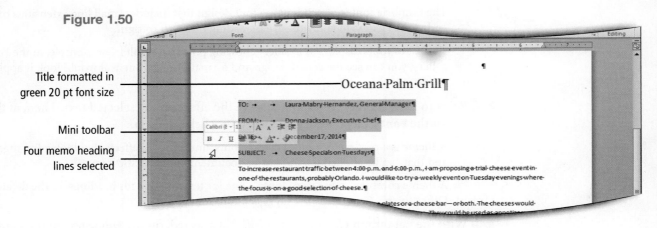 pointer, hold down the left mouse button, and then drag down to select the four memo headings. Compare your screen with Figure 1.50.

> Use this technique to select complete paragraphs from the margin area—dragging downward to select multiple-line paragraphs—which is faster and more efficient than dragging through text.

Figure 1.50

Title formatted in green 20 pt font size

Mini toolbar

Four memo heading lines selected

Oceana·Palm·Grill¶

TO: → → Laura·Mabry·Hernandez,·General·Manager¶
FROM: → → Donna·Jackson,·Executive·Chef¶
DATE: → → December·17,·2014¶
SUBJECT: → Cheese·Specials·on·Tuesdays¶

To·increase·restaurant·traffic·between·4:00·p.m.·and·6:00·p.m.,·I·am·proposing·a·trial·cheese·event·in·one·of·the·restaurants,·probably·Orlando.·I·would·like·to·try·a·weekly·event·on·Tuesday·evenings·where·the·focus·is·on·a·good·selection·of·cheese.¶

9 With the four paragraphs selected, on the Mini toolbar, click the **Font Color** button, which now displays a dark green bar instead of a red bar.

> The font color button retains its most recently used color—Olive Green, Accent 3, Darker 50%. As you progress in your study of Microsoft Office, you will use other buttons that behave in this manner; that is, they retain their most recently used format.

> The purpose of the Mini toolbar is to place commonly used commands close to text or objects that you select. By selecting a command on the Mini toolbar, you reduce the distance that you must move your mouse to access a command.

10 Click anywhere in the paragraph that begins *To increase*, and then ***triple-click***—click the left mouse button three times—to select the entire paragraph. If the entire paragraph is not selected, click in the paragraph and begin again.

11 With the entire paragraph selected, on the Mini toolbar, click the **Font Color button arrow**, and then under **Theme Colors**, in the sixth column, click the first color—**Red, Accent 2**.

> It is convenient to have commonly used commands display on the Mini toolbar so that you do not have to move your mouse to the top of the screen to access the command from the Ribbon.

12 Select the text *TO:* and then on the displayed Mini toolbar, click the **Bold** button **B** and the **Italic** button *I*.

> ***Font styles*** include bold, italic, and underline. Font styles emphasize text and are a visual cue to draw the reader's eye to important text.

13 On the displayed Mini toolbar, click the **Italic** button *I* again to turn off the Italic formatting. Notice that the Italic button no longer glows orange.

> A button that behaves in this manner is referred to as a ***toggle button***, which means it can be turned on by clicking it once, and then turned off by clicking it again.

14 With *TO:* still selected, on the Mini toolbar, click the **Format Painter** button ![icon]. Then, move your mouse under the word *Laura*, and notice the ![icon] mouse pointer. Compare your screen with Figure 1.51.

> You can use the *Format Painter* to copy the formatting of specific text or of a paragraph and then apply it in other locations in your document.

> The pointer takes the shape of a paintbrush, and contains the formatting information from the paragraph where the insertion point is positioned. Information about the Format Painter and how to turn it off displays in the status bar.

Figure 1.51

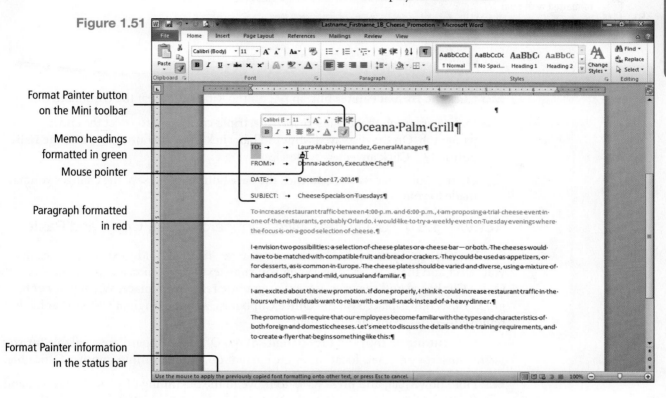

Format Painter button on the Mini toolbar

Memo headings formatted in green

Mouse pointer

Paragraph formatted in red

Format Painter information in the status bar

15 With the ![icon] pointer, drag to select the text *FROM:* and notice that the Bold formatting is applied. Then, point to the selected text *FROM:* and on the Mini toolbar, *double-click* the **Format Painter** button ![icon].

16 Select the text *DATE:* to copy the Bold formatting, and notice that the pointer retains the ![icon] shape.

> When you *double-click* the Format Painter button, the Format Painter feature remains active until you either click the Format Painter button again, or press [Esc] to cancel it—as indicated on the status bar.

17 With Format Painter still active, select the text *SUBJECT:*, and then on the Ribbon, on the **Home tab**, in the **Clipboard group**, notice that the **Format Painter** button ![icon] is glowing orange, indicating that it is active. Compare your screen with Figure 1.52.

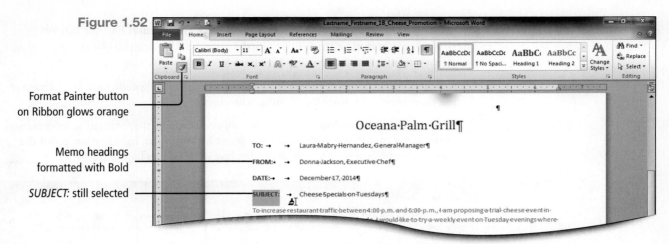

Figure 1.52

Format Painter button on Ribbon glows orange

Memo headings formatted with Bold

SUBJECT: still selected

18 Click the **Format Painter** button on the Ribbon to turn the command off.

19 In the paragraph that begins *To increase*, triple-click again to select the entire paragraph. On the displayed Mini toolbar, click the **Bold** button **B** and the **Italic** button *I*. Click anywhere to deselect.

20 On the Quick Access Toolbar, click the **Save** button to save the changes you have made to your document.

Activity 1.13 | Using the Office Clipboard to Cut, Copy, and Paste

The ***Office Clipboard*** is a temporary storage area that holds text or graphics that you select and then cut or copy. When you ***copy*** text or graphics, a copy is placed on the Office Clipboard and the original text or graphic remains in place. When you ***cut*** text or graphics, a copy is placed on the Office Clipboard, and the original text or graphic is removed—cut—from the document.

After cutting or copying, the contents of the Office Clipboard are available for you to ***paste***—insert—in a new location in the current document, or into another Office file.

1 Hold down Ctrl and press Home to move to the beginning of your document, and then take a moment to study the table in Figure 1.53, which describes similar keyboard shortcuts with which you can navigate quickly in a document.

To Move	Press
To the beginning of a document	Ctrl + Home
To the end of a document	Ctrl + End
To the beginning of a line	Home
To the end of a line	End
To the beginning of the previous word	Ctrl + ←
To the beginning of the next word	Ctrl + →
To the beginning of the current word (if insertion point is in the middle of a word)	Ctrl + ←
To the beginning of a paragraph	Ctrl + ↑
To the beginning of the next paragraph	Ctrl + ↓
To the beginning of the current paragraph (if insertion point is in the middle of a paragraph)	Ctrl + ↑
Up one screen	PgUp
Down one screen	PageDown

Figure 1.53

Another Way

Right-click the selection, and then click Copy on the shortcut menu; or, use the keyboard shortcut `Ctrl` + `C`.

2 To the left of *Oceana Palm Grill*, point in the left margin area to display the pointer, and then click one time to select the entire paragraph. On the **Home tab**, in the **Clipboard group**, click the **Copy** button.

Because anything that you select and then copy—or cut—is placed on the Office Clipboard, the Copy command and the Cut command display in the Clipboard group of commands on the Ribbon.

There is no visible indication that your copied selection has been placed on the Office Clipboard.

3 On the **Home tab**, in the **Clipboard group**, to the right of the group name *Clipboard*, click the **Dialog Box Launcher** button, and then compare your screen with Figure 1.54.

The Clipboard task pane displays with your copied text. In any Ribbon group, the *Dialog Box Launcher* displays either a dialog box or a task pane related to the group of commands.

It is not necessary to display the Office Clipboard in this manner, although sometimes it is useful to do so. The Office Clipboard can hold 24 items.

Figure 1.54

Copy button

Dialog Box Launcher in Clipboard group

Clipboard task pane displays

Selected text on the Office Clipboard

4 In the upper right corner of the **Clipboard** task pane, click the **Close** button.

Another Way

Right-click, on the shortcut menu under Paste Options, click the desired option button.

5 Press `Ctrl` + `End` to move to the end of your document. Press `Enter` one time to create a new blank paragraph. On the **Home tab**, in the **Clipboard group**, point to the **Paste** button, and then click the *upper* portion of this split button.

The Paste command pastes the most recently copied item on the Office Clipboard at the insertion point location. If you click the lower portion of the Paste button, a gallery of Paste Options displays.

6 Click the **Paste Options** button ⬚ that displays below the pasted text as shown in Figure 1.55.

> Here you can view and apply various formatting options for pasting your copied or cut text. Typically you will click Paste on the Ribbon and paste the item in its original format. If you want some other format for the pasted item, you can do so from the *Paste Options gallery*.

> The Paste Options gallery provides a Live Preview of the various options for changing the format of the pasted item with a single click. The Paste Options gallery is available in three places: on the Ribbon by clicking the lower portion of the Paste button—the Paste button arrow; from the Paste Options button that displays below the pasted item following the paste operation; or, on the shortcut menu if you right-click the pasted item.

Figure 1.55

Upper portion of Paste button

Paste button arrow on the Ribbon

Pasted text

Paste Options button

Paste Options gallery

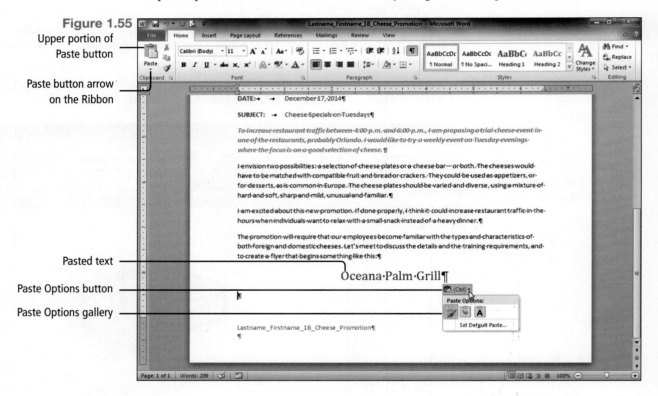

7 In the displayed **Paste Options** gallery, *point* to each option to see the Live Preview of the format that would be applied if you clicked the button.

> The contents of the Paste Options gallery are contextual; that is, they change based on what you copied and where you are pasting.

8 Press Esc to close the gallery; the button will remain displayed until you take some other screen action.

Another Way

On the Home tab, in the Clipboard group, click the Cut button; or, use the keyboard shortcut Ctrl + X.

9 Press Ctrl + Home to move to the top of the document, and then click the **cheese image** one time to select it. While pointing to the selected image, right-click, and then on the shortcut menu, click **Cut**.

> Recall that the Cut command cuts—removes—the selection from the document and places it on the Office Clipboard.

10 Press Del one time to remove the blank paragraph from the top of the document, and then press Ctrl + End to move to the end of the document.

11 With the insertion point blinking in the blank paragraph at the end of the document, right-click, and notice that the **Paste Options** gallery displays on the shortcut menu. Compare your screen with Figure 1.56.

Figure 1.56

Paste Options on shortcut menu

12 On the shortcut menu, under **Paste Options**, click the first button—**Keep Source Formatting**.

13 Click the picture to select it. On the **Home tab**, in the **Paragraph group**, click the **Center** button.

14 Above the cheese picture, click to position the insertion point at the end of the word *Grill*, press Spacebar one time, and then type **Tuesday Cheese Tastings** Compare your screen with Figure 1.57.

Figure 1.57

Heading

Picture inserted and centered

Activity 1.14 | Viewing Print Preview and Printing a Word Document

1 Press Ctrl + Home to move to the top of your document. Select the text *Oceana Palm Grill*, and then replace the selected text by typing **Memo**

2 Display **Backstage** view, on the right, click **Properties**, and then click **Show Document Panel**. Replace the existing author name with your first and last name. In the **Subject** box, type your course name and section number, and then in the **Keywords** box, type **cheese promotion** and then **Close** the **Document Information Panel**.

Another Way
Press Ctrl + F2 to display Print Preview.

3 On the Quick Access Toolbar, click **Save** 💾 to save the changes you have made to your document.

4 On the Quick Access Toolbar, click the **Print Preview** button 🔍 that you added. Compare your screen with Figure 1.58.

Figure 1.58

Memo typed

If no printer is attached to your system, OneNote is the default printer

Print tab active in Backstage view

Print Preview (if you have a non-color printer as your default printer, the preview may display in shades of gray)

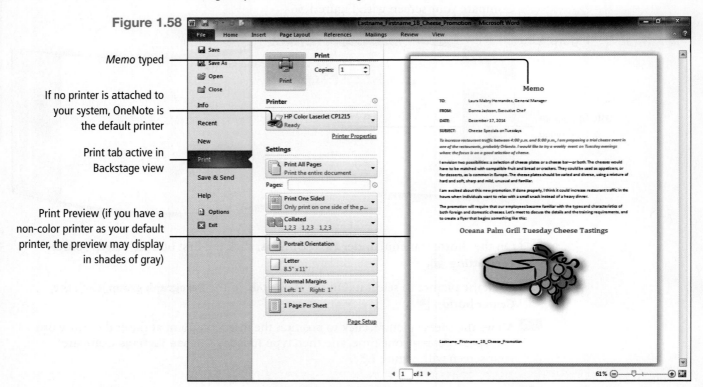

5 Examine the **Print Preview**. Under **Settings**, notice that in **Backstage** view, several of the same commands that are available on the Page Layout tab of the Ribbon also display.

> For convenience, common adjustments to Page Layout display here, so that you can make last-minute adjustments without closing Backstage view.

6 If you need to make any corrections, click the Home tab to return to the document and make any necessary changes.

> It is good practice to examine the Print Preview before printing or submitting your work electronically. Then, make any necessary corrections, re-save, and redisplay Print Preview.

7 If you are directed to do so, click Print to print the document; or, above the Info tab, click Close, and then submit your file electronically according to the directions provided by your instructor.

> If you click the Print button, Backstage view closes and the Word window redisplays.

8 On the Quick Access Toolbar, point to the **Print Preview icon** 🔍 you placed there, right-click, and then click **Remove from Quick Access Toolbar**.

> If you are working on your own computer and you want to do so, you can leave the icon on the toolbar; in a lab setting, you should return the software to its original settings.

9 At the right end of the title bar, click the program **Close** button ☒ .

10 If a message displays asking if you want the text on the Clipboard to be available after you quit Word, click **No**.

> This message most often displays if you have copied some type of image to the Clipboard. If you click Yes, the items on the Clipboard will remain for you to use.

Objective 11 | Use the Microsoft Office 2010 Help System

Within each Office program, the Help feature provides information about all of the program's features and displays step-by-step instructions for performing many tasks.

Activity 1.15 | Using the Microsoft Office 2010 Help System in Excel

In this activity, you will use the Microsoft Help feature to find information about formatting numbers in Excel.

> **Another Way**
>
> Press F1 to display Help.

1 **Start** the **Microsoft Excel 2010** program. In the upper right corner of your screen, click the **Microsoft Excel Help** button ❓ .

2 In the **Excel Help** window, click in the white box in upper left corner, type **formatting numbers** and then click **Search** or press Enter .

3 On the list of results, click **Display numbers as currency**. Compare your screen with Figure 1.59.

Figure 1.59

Excel Help window —
Search term —
Print button —
Search button —

Help information —

Excel Help button —

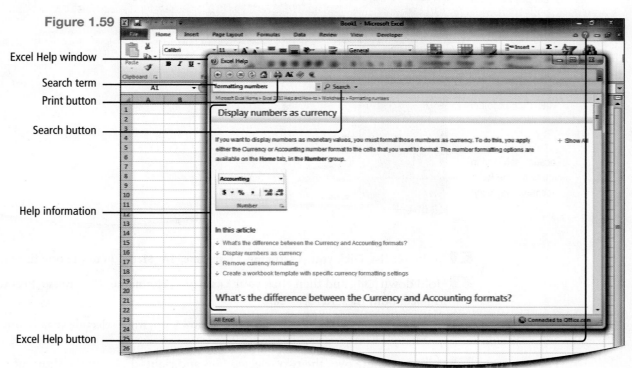

4 If you want to do so, on the toolbar at the top of the **Excel Help** window, click the Print 🖨 button to print a copy of this information for your reference.

5 On the title bar of the Excel Help window, click the **Close** button [×]. On the right side of the Microsoft Excel title bar, click the **Close** button [×] to close Excel.

Objective 12 | Compress Files

A *compressed file* is a file that has been reduced in size. Compressed files take up less storage space and can be transferred to other computers faster than uncompressed files. You can also combine a group of files into one compressed folder, which makes it easier to share a group of files.

Activity 1.16 | Compressing Files

In this activity, you will combine the two files you created in this chapter into one compressed file.

1 On the Windows taskbar, click the **Start** button ⊕, and then on the right, click **Computer**.

2 On the left, in the **navigation pane**, click the location of your two files from this chapter—your USB flash drive or other location—and display the folder window for your **Common Features Chapter 1** folder. Compare your screen with Figure 1.60.

Figure 1.60

Address bar displays path ⎯

Your chapter files in file list (your name displays) ⎯

Folder window for your chapter folder ⎯

Location selected in navigation pane (your location may vary) ⎯

3 In the **file list**, click your **Lastname_Firstname_1A_Menu_Plan** file one time to select it.

4 Hold down [Ctrl], and then click your **Lastname_Firstname_1B_Cheese_Promotion** file to select both files. Release [Ctrl].

In any Windows-based program, holding down [Ctrl] while selecting enables you to select multiple items.

5 Point anywhere over the two selected files and right-click. On the shortcut menu, point to **Send to**, and then compare your screen with Figure 1.61.

Figure 1.61

Two files selected

Send to submenu

Shortcut menu
(yours may vary)

6 On the shortcut submenu, click **Compressed (zipped) folder**.

Windows creates a compressed folder containing a *copy* of each of the selected files. The folder name is the name of the file or folder to which you were pointing, and is selected—highlighted in blue—so that you can rename it.

7 Using your own name, type **Lastname_Firstname_Common_Features_Ch1** and press [Enter].

The compressed folder is now ready to attach to an e-mail or share in some other electronic format.

8 **Close** [✕] the folder window. If directed to do so by your instructor, submit your compressed folder electronically.

More Knowledge | Extracting Compressed Files

Extract means to decompress, or pull out, files from a compressed form. When you extract a file, an uncompressed copy is placed in the folder that you specify. The original file remains in the compressed folder.

End **You have completed Project 1B** ————————————————

Content-Based Assessments

Summary

In this chapter, you used Windows Explorer to navigate the Windows file structure. You also used features that are common across the Microsoft Office 2010 programs.

Key Terms

Address bar 5

Alignment 34

All Programs.......................7

Application 6

AutoPlay 3

Back and Forward buttons 5

Backstage tabs 14

Backstage view 14

Center alignment 34

Click 4

Command 5

Common dialog boxes...............................22

Compressed file 44

Context sensitive command 11

Contextual tabs 30

Copy 38

Cut.....................................38

Default................................9

Deselect 29

Desktop..............................3

Details pane 5

Dialog box.........................11

Dialog Box Launcher 39

Document properties......14

Double-click 5

Drag...................................10

Edit 9

Ellipsis...............................11

Enhanced ScreenTip 28

Extract................................45

File..3

File list..................................5

Fill 12

Folder 3

Folder window 4

Font 35

Font styles 36

Footer 33

Format Painter 37

Formatting 32

Formatting marks.............25

Gallery 12

Groups...............................26

Header................................33

Icons 5

Info tab 14

Insertion point 9

Keyboard shortcut 10

KeyTip 31

Landscape orientation.....................33

Library..................................4

Live Preview 31

Location 13

Metadata............................14

Microsoft Access..............7

Microsoft Excel 7

Microsoft InfoPath............7

Microsoft Office 2010 6

Microsoft OneNote 7

Microsoft Outlook 7

Microsoft PowerPoint 7

Microsoft Publisher 7

Microsoft SharePoint Workspace 7

Microsoft Word.................7

Mini toolbar......................10

Navigate 3

Navigation pane 5

Nonprinting characters.....................25

Office Clipboard 38

Open dialog box 22

Option button 12

Options dialog box..........25

Paragraph symbol 28

Paste 38

Paste Options 40

PDF (Portable Document Format) file 20

Point 4

Pointer.................................9

Points 35

Portrait orientation..........33

Preview pane button 5

Print Preview 18

Program 6

Program-level control buttons 8

Protected View 24

Pt..35

Quick Access Toolbar 27

Quick Commands 14

Read-Only.........................23

Ribbon...............................26

Ribbon tabs 8

Right-click..........................11

Sans serif 35

ScreenTip 12

Scroll bar...........................16

Scroll box 16

Search box 5

Select 10

Serif....................................35

Shortcut menu 11

Split button 5

Start button 4

Start menu 4

Status bar 8

Subfolder 3

Tabs....................................26

Tags......................................5

Task pane 28

Theme 35

Title bar................................8

Toggle button 36

Triple-click 36

Trusted Documents 24

USB flash drive..................6

Views button.......................5

Window 3

Windows Explorer 3

Windows taskbar 4

Zoom 18

Content-Based Assessments

Matching

Match each term in the second column with its correct definition in the first column by writing the letter of the term on the blank line in front of the correct definition.

A Address bar

B Command

C File

D Folder

E Folder window

F Icons

G Keyboard shortcut

H Library

I Microsoft Excel

J Program

K Ribbon

L Start menu

M Subfolder

N Title bar

O Windows Explorer

_____ 1. A collection of information stored on a computer under a single name.

_____ 2. A container in which you store files.

_____ 3. A folder within a folder.

_____ 4. The program that displays the files and folders on your computer.

_____ 5. The Windows menu that is the main gateway to your computer.

_____ 6. In Windows 7, a window that displays the contents of the current folder, library, or device, and contains helpful parts so that you can navigate.

_____ 7. In Windows, a collection of items, such as files and folders, assembled from various locations that might be on your computer.

_____ 8. The bar at the top of a folder window with which you can navigate to a different folder or library, or go back to a previous one.

_____ 9. An instruction to a computer program that carries out an action.

_____ 10. Small pictures that represent a program, a file, a folder, or an object.

_____ 11. A set of instructions that a computer uses to perform a specific task.

_____ 12. A spreadsheet program used to calculate numbers and create charts.

_____ 13. The user interface that groups commands on tabs at the top of the program window.

_____ 14. A bar at the top of the program window displaying the current file and program name.

_____ 15. One or more keys pressed to perform a task that would otherwise require a mouse.

Multiple Choice

Circle the correct answer.

1. A small toolbar with frequently used commands that displays when selecting text or objects is the:
    A. Quick Access Toolbar   B. Mini toolbar   C. Document toolbar

2. In Office 2010, a centralized space for file management tasks is:
    A. a task pane   B. a dialog box   C. Backstage view

3. The commands Save, Save As, Open, and Close in Backstage view are located:
    A. above the Backstage tabs   B. below the Backstage tabs   C. under the screen thumbnail

4. The tab in Backstage view that displays information about the current file is the:
    A. Recent tab   B. Info tab   C. Options tab

5. Details about a file, including the title, author name, subject, and keywords are known as:
    A. document properties   B. formatting marks   C. KeyTips

6. An Office feature that displays a list of potential results is:
    A. Live Preview   B. a contextual tab   C. a gallery

7. A type of formatting emphasis applied to text such as bold, italic, and underline, is called:

A. a font style   **B.** a KeyTip   **C.** a tag

8. A technology showing the result of applying formatting as you point to possible results is called:

A. Live Preview   **B.** Backstage view   **C.** gallery view

9. A temporary storage area that holds text or graphics that you select and then cut or copy is the:

A. paste options gallery   **B.** ribbon   **C.** Office clipboard

10. A file that has been reduced in size is:

A. a compressed file   **B.** an extracted file   **C.** a PDF file

Creating Documents with Microsoft Word 2010

OUTCOMES
At the end of this chapter you will be able to:

OBJECTIVES
Mastering these objectives will enable you to:

PROJECT 1A
Create a flyer with a picture.

1. Create a New Document and Insert Text (p. 51)
2. Insert and Format Graphics (p. 53)
3. Insert and Modify Text Boxes and Shapes (p. 58)
4. Preview and Print a Document (p. 62)

PROJECT 1B
Format text, paragraphs, and documents.

5. Change Document and Paragraph Layout (p. 67)
6. Create and Modify Lists (p. 73)
7. Set and Modify Tab Stops (p. 78)
8. Insert a SmartArt Graphic (p. 80)

Joy Brown/Shutterstock

In This Chapter

In this chapter, you will use Microsoft Word, which is one of the most common programs found on computers and one that almost everyone has a reason to use. You will use many of the new tools found in Word 2010. When you learn word processing, you are also learning skills and techniques that you need to work efficiently on a computer. You can use Microsoft Word to perform basic word processing tasks such as writing a memo, a report, or a letter. You can also use Word to complete complex word processing tasks, such as creating sophisticated tables, embedding graphics, writing blogs, creating publications, and inserting links into other documents and the Internet. Word is a program that you can learn gradually, and then add more advanced skills one at a time.

The projects in this chapter relate to **Laurel College**. The college offers this diverse geographic area a wide range of academic and career programs, including associate degrees, certificate programs, and non-credit continuing education and personal development courses. The college makes positive contributions to the community through cultural and athletic programs and partnerships with businesses and nonprofit organizations. The college also provides industry-specific training programs for local businesses through its growing Economic Development Center.

Project 1A Flyer

Project Activities

In Activities 1.01 through 1.12, you will create a flyer announcing a new rock climbing class offered by the Physical Education Department at Laurel College. Your completed document will look similar to Figure 1.1.

Project Files

For Project 1A, you will need the following files:

New blank Word document
w01A_Fitness_Flyer
w01A_Rock_Climber

You will save your document as:

Lastname_Firstname_1A_Fitness_Flyer

Project Results

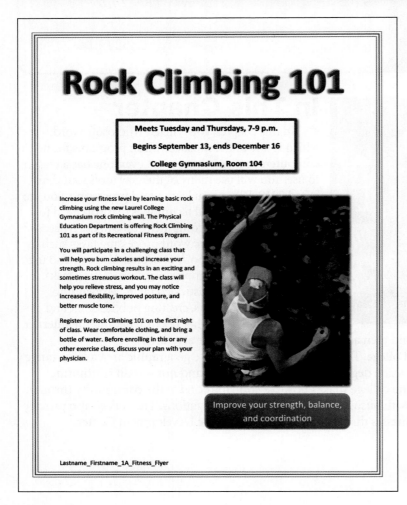

Figure 1.1
Project 1A Fitness Flyer

Objective 1 | Create a New Document and Insert Text

When you create a new document, you can type all of the text, or you can type some of the text and then insert additional text from another source.

Activity 1.01 | Starting a New Word Document and Inserting Text

1 **Start** Word and display a new blank document. On the **Home tab**, in the **Paragraph group**, if necessary click the Show/Hide button ¶ so that it is active (glows orange) to display the formatting marks. If the rulers do not display, click the View tab, and then in the Show group, select the Ruler check box.

2 Type **Rock Climbing 101** and then press [Enter] two times. As you type the following text, press the [Spacebar] only one time at the end of a sentence: **Increase your fitness level by learning basic rock climbing using the new Laurel College Gymnasium rock climbing wall. The Physical Education Department is offering Rock Climbing 101 as part of its Recreational Fitness Program.**

As you type, the insertion point moves to the right, and when it approaches the right margin, Word determines whether the next word in the line will fit within the established right margin. If the word does not fit, Word moves the entire word down to the next line. This feature is called ***wordwrap*** and means that you press [Enter] *only* when you reach the end of a paragraph—it is not necessary to press [Enter] at the end of each line of text.

Note | Spacing Between Sentences

Although you might have learned to add two spaces following end-of-sentence punctuation, the common practice now is to space only one time at the end of a sentence.

---

3 Press [Enter] one time. Take a moment to study the table in Figure 1.2 to become familiar with the default document settings in Microsoft Word, and then compare your screen with Figure 1.3.

When you press [Enter], [Spacebar], or [Tab] on your keyboard, characters display in your document to represent these keystrokes. These characters do not print and are referred to as ***formatting marks*** or ***nonprinting characters***. These marks will display throughout this instruction.

Default Document Settings in a New Word Document

Setting	Default format
Font and font size	The default font is Calibri and the default font size is 11.
Margins	The default left, right, top, and bottom page margins are 1 inch.
Line spacing	The default line spacing is 1.15, which provides slightly more space between lines than single spacing does—an extra 1/6 of a line added between lines than single spacing.
Paragraph spacing	The default spacing after a paragraph is 10 points, which is slightly less than the height of one blank line of text.
View	The default view is Print Layout view, which displays the page borders and displays the document as it will appear when printed.

Figure 1.2

Figure 1.3

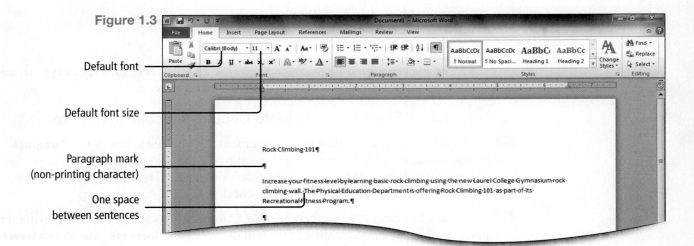

Default font

Default font size

Paragraph mark
(non-printing character)

One space
between sentences

4 On the Ribbon, click the **Insert tab**. In the **Text group**, click the **Object button arrow**, and then click **Text from File**.

Alert! | Does the Object Dialog Box Display?

If the Object dialog box displays, you probably clicked the Object *button* instead of the Object *button arrow*. Close the Object dialog box, and then in the Text group, click the Object button arrow, as shown in Figure 1.4. Click *Text from File*, and then continue with Step 5.

Another Way

Open the file, copy the required text, close the file, and then paste the text into the current document.

5 In the **Insert File** dialog box, navigate to the student files that accompany this textbook, locate and select **w01A_Fitness_Flyer**, and then click **Insert**. Compare your screen with Figure 1.4.

A *copy* of the text from the w01A_Fitness_Flyer file displays at the insertion point location; the text is not removed from the original file.

Figure 1.4

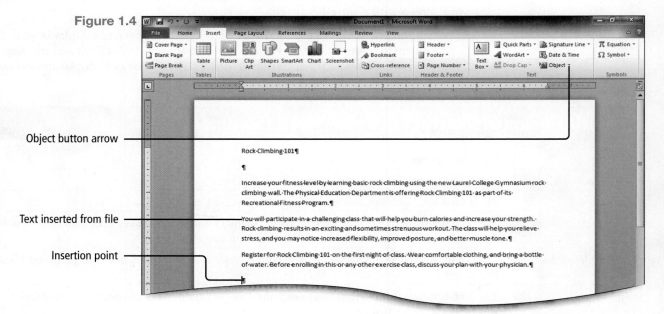

Object button arrow

Text inserted from file

Insertion point

6 On the **Quick Access Toolbar**, click the **Save** button. In the **Save As** dialog box, navigate to the location where you are saving your files for this chapter, and then create and open a new folder named **Word Chapter 1** In the **File name** box, replace the existing text with **Lastname_Firstname_1A_Fitness_Flyer** and then click **Save**.

Objective 2 | Insert and Format Graphics

To add visual interest to a document, insert **graphics**. Graphics include pictures, clip art, charts, and **drawing objects**—shapes, diagrams, lines, and so on. For additional visual interest, you can convert text to an attractive graphic format; add, resize, move, and format pictures; and add an attractive page border.

Activity 1.02 | Formatting Text Using Text Effects

Text effects are decorative formats, such as shadowed or mirrored text, text glow, 3-D effects, and colors that make text stand out.

1 Including the paragraph mark, select the first paragraph of text—*Rock Climbing 101*. On the **Home tab**, in the **Font group**, click the **Text Effects** button ⓐ.

2 In the displayed **Text Effects** gallery, in the first row, point to the second effect to display the ScreenTip *Fill - None, Outline - Accent 2* and then click this effect.

3 With the text still selected, in the **Font group**, click in the **Font Size** box 11 ⌄ to select the existing font size. Type **60** and then press Enter.

When you want to change the font size of selected text to a size that does not display in the Font Size list, type the number in the Font Size button box and press Enter to confirm the new font size.

4 With the text still selected, in the **Paragraph group**, click the **Center** button ≡ to center the text. Compare your screen with Figure 1.5.

Figure 1.5

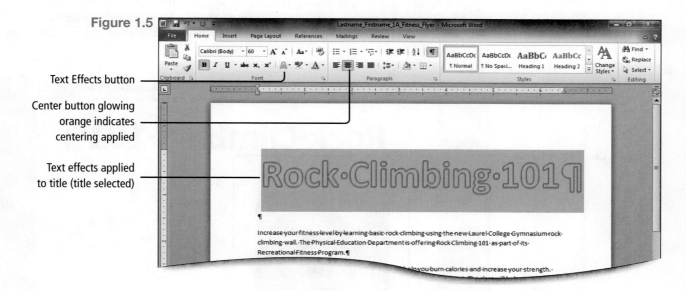

Text Effects button

Center button glowing orange indicates centering applied

Text effects applied to title (title selected)

5 With the text still selected, in the **Font group**, click the **Text Effects** button ⓐ. Point to **Shadow**, and then under **Outer**, in the second row, click the third style—**Offset Left**.

6 With the text still selected, in the **Font group**, click the **Font Color button arrow** ⓐ. Under **Theme Colors**, in the fourth column, click the first color—**Dark Blue, Text 2**.

7 Click anywhere in the document to deselect the text, and then compare your screen with Figure 1.6.

Figure 1.6

Title color changed
and shadow added

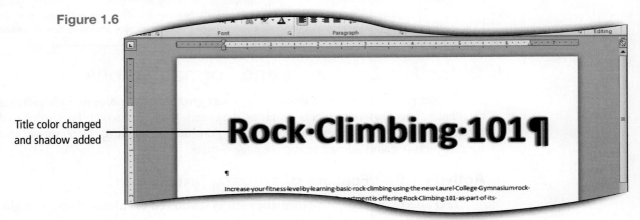

Rock·Climbing·101¶

¶

Increase·your·fitness·level·by·learning·basic·rock·climbing·using·the·new·Laurel·College·Gymnasium·rock-
····················artment·is·offering·Rock·Climbing·101·as·part·of·its·

8 **Save** 💾 your document.

Activity 1.03 | Inserting and Resizing Pictures

1 In the paragraph that begins *Increase your fitness*, click to position the insertion point at the beginning of the paragraph.

2 On the **Insert tab**, in the **Illustrations group**, click the **Picture** button. In the **Insert Picture** dialog box, navigate to your student data files, locate and click **w01A_Rock_Climber**, and then click **Insert**.

Word inserts the picture as an ***inline object***; that is, the picture is positioned directly in the text at the insertion point, just like a character in a sentence. Sizing handles surround the picture indicating it is selected.

3 If necessary, scroll to view the entire picture. Notice the round and square sizing handles around the border of the selected picture, as shown in Figure 1.7.

The round corner sizing handles resize the graphic proportionally. The square sizing handles resize a graphic vertically or horizontally only; however, sizing with these will distort the graphic. A green rotate handle, with which you can rotate the graphic to any angle, displays above the top center sizing handle.

Figure 1.7

Center sizing handle
Rotate handle

Corner sizing handles

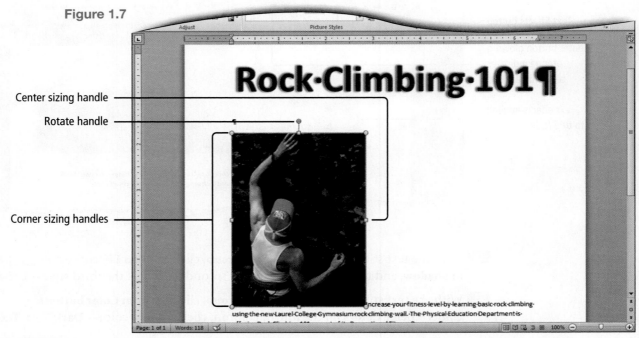

Rock·Climbing·101¶

ncrease·your·fitness·level·by·learning·basic·rock·climbing·
using·the·new·Laurel·College·Gymnasium·rock·climbing·wall.·The·Physical·Education·Department·is-

4 At the lower right corner of the picture, point to the round sizing handle until the ⬚ pointer displays. Drag upward and to the left until the bottom of the graphic is aligned at approximately **4 inches on the vertical ruler**. Compare your screen with Figure 1.8. Notice that the graphic is proportionally resized.

Figure 1.8

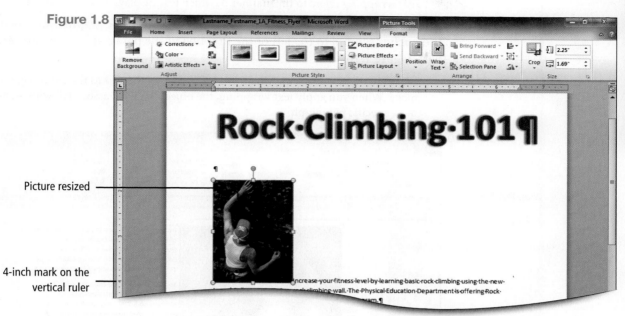

Picture resized

4-inch mark on the
vertical ruler

5 On the **Format tab**, in the **Adjust group**, click the **Reset Picture button arrow** 🖼, and then click **Reset Picture & Size**.

6 In the **Size group**, click the **Shape Height spin box up arrow** 〔 1.5" 〕 as necessary to change the height of the picture to **4.5"**. Scroll down to view the entire picture on your screen, compare your screen with Figure 1.9, and then **Save** 💾 your document.

When you use the Height and Width **spin boxes** to change the size of a graphic, the graphic will always resize proportionally; that is, the width adjusts as you change the height and vice versa.

Figure 1.9

Picture height increased
to 4.5 inches

Activity 1.04 | Wrapping Text Around a Picture

Graphics inserted as inline objects are treated like characters in a sentence, which can result in unattractive spacing. You can change an inline object to a *floating object*—a graphic that can be moved independently of the surrounding text characters.

1 Be sure the picture is selected—you know it is selected if the sizing handles display.

2 On the **Format tab**, in the **Arrange group**, click the **Wrap Text** button to display a gallery of text wrapping arrangements.

Text wrapping refers to the manner in which text displays around an object.

3 From the gallery, click **Square** to wrap the text around the graphic, and then notice the *anchor* symbol to the left of the first line of the paragraph. Compare your screen with Figure 1.10.

Select square text wrapping when you want to wrap the text to the left or right of the image. When you apply text wrapping, the object is always associated with—anchored to—a specific paragraph.

Figure 1.10

Wrap Text button

Anchor symbol

Text wrapped around picture

4 **Save** your document.

Activity 1.05 | Moving a Picture

1 Point to the rock climber picture to display the pointer.

2 Hold down Shift and drag the picture to the right until the right edge of the picture aligns at approximately **6.5 inches on the horizontal ruler**. Notice that the picture moves in a straight line when you hold down Shift. Compare your screen with Figure 1.11.

Figure 1.11

Right edge aligned with right margin

Top edge aligned with top of paragraph

3 If necessary, press any of the arrow keys on your keyboard to *nudge*—move in small increments—the picture in any direction so that the text wraps to match Figure 1.11. **Save** 🖫 your document.

Activity 1.06 | Applying Picture Styles and Artistic Effects

Picture styles include shapes, shadows, frames, borders, and other special effects with which you can stylize an image. *Artistic effects* are formats that make pictures look more like sketches or paintings.

1 Be sure the rock climber picture is selected. On the **Format tab**, in the **Picture Styles group**, click the **Picture Effects** button. Point to **Soft Edges**, and then click **5 Point**.

> The Soft Edges feature fades the edges of the picture. The number of points you choose determines how far the fade goes inward from the edges of the picture.

2 On the **Format tab**, in the **Adjust group**, click the **Artistic Effects** button. In the first row of the gallery, point to, but do not click, the third effect—**Pencil Grayscale**.

> Live Preview displays the picture with the *Pencil Grayscale* effect added.

3 In the second row of the gallery, click the third effect—**Paint Brush**. Notice that the picture looks like a painting, rather than a photograph, as shown in Figure 1.12. **Save** 🖫 your document.

Figure 1.12

Paint Brush artistic effect applied to picture

Activity 1.07 | Adding a Page Border

Page borders frame a page and help to focus the information on the page.

1 Click anywhere outside the picture to deselect it. On the **Page Layout tab**, in the **Page Background group**, click the **Page Borders** button.

2 In the **Borders and Shading** dialog box, under **Setting**, click **Box**. Under **Style**, scroll down the list about a third of the way and click the heavy top line with the thin bottom line—check the **Preview** area to be sure the heavier line is the nearest to the edges of the page.

3 Click the **Color arrow**, and then in the fourth column, click the first color—**Dark Blue, Text 2**.

4 Under **Apply to**, be sure *Whole document* is selected, and then compare your screen with Figure 1.13.

Figure 1.13

Page Borders button

Page border preview

Box setting

Border style

Border color

5 At the bottom of the **Borders and Shading** dialog box, click **OK**.

6 Press [Ctrl] + [Home] to move to the top of the document, and then compare your page border with Figure 1.14. **Save** 💾 your document.

Figure 1.14

Page Border added to document

Objective 3 | Insert and Modify Text Boxes and Shapes

Word provides predefined ***shapes*** and ***text boxes*** that you can add to your documents. A shape is an object such as a line, arrow, box, callout, or banner. A text box is a movable, resizable container for text or graphics. Use these objects to add visual interest to your document.

Activity 1.08 | Inserting a Shape

1 Press [↓] one time to move to the blank paragraph below the title. Press [Enter] four times to make space for a text box, and notice that the picture anchored to the paragraph moves with the text.

2 Press [Ctrl] + [End] to move to the bottom of the document, and notice that your insertion point is positioned in the empty paragraph at the end of the document.

3 Click the **Insert tab**, and then in the **Illustrations group**, click the **Shapes** button to display the gallery. Compare your screen with Figure 1.15.

Figure 1.15

Shapes button

Rounded Rectangle shape

Shapes gallery

4 Under **Rectangles**, click the second shape—**Rounded Rectangle**, and then move your pointer. Notice that the ⊞ pointer displays.

5 Position the ⊞ pointer just under the lower left corner of the picture, and then drag down approximately **1 inch** and to the right edge of the picture.

6 Point to the shape and right-click, and then from the shortcut menu, click **Add Text**.

7 With the insertion point blinking inside the shape, point inside the shape and right-click, and then on the Mini toolbar, change the **Font Size** to **16**, and be sure **Center** ≣ alignment is selected.

8 Click inside the shape again, and then type **Improve your strength, balance, and coordination** If necessary, use the lower middle sizing handle to enlarge the shape to view your text. Compare your screen with Figure 1.16. **Save** 🖫 your document.

Figure 1.16

Rounded Rectangle shape inserted and formatted, text added

Activity 1.09 | Inserting a Text Box

A text box is useful to differentiate portions of text from other text on the page. You can move a text box anywhere on the page.

1 Press Ctrl + Home to move to the top of the document.

2 On the **Insert tab**, in the **Text group**, click the **Text Box** button. At the bottom of the gallery, click **Draw Text Box**.

3 Position the ➕ pointer below the letter *k* in *Rock*—at approximately **1.5 inches on the vertical ruler**. Drag down and to the right to create a text box approximately **1.5 inches** high and **3 inches** wide—the exact size and location need not be precise.

4 With the insertion point blinking in the text box, type the following, pressing Enter after each line to create a new paragraph:

Meets Tuesdays and Thursdays, 7-9 p.m.

Begins September 13, ends December 16

College Gymnasium, Room 104

5 Compare your screen with Figure 1.17.

Figure 1.17

Text box with inserted text

6 **Save** 💾 your document.

Activity 1.10 | Moving, Resizing, and Formatting Shapes and Text Boxes

1 In the text box you just created in the upper portion of the flyer, select all of the text. From the Mini toolbar, change the **Font Size** to **14**, apply **Bold** **B**, and then **Center** ≡ the text.

2 On the **Format tab**, in the **Size group**, if necessary, click the **Size** button. Click the **Shape Height spin arrows** as necessary to set the height of the text box to **1.2"**. Click the **Shape Width spin arrows** as necessary to set the width of the text box to **4"**.

3 In the **Shape Styles group**, click the **Shape Effects** button. Point to **Shadow**, and then under **Outer**, in the first row, click the first style—**Offset Diagonal Bottom Right**.

4 In the **Shape Styles group**, click the **Shape Outline button arrow**. In the fourth column, click the first color—**Dark Blue, Text 2** to change the color of the text box border.

5 Click the **Shape Outline button arrow** again, point to **Weight**, and then click **3 pt**.

6 Click anywhere in the document to deselect the text box. Notice that with the text box deselected, you can see all the measurements on the horizontal ruler.

7 Click anywhere in the text box and point to the text box border to display the pointer. By dragging, visually center the text box vertically and horizontally in the space below the *Rock Climbing 101* title. Then, if necessary, press any of the arrow keys on your keyboard to nudge the text box in precise increments to match Figure 1.18.

Figure 1.18

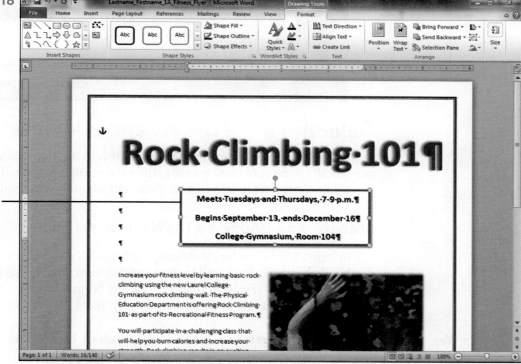

Text formatted and centered in text box, shadow added, border color and weight changed

8 Press Ctrl + End to move to the bottom of the document. Click on the border of the rounded rectangular shape to select it.

9 On the **Format tab**, in the **Size group**, if necessary, click the **Size** button. Click the **Shape Height spin arrows** as necessary to change the height of the shape to **0.8"**.

10 In the **Shape Styles group**, click the **Shape Fill button arrow**, and then at the bottom of the gallery, point to **Gradient**. Under **Dark Variations**, in the third row click the first gradient—**Linear Diagonal - Bottom Left to Top Right**.

11 In the **Shape Styles group**, click the **Shape Outline button arrow**. In the sixth column, click the first color—**Red, Accent 2**.

12 Click the **Shape Outline button arrow** again, point to **Weight**, and then click **1 1/2 pt**. Click anywhere in the document to deselect the shape. Compare your screen with Figure 1.19, and then **Save** 📁 your document.

Figure 1.19

Gradient fill added, shape outline formatted

Objective 4 | Preview and Print a Document

While you are creating your document, it is useful to preview your document periodically to be sure that you are getting the result you want. Then, before printing, make a final preview to be sure the document layout is what you intended.

Activity 1.11 | Adding a File Name to the Footer

Information in headers and footers helps to identify a document when it is printed or displayed electronically. Recall that a header is information that prints at the top of every page; a footer is information that prints at the bottom of every page. In this textbook, you will insert the file name in the footer of every Word document.

Another Way

At the bottom edge of the page, right-click; from the shortcut menu, click Edit Footer.

1 Click the **Insert tab**, and then, in the **Header & Footer group**, click the **Footer** button.

2 At the bottom of the **Footer** gallery, click **Edit Footer**.

The footer area displays with the insertion point blinking at the left edge, and on the Ribbon, the Header & Footer Tools display and add the Design tab.

3 On the **Design tab**, in the **Insert group**, click the **Quick Parts** button, and then click **Field**. In the **Field** dialog box, under **Field names**, use the vertical scroll bar to examine the items that you can insert in a header or footer.

A *field* is a placeholder that displays preset content such as the current date, the file name, a page number, or other stored information.

4 In the **Field names** list, scroll as necessary to locate and then click **FileName**. Compare your screen with Figure 1.20.

Figure 1.20

Quick Parts button

Field dialog box

FileName field

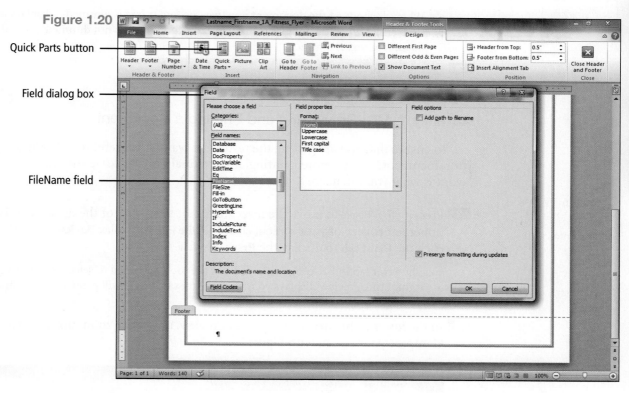

5 In the lower right corner of the **Field** dialog box, click **OK**, and then compare your screen with Figure 1.21.

Figure 1.21

Document text and image dimmed when footer is open

File name in footer

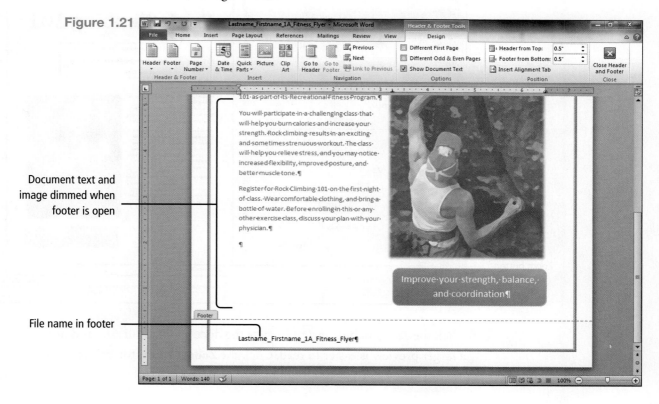

Another Way
Double-click anywhere in the document to close the footer area.

> **6** On the **Design tab**, at the far right in the **Close group**, click the **Close Header and Footer** button.

> When the body of the document is active, the footer text is dimmed—displays in gray. Conversely, when the footer area is active, the footer text is not dimmed; instead, the document text is dimmed.

> **7 Save** 🖫 your document.

Activity 1.12 | Previewing and Printing a Document

To ensure that you are getting the result you want, it is useful to periodically preview your document. Then, before printing, make a final preview to be sure the document layout is what you intended.

Another Way
Press Ctrl + F2 to display Print Preview.

> **1** Press Ctrl + Home to move the insertion point to the top of the document. In the upper left corner of your screen, click the **File tab** to display **Backstage** view, and then click the **Print tab** to display the **Print Preview**.

> The Print tab in Backstage view displays the tools you need to select your settings. On the right, Print Preview displays your document exactly as it will print; the formatting marks do not display.

> **2** In the lower right corner of the **Print Preview**, notice the zoom buttons that display. Compare your screen with Figure 1.22.

Figure 1.22

Print tab

Print Preview of document

Zoom buttons

> **3** Click the **Zoom In** button ⊕ to view the document at full size, and notice that a larger preview is easier to read. Click the **Zoom Out** button ⊖ to view the entire page.

4 Click the **Info tab**. On the right, under the screen thumbnail, click **Properties**, and then click **Show Document Panel**.

Here you can adjust the document properties.

5 In the **Author** box, delete any text and then type your firstname and lastname. In the **Subject** box type your course name and section number, and in the **Keywords** box type **fitness, rock climbing Close** the Document Panel.

6 **Save** your document. To print, display **Backstage** view, and then on the **navigation bar**, click **Print**. In the **Settings** group, be sure the correct printer is selected, and then in the **Print group**, click the **Print** button. Or, submit your document electronically as directed by your instructor.

7 In **Backstage** view, click **Exit** to close the document and exit Word.

End **You have completed Project 1A** ────────────────────────

Project 1B Information Handout

myitlab
Project 1B Training

Project Activities

In Activities 1.13 through 1.23, you will format and add lists to an information handout that describes student activities at Laurel College. Your completed document will look similar to Figure 1.23.

Project Files

For Project 1B, you will need the following file:

w01B_Student_Activities

You will save your document as:

Lastname_Firstname_1B_Student_Activities

Project Results

Every spring, students vote for the President, Vice President, Treasurer, Secretary, and Student Trustee for the following year. Executive Officers work with the college administration to manage campus activities and to make changes to policies and procedures. For example, the Student Trustee is a
h consists of elected members from the
college budget, and employee hiring.
the Board to vote for a proposal to
ocations in Laurelton and outlying areas.

lubs and academic organizations vote for
on information and applications on the
mpus and in the student newspaper.

f interests, including academic, political,
currently in existence at Laurel College. A
oin a club, you may enjoy being a member
or you may decide to take a leadership role

fice in the Campus Center, Room CC208, or
d complete the form online. Clubs accept
e following are the first meeting dates and

. October 8, 2:00 p.m., Room CC214
ctober 5, 5:00 p.m., Computer Café
7, 3:00 p.m., Field House, Room 2A
. October 6, 2:00 p.m., Room CC212
6, 4:00 p.m., Math Tutoring Lab, L35
. October 8, 3:00 p.m., Room CC214
4, 5:30 p.m., Photo Lab, Foster Hall
.......October 8, 5:00 p.m., Room L24
. October 7, 4:30 p.m., Room CC214
.October 4, 3:00 p.m., Little Theater

listed here, are great, but your goals are
ing a degree or certificate. Maybe you want
ou leave Laurel College. Whatever your
ur education, work experience, and
lly ones in which you had a leadership role,

Associated Students of Laurel College

Get Involved in Student Activities

Your experience at Laurel College will be richer and more memorable if you get involved in activities that take you beyond the classroom. You will have the opportunity to meet other students, faculty, and staff members and will participate in organizations that make valuable contributions to your college and to the community.

Consider becoming involved in student government or joining a club. You might take part in activities such as these:

✓ Volunteering to help with a blood drive
✓ Traveling to a foreign country to learn about other cultures
✓ Volunteering to assist at graduation
✓ Helping to organize a community picnic
✓ Planning and implementing advertising for a student event
✓ Meeting with members of the state legislature to discuss issues that affect college students—for example, tuition costs and financial aid

Student Government

As a registered student, you are eligible to attend meetings of the Executive Officers of the Associated Students of Laurel College. At the meetings, you will have the opportunity to learn about college issues that affect students. At the conclusion of each meeting, the Officers invite students to voice their opinions. Eventually, you might decide to run for an office yourself. Running for office is a three-step process:

1. Pick up petitions at the Student Government office.
2. Obtain 100 signatures from current students.
3. Turn in petitions and start campaigning.

Lastname_Firstname_1B_Student_Activities

Figure 1.23
Project 1B Student Activities

Objective 5 | Change Document and Paragraph Layout

Document layout includes *margins*—the space between the text and the top, bottom, left, and right edges of the paper. Paragraph layout includes line spacing, indents, and tabs. In Word, the information about paragraph formats is stored in the paragraph mark at the end of a paragraph. When you press the [Enter], the new paragraph mark contains the formatting of the previous paragraph, unless you take steps to change it.

Activity 1.13 | Setting Margins

1 **Start** Word. From **Backstage** view, display the **Open** dialog box. From your student files, locate and open the document **w01B_Student_Activities**. On the **Home tab**, in the **Paragraph group**, be sure the **Show/Hide** button [¶] is active—glows orange—so that you can view the formatting marks.

2 From **Backstage** view, display the **Save As** dialog box. Navigate to your **Word Chapter 1** folder, and then **Save** the document as **Lastname_Firstname_1B_Student_Activities**

3 Click the **Page Layout tab**. In the **Page Setup group**, click the **Margins** button, and then take a moment to study the buttons in the Margins gallery.

The top button displays the most recent custom margin settings, while the other buttons display commonly used margin settings.

4 At the bottom of the **Margins** gallery, click **Custom Margins**.

5 In the **Page Setup** dialog box, press [Tab] as necessary to select the value in the **Left** box, and then, with *1.25"* selected, type **1**

This action will change the left margin to 1 inch on all pages of the document. You do not need to type the inch (") mark.

6 Press [Tab] to select the margin in the **Right** box, and then type **1** At the bottom of the dialog box, notice that the new margins will apply to the **Whole document**. Compare your screen with Figure 1.24.

Figure 1.24

Margins button —

Left and Right margins changed —

Changes applied to entire document —

Another Way

Click the View tab, and then in the Show group, select the Ruler check box.

7 Click **OK** to apply the new margins and close the dialog box. If the ruler below the Ribbon is not displayed, at the top of the vertical scroll bar, click the View Ruler button 🔲.

8 Scroll to view the bottom of **Page 1** and the top of **Page 2**. Notice that the page edges display, and the page number and total number of pages display on the left side of the status bar.

9 Near the bottom edge of **Page 1**, point anywhere in the margin area, right-click, and then click **Edit Footer** to display the footer area.

10 On the **Design tab**, in the **Insert group**, click the **Quick Parts** button, and then click **Field**. In the **Field** dialog box, under **Field names**, locate and click **FileName**, and then click **OK**.

11 Double-click anywhere in the document to close the footer area, and then **Save** 🔲 your document.

Activity 1.14 | Aligning Text

Alignment refers to the placement of paragraph text relative to the left and right margins. Most paragraph text uses *left alignment*—aligned at the left margin, leaving the right margin uneven. Three other types of paragraph alignment are: *center alignment*—centered between the left and right margins; *right alignment*—aligned at the right margin with an uneven left margin; and *justified alignment*—text aligned evenly at both the left and right margins. See the table in Figure 1.25.

Paragraph Alignment Options		
Alignment	**Button**	**Description and Example**
Align Text Left	▤	Align Text Left is the default paragraph alignment in Word. Text in the paragraph aligns at the left margin, and the right margin is uneven.
Center	▤	Center alignment aligns text in the paragraph so that it is centered between the left and right margins.
Align Text Right	▤	Align Text Right aligns text at the right margin. Using Align Text Right, the left margin, which is normally even, is uneven.
Justify	▤	The Justify alignment option adds additional space between words so that both the left and right margins are even. Justify is often used when formatting newspaper-style columns.

Figure 1.25

1 Scroll to position the middle of **Page 2** on your screen, look at the left and right margins, and notice that the text is justified—both the right and left margins of multiple-line paragraphs are aligned evenly at the margins. On the **Home tab**, in the **Paragraph group**, notice that the **Justify** button ▤ is active.

2 In the paragraph that begins *Every spring, students vote*, in the first line, look at the space following the word *Every*, and then compare it with the space following the word *Trustee* in the second line. Notice how some of the spaces between words are larger than others.

To achieve a justified right margin, Word adjusts the size of spaces between words in this manner, which can result in unattractive spacing in a document that spans the width of a page. Many individuals find such spacing difficult to read.

Another Way

On the Home tab, in the Editing group, click the Select button, and then click Select All.

3 Press Ctrl + A to select all of the text in the document, and then on the **Home tab**, in the **Paragraph group**, click the **Align Text Left** button 📄.

4 Press Ctrl + Home. At the top of the document, in the left margin area, point to the left of the first paragraph—*Associated Students of Laurel College*—until the 📄 pointer displays, and then click one time to select the paragraph. On the Mini toolbar, change the **Font Size** to **26**.

> Use this technique to select entire lines of text.

5 Point to the left of the first paragraph—*Associated Students of Laurel College*—to display the 📄 pointer again, and then drag down to select the first two paragraphs, which form the title and subtitle of the document.

6 On the Mini toolbar, click the **Center** button 📄 to center the title and subtitle between the left and right margins, and then compare your screen with Figure 1.26.

Figure 1.26

Title centered and font size set to 26

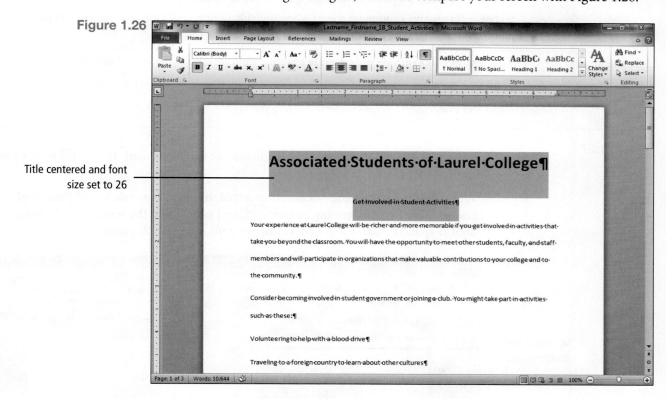

7 Scroll down to view the bottom of **Page 1**, and then locate the first bold subheading—*Student Government*. Point to the left of the paragraph to display the 📄 pointer, and then click one time.

8 With *Student Government* selected, use your mouse wheel or the vertical scroll bar to bring the lower portion of **Page 2** into view. Locate the subheading *Clubs*. Move the pointer to the left of the paragraph to display the 📄 pointer, hold down Ctrl, and then click one time.

> Two subheadings are selected; in Windows-based programs, you can hold down Ctrl to select multiple items.

9 On the Mini toolbar, click the **Center** button 📄 to center both subheadings, and then click **Save** 💾.

Activity 1.15 | Changing Line Spacing

Line spacing is the distance between lines of text in a paragraph. Three of the most commonly used line spacing options are shown in the table in Figure 1.27.

Line Spacing Options	
Alignment	**Description, Example, and Information**
Single spacing	**This text in this example uses single spacing**. Single spacing was once the most commonly used spacing in business documents. Now, because so many documents are read on a computer screen rather than on paper, single spacing is becoming less popular.
Multiple 1.15 spacing	**This text in this example uses multiple 1.15 spacing**. The default line spacing in Microsoft Word 2010 is 1.15, which is equivalent to single spacing with an extra 1/6 line added between lines to make the text easier to read on a computer screen. Many individuals now prefer this spacing, even on paper, because the lines of text appear less crowded.
Double spacing	**This text in this example uses double spacing**. College research papers and draft documents that need space for notes are commonly double-spaced; there is space for a full line of text between each document line.

Figure 1.27

1 Press Ctrl + Home to move to the beginning of the document. Press Ctrl + A to select all of the text in the document.

2 With all of the text in the document selected, on the **Home tab**, in the **Paragraph group**, click the **Line Spacing** button, and notice that the text in the document is double spaced—**2.0** is checked. Compare your screen with Figure 1.28.

Figure 1.28

Document text double-spaced

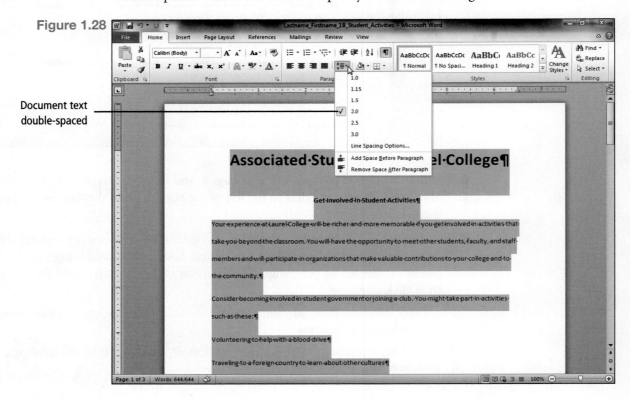

3 On the **Line Spacing** menu, click the *second* setting—**1.15**—and then click anywhere in the document. Compare your screen with Figure 1.29, and then **Save** 🖫 your document.

Double spacing is most commonly used in research papers and rough draft documents. Recall that 1.15 is the default line spacing for new Word documents. Line spacing of 1.15 has slightly more space between the lines than single spacing. On a computer screen, spacing of 1.15 is easier to read than single spacing. Because a large percentage of Word documents are read on a computer screen, 1.15 is the default spacing for a new Word document.

Figure 1.29

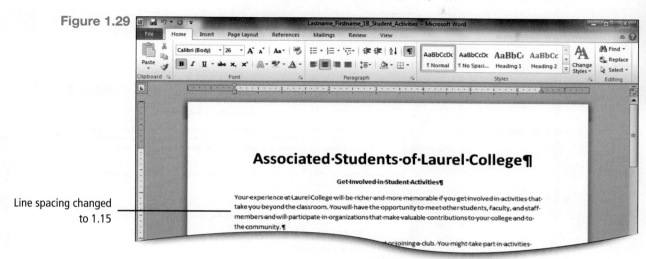

Line spacing changed to 1.15

Activity 1.16 | Indenting Text and Adding Space After Paragraphs

Common techniques to distinguish paragraphs include adding space after each paragraph, indenting the first line of each paragraph, or both.

1 Below the title and subtitle of the document, click anywhere in the paragraph that begins *Your experience*.

2 On the **Home tab**, in the **Paragraph group**, click the **Dialog Box Launcher** 🔲.

3 In the **Paragraph** dialog box, on the **Indents and Spacing tab**, under **Indentation**, click the **Special arrow**, and then click **First line** to indent the first line by 0.5″, which is the default indent setting. Compare your screen with Figure 1.30.

Figure 1.30

First line indent applied

4 Click **OK**, and then click anywhere in the next paragraph, which begins *Consider becoming*. On the ruler under the Ribbon, drag the **First Line Indent** button ⬇ to **0.5 inches on the horizontal ruler**, and then compare your screen with Figure 1.31.

Figure 1.31

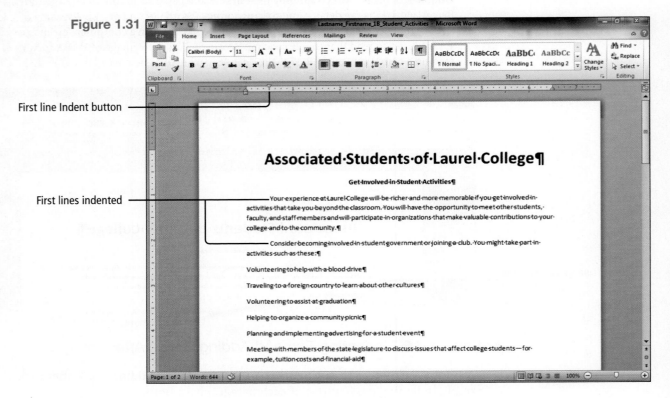

First line Indent button

First lines indented

5 By using either of the techniques you just practiced, or by using the Format Painter, apply a first line indent of **0.5″** in the paragraph that begins *As a registered* to match the indent of the remaining paragraphs in the document.

6 Press Ctrl + A to select all of the text in the document. Click the **Page Layout tab**, and then in the **Paragraph group**, under **Spacing**, click the **After spin box down arrow** one time to change the value to **6 pt**.

To change the value in the box, you can also select the existing number, type a new number, and then press Enter. This document will use 6 pt spacing after paragraphs.

7 Press Ctrl + Home, and then compare your screen with Figure 1.32.

Figure 1.32

Spacing After set to 6 pt

8 Scroll to view the lower portion of **Page 1**. Select the subheading *Student Government*, including the paragraph mark following it, hold down Ctrl, and then select the subheading *Clubs*.

9 With both subheadings selected, in the **Paragraph group**, under **Spacing**, click the **Before up spin box arrow** two times to set the **Spacing Before** to **12 pt**. Compare your screen with Figure 1.33, and then **Save** 🖫 your document.

> This action increases the amount of space above each of the two subheadings, which will make them easy to distinguish in the document. The formatting is applied only to the two selected paragraphs.

Figure 1.33
Spacing before set to 12 pt.

12-point spacing before paragraphs

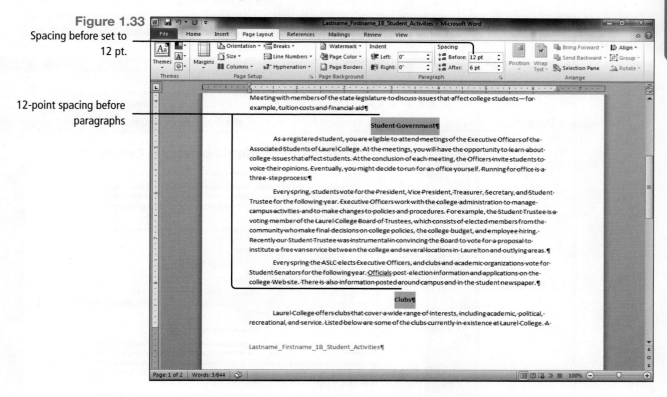

Objective 6 | Create and Modify Lists

To display a list of information, you can choose a ***bulleted list***, which uses ***bullets***—text symbols such as small circles or check marks—to introduce each item in a list. You can also choose a ***numbered list***, which uses consecutive numbers or letters to introduce each item in a list.

Use a bulleted list if the items in the list can be introduced in any order; use a numbered list for items that have definite steps, a sequence of actions, or are in chronological order.

Activity 1.17 | Creating a Bulleted List

1 In the upper portion of **Page 1**, locate the paragraph that begins *Volunteering to help*, and then point to this paragraph from the left margin area to display the 🔖 pointer. Drag down to select this paragraph and the next five paragraphs.

2 On the **Home tab**, in the **Paragraph group**, click the **Bullets** button 📋▾ to change the selected text to a bulleted list.

> The spacing between each of the bulleted points changes to the spacing between lines in a paragraph—in this instance, 1.15 line spacing. The spacing after the last item in the list is the same as the spacing after each paragraph—in this instance, 6 pt. Each bulleted item is automatically indented.

3 On the ruler, point to the **First Line Indent** button ▽ and read the ScreenTip, and then point to the **Hanging Indent** button △. Compare your screen with Figure 1.34.

> By default, Word formats bulleted items with a first line indent of 0.25″ and adds a Hanging Indent at 0.5″. The hanging indent maintains the alignment of text when a bulleted item is more than one line, for example, the last bulleted item in this list.

Figure 1.34

Hanging Indent button on ruler

Bulleted list

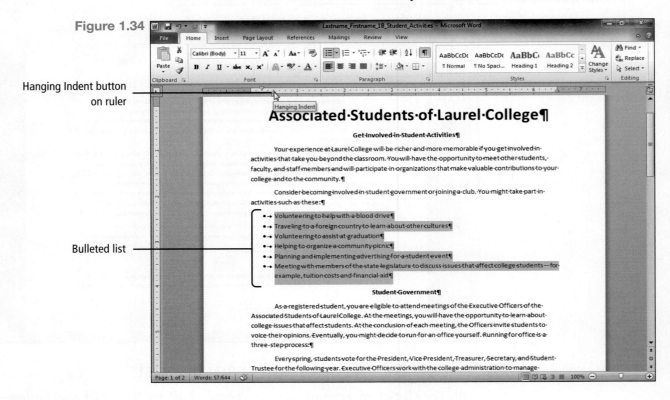

4 Scroll down to view **Page 2**. By using the 🖈 pointer from the left margin area, select all of the paragraphs that indicate the club names and meeting dates, beginning with *Chess Club* and ending with *Theater Club*.

5 In the **Paragraph group**, click the **Bullets** button 📋▾, and then **Save** 💾 your document.

Activity 1.18 | Creating a Numbered List

1 Scroll to view **Page 1**, and then under the subheading *Student Government*, in the paragraph that begins *As a registered student*, click to position the insertion point at the *end* of the paragraph following the colon. Press Enter to create a blank paragraph.

2 Notice that the paragraph is indented, because the First Line Indent from the previous paragraph carried over to the new paragraph.

3 To change the indent formatting for this paragraph, on the ruler, drag the **First Line Indent** button ▽ to the left so that it is positioned directly above the lower button. Compare your screen with Figure 1.35.

Figure 1.35

First Line Indent button ⎯⎯⎯

Paragraph with no first line indent ⎯⎯⎯

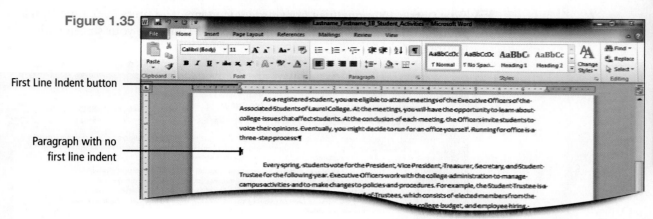

4 Being sure to include the period, type **1.** and press Spacebar.

Word determines that this paragraph is the first item in a numbered list and formats the new paragraph accordingly, indenting the list in the same manner as the bulleted list. The space after the number changes to a tab, and the AutoCorrect Options button displays to the left of the list item. The tab is indicated by a right arrow formatting mark.

Alert! | Activating Automatic Numbered Lists

If a numbered list does not begin automatically, display Backstage view, and then click the Options tab. On the left side of the Word Options dialog box, click Proofing. Under AutoCorrect options, click the AutoCorrect Options button. In the AutoCorrect dialog box, click the AutoFormat As You Type tab. Under *Apply as you type*, select the *Automatic numbered lists* check box, and then click OK two times to close both dialog boxes.

---

5 Click the **AutoCorrect Options** button 🖅 ▾, and then compare your screen with Figure 1.36.

From the displayed list, you can remove the automatic formatting here, or stop using the automatic numbered lists option in this document. You also have the option to open the AutoCorrect dialog box to *Control AutoFormat Options*.

Figure 1.36

AutoCorrect Options button ⎯⎯⎯

6 Click the **AutoCorrect Options** button again to close the menu without selecting any of the commands. Type **Pick up petitions at the Student Government office.** and press [Enter]. Notice that the second number and a tab are added to the next line.

7 Type **Obtain 100 signatures from current students.** and press [Enter]. Type **Turn in petitions and start campaigning.** and press [Enter]. Compare your screen with Figure 1.37.

Figure 1.37

Numbered list

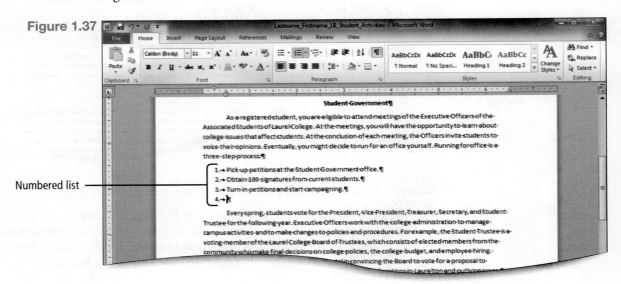

8 Press [←Bksp] to turn off the list numbering. Then, press [←Bksp] three more times to remove the blank paragraph. Compare your screen with Figure 1.38.

Figure 1.38

Three items in the list, item 4 deleted

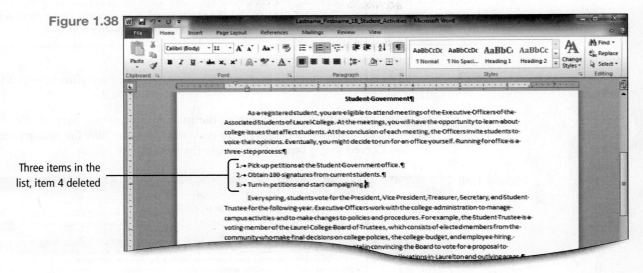

9 **Save** 🖫 your document.

More Knowledge | To End a List

To turn a list off, you can press [←Bksp], click the Numbering or Bullets button, or press [Enter] a second time. Both list buttons—Numbering and Bullets—act as *toggle buttons*; that is, clicking the button one time turns the feature on, and clicking the button again turns the feature off.

Activity 1.19 | Customizing Bullets

1 Press [Ctrl] + [End] to move to the end of the document, and then scroll up as necessary to display the bulleted list containing the list of clubs.

2 Point to the left of the first list item to display the 🔏 pointer, and then drag down to select all the clubs in the list—the bullet symbols are not highlighted.

3 Point to the selected list and right-click. From the shortcut menu, point to **Bullets**, and then compare your screen with Figure 1.39.

Figure 1.39

Check mark bullet

4 Under **Bullet Library**, click the **check mark** symbol. If the check mark is not available, choose another bullet symbol.

> **Another Way**
>
> On the Home tab, in the Clipboard group, click the Format Painter button.

5 With the bulleted list still selected, right-click over the list, and then on the Mini toolbar, click the **Format Painter** button 🖌.

6 Use the vertical scroll bar or your mouse wheel to scroll to view **Page 1**. Move the pointer to the left of the first item in the bulleted list to display the 🔏 pointer, and then drag down to select all of the items in the list and to apply the format of the second bulleted list to this list. Compare your screen with Figure 1.40, and then **Save** 💾 your document.

Figure 1.40

Bullet symbol changed

Objective 7 | Set and Modify Tab Stops

Tab stops mark specific locations on a line of text. Use tab stops to indent and align text, and use the Tab key to move to tab stops.

Activity 1.20 | Setting Tab Stops

1 Scroll to view the middle of **Page 2**, and then by using the 🔏 pointer at the left of the first item, select all of the items in the bulleted list. Notice that there is a tab mark between the name of the club and the date.

> The arrow that indicates a tab is a nonprinting formatting mark.

2 To the left of the horizontal ruler, point to the **Tab Alignment** button 🔲 to display the *Left Tab* ScreenTip, and then compare your screen with Figure 1.41.

Figure 1.41

Tab Alignment button

Left Tab ScreenTip

Tab mark

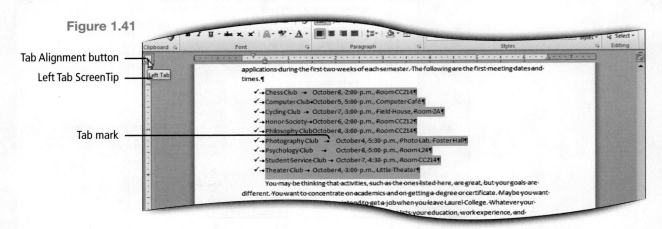

3 Click the **Tab Alignment** button 🔲 several times to view the tab alignment options shown in the table in Figure 1.42.

Tab Alignment Options

Type	Tab Alignment Button Displays This Marker	Description
Left	🔲	Text is left aligned at the tab stop and extends to the right.
Center	🔲	Text is centered around the tab stop.
Right	🔲	Text is right aligned at the tab stop and extends to the left.
Decimal	🔲	The decimal point aligns at the tab stop.
Bar	🔲	A vertical bar displays at the tab stop.
First Line Indent	▽	Text in the first line of a paragraph indents.
Hanging Indent	△	Text in all lines except the first line in the paragraph indents.
Left Indent	🔲	Moves both the First Line Indent and Hanging Indent buttons.

Figure 1.42

4 Display the **Left Tab** button 🔲. Along the lower edge of the horizontal ruler, point to and then click at **3 inches on the horizontal ruler**. Notice that all of the dates left align at the new tab stop location, and the right edge of the column is uneven.

5 Compare your screen with Figure 1.43, and then **Save** 🖫 your document.

Figure 1.43

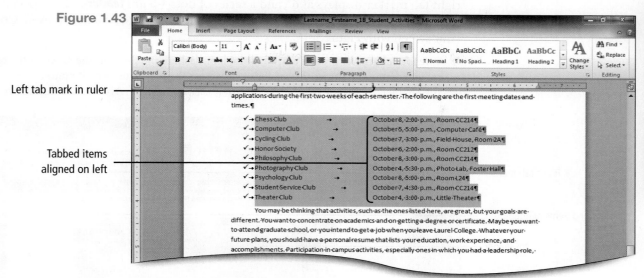

Left tab mark in ruler

Tabbed items aligned on left

Activity 1.21 | Modifying Tab Stops

Tab stops are a form of paragraph formatting, and thus, the information about tab stops is stored in the paragraph mark in the paragraphs to which they were applied.

1 With the bulleted list still selected, on the ruler, point to the new tab marker, and then when the *Left Tab* ScreenTip displays, drag the tab marker to **3.5 inches on the horizontal ruler**.

> In all of the selected lines, the text at the tab stop left aligns at 3.5 inches.

Another Way

On the Home tab, in the Paragraph group, click the Dialog Box Launcher. At the bottom of the Paragraph dialog box, click the Tabs button.

2 On the ruler, point to the tab marker to display the ScreenTip, and then double-click to display the **Tabs** dialog box.

3 In the **Tabs** dialog box, under **Tab stop position**, if necessary select *3.5″* and then type **6**

4 Under **Alignment**, click the **Right** option button. Under **Leader**, click the **2** option button. Near the bottom of the **Tabs** dialog box, click **Set**.

> Because the Right tab will be used to align the items in the list, the tab stop at 3.5″ is no longer necessary.

5 In the **Tabs** dialog box, in the **Tab stop position** box, click **3.5″** to select this tab stop, and then in the lower portion of the **Tabs** dialog box, click the **Clear** button to delete this tab stop, which is no longer necessary. Compare your screen with Figure 1.44.

Figure 1.44

Tab stop position

Right tab selected

Leader 2 selected

6 Click **OK**. On the ruler, notice that the left tab marker at *3.5"* no longer displays, a right tab marker displays at *6"*, and a series of dots—a *dot leader*—displays between the columns of the list. Notice also that the right edge of the column is even. Compare your screen with Figure 1.45.

A *leader character* creates a solid, dotted, or dashed line that fills the space to the left of a tab character and draws the reader's eyes across the page from one item to the next. When the character used for the leader is a dot, it is commonly referred to as a dot leader.

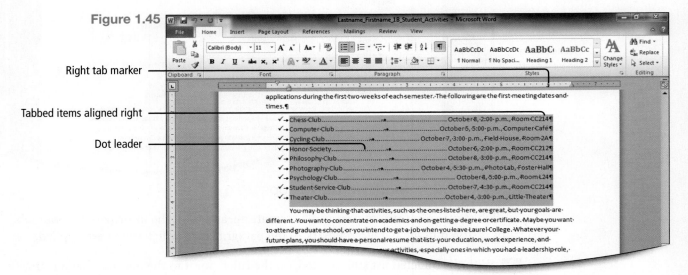

Figure 1.45

Right tab marker

Tabbed items aligned right

Dot leader

7 In the bulleted list that uses dot leaders, locate the *Honor Society* item, and then click to position the insertion point at the end of that line. Press **Enter** to create a new blank bullet item.

8 Type **Math Club** and press **Tab**. Notice that a dot leader fills the space to the tab marker location.

9 Type **October 6, 4:00 p.m., Math Tutoring Lab, L35** and notice that the text moves to the left to maintain the right alignment of the tab stop.

10 **Save** 💾 your document.

Objective 8 | Insert a SmartArt Graphic

SmartArt graphics are designer-quality visual representations of information, and Word provides many different layouts from which you can choose. A SmartArt graphic can communicate your messages or ideas more effectively than plain text and adds visual interest to a document or Web page.

Activity 1.22 | Inserting a SmartArt Graphic

1 Press **Ctrl** + **Home** to move to the top of the document. Press **End** to move to the end of the first paragraph—the title—and then press **Enter** to create a blank paragraph.

Because the paragraph above is 26 pt font size, the new paragraph mark displays in that size.

2 Click the **Insert tab**, and then in the **Illustrations group**, point to the **SmartArt** button to display its ScreenTip. Read the ScreenTip, and then click the button.

3 In the center portion of the **Choose a SmartArt Graphic** dialog box, scroll down and examine the numerous types of SmartArt graphics available.

4 On the left, click **Hierarchy**, and then in the first row, click the first graphic—**Organization Chart**.

At the right of the dialog box, a preview and description of the graphic displays.

5 Compare your screen with Figure 1.46.

Figure 1.46

SmartArt button

Preview of selected SmartArt

Hierarchy category

6 Click **OK**. If the pane indicating *Type your text here* does not display on the left side of the graphic, on the Design tab, in the Create Graphic group, click the Text Pane button. **Save** 🖫 your document.

The SmartArt graphic displays at the insertion point location and consists of two parts—the graphic itself, and the Text Pane. On the Ribbon, the SmartArt Tools add the Design tab and the Format tab. You can type directly into the graphics, or type in the Text Pane. By typing in the Text Pane, you might find it easier to organize your layout.

Activity 1.23 | Modifying a SmartArt Graphic

1 In the SmartArt graphic, in the second row, click the border of the *[Text]* box to display a *solid* border and sizing handles, and then press Del. Repeat this procedure in the bottom row to delete the middle *[Text]* box.

Another Way

Close the Text Pane and type the text directly in the SmartArt boxes.

2 In the **Text Pane**, click in the top bulleted point, and then type **Student Activities** Notice that the first bulleted point aligns further to the left than the other points.

The *top-level points* are the main points in a SmartArt graphic. *Subpoints* are indented second-level bullet points.

Project 1B: Information Handout | **Word** 81

3 Press ↓. Type **Government** and then press ↓ again. Type **Clubs** and then compare your screen with Figure 1.47.

Figure 1.47

SmartArt graphic —

Text Pane —

Top-level point —

Subpoints —

4 In the upper right corner of the **Text Pane**, click the **Close** button 🗙.

5 Click the border of the SmartArt graphic—a pale border surrounds it. Click the **Format tab**, and then in the **Size group**, if necessary click the **Size** button to display the **Shape Height** and **Shape Width** boxes.

6 Set the **Height** to **2.5″** and the **Width** to **4.2″**, and then compare your screen with Figure 1.48.

Figure 1.48

Size button —

Height and Width set —

7 With the SmartArt graphic still selected, click the **Design tab**, and then in the **SmartArt Styles group**, click the **Change Colors** button. Under **Colorful**, click the second style—**Colorful Range - Accent Colors 2 to 3**.

8 On the **Design tab**, in the **SmartArt Styles group**, click the **More** button ⏷. Under **3-D**, click the first style—**Polished**. Compare your screen with Figure 1.49.

Figure 1.49

Polished style selected

SmartArt color and style changed

9 Click outside of the graphic to deselect it. Display **Backstage** view. On the right, under the screen thumbnail, click **Properties**, and then click **Show Document Panel**. In the **Author** box, delete any text and then type your firstname and lastname. In the **Subject** box, type your course name and section number, and in the **Keywords** box type **Student Activities, Associated Students Close** ☒ the Document Panel and **Save** 🖫 your document.

10 Display **Backstage** view, and then click **Print** to display **Print Preview**. At the bottom of the preview, click the **Next Page** ▶ and **Previous Page** ◀ buttons to move between pages. If necessary, return to the document and make any necessary changes.

11 As directed by your instructor, print your document or submit it electronically. **Close** ☒ Word.

More Knowledge | Changing the Bullet Level in a SmartArt Graphic

To increase or decrease the level of an item, on the Design tab, in the Create Graphic group, click either the Promote or the Demote button.

End **You have completed Project 1B**——————————————————————

Content-Based Assessments

Summary

In this chapter, you created and formatted documents using Microsoft Word 2010. You inserted and formatted graphics, created and formatted bulleted and numbered lists, and created and formatted text boxes. You also created lists using tab stops with dot leaders, and created and modified a SmartArt graphic.

Key Terms

Alignment 68

Anchor................................56

Artistic effects 57

Bar tab stop 78

Bulleted list.......................73

Bullets 73

Center alignment 68

Center tab stop 78

Decimal tab stop 78

Dot leader 80

Drawing objects 53

Field...................................62

Floating object 55

Formatting marks.............51

Graphics 53

Inline object 54

Justified alignment..........68

Leader characters 80

Left alignment..................68

Left tab stop 78

Line spacing 70

Margins 67

Nonprinting
   characters....................51

Nudge 57

Numbered list 73

Picture styles 57

Right alignment 68

Right tab stop..................78

Shapes 58

SmartArt 80

Spin box 55

Subpoints 81

Tab stop.............................78

Text box............................58

Text effects 53

Text wrapping 56

Toggle button 76

Top-level points 81

Wordwrap 51

Matching

Match each term in the second column with its correct definition in the first column by writing the letter of the term on the blank line in front of the correct definition.

_____ 1. Formats that make pictures look more like sketches or paintings.

_____ 2. A small box with an upward- and downward-pointing arrow that enables you to move rapidly through a set of values by clicking.

_____ 3. Small circles in the corners of a selected graphic with which you can resize the graphic proportionally.

_____ 4. The manner in which text displays around an object.

_____ 5. An object or graphic that can be moved independently of the surrounding text.

_____ 6. The process of using the arrow keys to move an object in small precise increments.

_____ 7. An object or graphic inserted in a document that acts like a character in a sentence.

_____ 8. Frames, shapes, shadows, borders, and other special effects that can be added to an image to create an overall visual style for the image.

_____ 9. Predefined drawing objects, such as stars, banners, arrows, and callouts, included with Microsoft Office, and that can be inserted into documents.

A Artistic effects

B Bullets

C Floating object

D Inline object

E Justified alignment

F Left alignment

G Line spacing

H Nudge

I Picture styles

J Shapes

K Sizing handles

L SmartArt

M Spin box

N Tab stop

O Text wrapping

_____ 10. A commonly used alignment of text in which text is aligned at the left margin, leaving the right margin uneven.

_____ 11. An alignment of text in which the text is evenly aligned on both the left and right margins.

_____ 12. The distance between lines of text in a paragraph.

_____ 13. Text symbols such as small circles or check marks that introduce items in a list.

_____ 14. A mark on the ruler that indicates the location where the insertion point will be placed when you press the Tab key.

_____ 15. A designer-quality graphic used to create a visual representation of information.

Multiple Choice

Circle the correct answer.

1. Characters that display on the screen to show the location of paragraphs, tabs, and spaces, but that do not print, are called:
   A. text effects   B. bullets   C. formatting marks

2. The placement of paragraph text relative to the left and right margins is referred to as:
   A. alignment   B. spacing   C. indents

3. The symbol that indicates to which paragraph an image is attached is:
   A. a small arrow   B. an anchor   C. a paragraph mark

4. A movable, resizable container for text or graphics is a:
   A. text box   B. dialog box   C. SmartArt graphic

5. A banner is an example of a predefined:
   A. paragraph   B. format   C. shape

6. A placeholder that displays preset content, such as the current date, the file name, a page number, or other stored information is:
   A. a leader   B. a field   C. a tab

7. The space between the text and the top, bottom, left, and right edges of the paper are referred to as:
   A. alignment   B. margins   C. spacing

8. A group of items in which items are displayed in order to indicate definite steps, a sequence of actions, or chronological order is a:
   A. numbered list   B. bulleted list   C. outline list

9. A series of dots following a tab that serve to guide the reader's eye is a:
   A. leader   B. field   C. shape

10. Tab stops are a form of:
    A. line formatting   B. document formatting   C. paragraph formatting

Content-Based Assessments

Apply **1A** skills from these Objectives:

1 Create a New Document and Insert Text

2 Insert and Format Graphics

3 Insert and Modify Text Boxes and Shapes

4 Preview and Print a Document

Skills Review | Project **1C** Welcome Week

In the following Skills Review, you will create and edit a flyer for the Laurel College New Student Welcome Week. Your completed document will look similar to Figure 1.50.

Project Files

For Project 1C, you will need the following files:

New blank Word document
w01C_Welcome_Text
w01C_Welcome_Picture

You will save your document as:

Lastname_Firstname_1C_Welcome_Week

Project Results

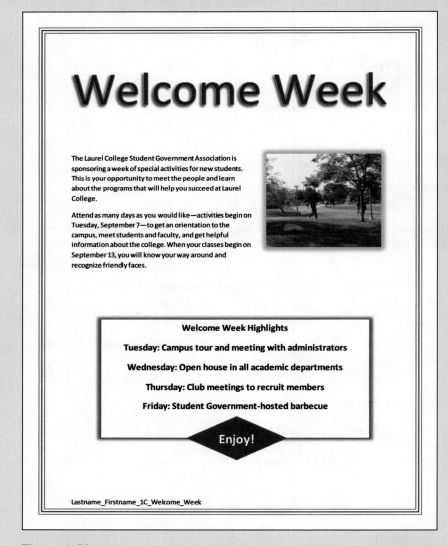

Figure 1.50

(Project 1C Welcome Week continues on the next page)

Content-Based Assessments

1 **Start** Word and display a new blank document. On the **Home tab**, in the **Paragraph group**, be sure the **Show/Hide ¶** button is active so that you can view formatting marks. In the **Quick Access Toolbar**, click the **Save** button, navigate to your **Word Chapter 1** folder, and then **Save** the document as Lastname_Firstname_1C_Welcome_Week

a. Type **Welcome Week** and then press Enter two times.

b. Type **The Laurel College Student Government Association is sponsoring a week of special activities for new students. This is your opportunity to meet the people and learn about the programs that will help you succeed at Laurel College.**

c. Press Enter one time. Click the **Insert tab**. In the **Text group**, click the **Object button arrow**, and then click **Text from File**. Navigate to your student files, select the file **w01C_Welcome_Text**, and then at the bottom of the **Insert File** dialog box, click **Insert**. **Save** your document.

2 At the top of the document, in the left margin area, point to the left of the first paragraph—*Welcome Week*—until the 🔏 pointer displays, and then click one time to select the paragraph. On the **Home tab**, in the **Font group**, click the **Text Effects** button. In the displayed **Text Effects** gallery, in the first row, click the fourth effect—**Fill - White, Outline - Accent 1**.

a. With the text still selected, in the **Font group**, click the **Font Size button arrow**, and then click **72**. In the **Paragraph group**, click the **Center** button.

b. With the text still selected, in the **Font group**, click the **Text Effects** button. Point to **Shadow**, and then under **Outer**, in the first row click the third style— **Offset Diagonal Bottom Left**. In the **Font group**, click the **Font Color button arrow**. Under **Theme Colors**, in the fourth column, click the first color— **Dark Blue, Text 2**.

c. In the paragraph that begins *The Laurel College*, click to position the insertion point at the beginning of the paragraph. On the **Insert tab**, in the **Illustrations group**, click the **Picture** button. From your student data files, **Insert** the file **w01C_Welcome_Picture**. On the **Format tab**, in the **Size group**, click the **Shape Height down spin arrow** as necessary to change the height of the picture to **2"**.

d. With the picture still selected, on the **Format tab**, in the **Arrange group**, click the **Wrap Text** button. From the **Wrap Text** gallery, click **Square**.

e. Hold down Shift and point anywhere in the picture to display the 🖼 pointer. Drag the picture to align the right edge of the picture just to the left of the right margin.

f. On the **Format tab**, in the **Picture Styles group**, click the **Picture Effects** button. Point to **Glow**, and then under **Glow Variations**, in the third row, click the first style—**Blue, 11 pt glow, Accent color 1**. Nudge as necessary to match the picture position shown in Figure 1.50.

g. Click anywhere to deselect the picture. Click the **Page Layout tab**, and then in the **Page Background group**, click the **Page Borders** button. In the **Borders and Shading** dialog box, under **Setting**, click **Box**. Under **Style**, scroll down the list. About two-thirds down the list, click the style with a thin top and bottom line and a slightly thicker middle line.

h. Click the **Color arrow**, and then under **Theme Colors**, in the fourth column, click the first color— **Dark Blue, Text 2**. Click **OK**, and then **Save** your document.

3 Press Ctrl + End to move to the bottom of the document. On the **Insert tab**, in the **Text group**, click the **Text Box** button. At the bottom of the **Text Box** gallery, click **Draw Text Box**.

a. At the bottom of the document, position the ➕ pointer in an open area near the left margin, and then drag down and to the right to create a text box approximately **2.5 inches** high and **5.5 inches** wide; you need not be precise.

b. With the insertion point positioned in the text box, type the following:

Welcome Week Highlights

Tuesday: Campus tour and meeting with administrators

Wednesday: Open house in all academic departments

Thursday: Club meetings to recruit members

Friday: Student Government-hosted barbecue

(Project 1C Welcome Week continues on the next page)

c. In the text box, select all of the text. On the Mini toolbar, click the **Font Size button arrow**, and then click **14**. Click the **Bold** button, and then click the **Center** button.

d. On the **Format tab**, in the **Size group**, if necessary click the **Size** button. Click the **Shape Height spin arrows** as necessary to change the height of the text box to **2.5"**. Click the **Shape Width button up spin arrow** as necessary to widen the text box to **5.5"**.

e. In the **Shape Styles group**, click the **Shape Effects** button. Point to **Shadow**, and then under **Outer**, in the second row, click the second style—**Offset Center**. In the **Shape Styles group**, click the **Shape Outline button arrow**. Under **Theme Colors**, in the fourth column, click the first color—**Dark Blue, Text 2**.

f. If necessary, click anywhere inside the text box. Point to the text box border to display the ⬚ pointer. Drag the text box to align the left edge at approximately **0.5 inches on the horizontal ruler** and to align the top edge at approximately **5.5 inches on the vertical ruler**. You may have to click outside the text box several times to see the exact location on the rulers.

g. On the **Insert tab**, in the **Illustrations group**, click the **Shapes** button. Under **Basic Shapes**, in the first row, click the seventh shape—**Diamond**.

h. Position the ⊞ pointer slightly under the text box and at approximately **2 inches on the horizontal ruler**. Drag down approximately **1 inch** and to the right approximately **2 inches**. On the **Format tab**, in the **Size group**, adjust the **Shape Height** to **0.9"** and the **Shape Width** to **2"**.

i. Right-click the new shape, and then click **Add Text**. Type **Enjoy!** and then select the text you typed. On the Mini toolbar, click the **Font Size button arrow**, and then click **20**. Click the **Bold** button, and then if necessary, click the **Center** button.

j. On the **Format tab**, in the **Shape Styles group**, click the **Shape Fill button arrow**, and then under **Theme Colors**, in the fourth column, click the first color—**Dark Blue, Text 2**.

k. Point to the shape border until the ⬚ pointer displays, and then position the shape with its widest points aligned with the lower edge of the text box and approximately centered. As necessary, move the shape in small increments by pressing the arrow keys on your keyboard. Refer to Figure 1.50 for approximate placement. **Save** your document.

4 Click the **Insert tab**, and then, in the **Header & Footer group**, click the **Footer** button. At the bottom of the **Footer** gallery, click **Edit Footer**.

a. On the **Design tab**, in the **Insert group**, click the **Quick Parts** button, and then click **Field**. In the **Field names** list, scroll as necessary to locate and click **FileName**. Click **OK**, and then double-click anywhere in the document.

b. Press ⌃Ctrl + Home to move the insertion point to the beginning of the document. Display **Backstage** view. On the right, under the screen thumbnail, click **Properties**, and then click **Show Document Panel**. In the **Author** box, delete any text and then type your firstname and lastname. In the **Subject** box, type your course name and section number, and in the **Keywords** box type **Welcome Week**

c. **Close** the Document Panel. In **Backstage** view, click the **Print tab** to display the **Print Preview**. If necessary, return to the document to make any corrections or adjustments.

d. **Save** your document, print or submit electronically as directed by your instructor, and then **Close** Word.

End **You have completed Project 1C** ——————————

Content-Based Assessments

Apply 1B skills from these Objectives:

5 Change Document and Paragraph Layout

6 Create and Modify Lists

7 Set and Modify Tab Stops

8 Insert a SmartArt Graphic

Skills Review | Project **1D** Constitution

In the following Skills Review, you will edit the constitution of the Associated Students of Laurel College. Your completed document will look similar to Figure 1.51.

Project Files

For Project 1D, you will need the following file:

w01D_Constitution

You will save your document as:

Lastname_Firstname_1D_Constitution

Project Results

Figure 1.51

(Project 1D Constitution continues on the next page)

Skills Review | Project **1D** Constitution (continued)

1 **Start** Word. From your student files, locate and open the document **w01D_Constitution**. Display **Backstage** view, click **Save As**, and then navigate to your **Word Chapter 1** folder. **Save** the document as **Lastname_Firstname_1D_Constitution**

   a. On the **Home tab**, in the **Paragraph group**, be sure the **Show/Hide** button is active so you can view formatting marks. Click the **Page Layout tab**. In the **Page Setup group**, click the **Margins** button, and then at the bottom of the **Margins** gallery, at the bottom of the list, click **Custom Margins**. In the **Page Setup** dialog box, in the **Top** box, type **1** Press Tab as necessary to select the values in the **Bottom**, **Left**, and **Right** boxes and change all margins to **1**. Click **OK**.

   b. Press Ctrl + A to select all of the text in the document. On the **Home tab**, in the **Paragraph group**, click the **Align Text Left** button to change the alignment from justified to left aligned.

   c. With all of the text still selected, on the **Home tab**, in the **Paragraph group**, click the **Line Spacing** button, and then click **1.15**. Click the **Page Layout tab**, and then in the **Paragraph group**, under **Spacing**, set **After** to **6 pt** spacing after each paragraph.

   d. At the top of the document, click anywhere in the title, right-click, and then on the Mini toolbar, click **Center**. Near the top of **Page 1**, locate and select the paragraph that begins *ARTICLE 1*. Hold down Ctrl, and then use the vertical scroll bar to scroll through the document, and then select the other two paragraphs that begin *ARTICLE*. On the Mini toolbar, click **Center**.

   e. With the three subheadings that begin *ARTICLE* still selected, on the **Page Layout tab**, in the **Paragraph group**, under **Spacing**, set **Before** to **12 pt**.

   f. Scroll to view the bottom of **Page 1**, point anywhere in the bottom margin area, right-click, and then click **Edit Footer**. On the **Design tab**, in the **Insert group**, click the **Quick Parts** button, and then click **Field**. In the **Field names** list, scroll as necessary to locate and click **FileName**. Click **OK**, and then double-click anywhere in the document to exit the footer area.

2 Near the middle of **Page 1**, *above* the *ARTICLE II* subheading, locate the paragraph that begins *Executive Branch*, and then move the pointer into the left margin

area to display the pointer. Drag down to select this paragraph and the next two paragraphs. On the **Home tab**, in the **Paragraph group**, click the **Bullets** button.

   a. Scroll to view the bottom of **Page 1**, and then locate the paragraph that begins *Completion of at least*. Select that paragraph and the next two paragraphs. On the **Home tab**, in the **Paragraph group**, click the **Numbering** button.

   b. Locate the paragraph that begins *Section 4 Elections*. Click to position the insertion point at the *end* of that paragraph after the colon, and then press Enter.

   c. Type **1.** and press Spacebar. Type **Completion of at least 12 credit hours at Laurel College** and then press Enter. Type the following text for items 2 and 3 in the list:

   Minimum GPA of 2.75

   Enrollment in at least six credit hours each semester in office

   d. Near the middle of **Page 1**, select the three items in the bulleted list, right-click the list, and then point to **Bullets**. Under **Bullet Library**, click the **black square** symbol. If the black square is not available, choose another bullet symbol. **Save** your document.

3 Be sure the bulleted list is still selected. Point to the left tab marker at **2″ on the horizontal ruler**. When the *Left Tab* ScreenTip displays, double-click to open the **Tabs** dialog box.

   a. Under **Tab stop position**, with *2″* selected, at the bottom of the dialog box, click **Clear** to delete this tab stop. Then, type **5.5** in the **Tab stop position** box.

   b. Under **Alignment**, click the **Right** option button. Under **Leader**, click the **2** option button. At the bottom of the **Tabs** dialog box, click the **Set** button, and then click **OK**.

4 Press Ctrl + Home to move to the top of the document. Click at the end of the title, and then press Enter to insert a blank paragraph. Click the **Insert tab**, and then in the **Illustrations group**, click the **SmartArt** button.

   a. In the **Choose a SmartArt Graphic** dialog box, on the left, click **Hierarchy**, and in the second row, click the fourth style—**Table Hierarchy**. At the bottom of the **Choose a SmartArt Graphic** dialog box, click **OK**. If necessary, on the Design tab, in the Create Graphic group, activate the Text Pane button.

(Project 1D Constitution continues on the next page)

b. In the SmartArt graphic, in the second row, click the border of the first *[Text]* box, and then press Del. Press Del again to delete a second *[Text]* box. In the **Text Pane**, under **Type your text here** box, click in the last bulleted point. On the **Design tab**, in the **Create Graphic group**, click the **Promote** button to move the list item up one level.

c. In the **Text Pane**, click in the top bulleted point, type **Associated Students of Laurel College** and then press ↓. Type the following in the three remaining boxes:

Executive Officers

Student Senate

Judicial Review Committee

d. In the upper right corner of the **Text Pane**, click the **Close** button. Be sure the graphic is selected—a pale border surrounds the entire graphic, and then click the outside border one time. Click the **Format tab**, and then in the **Size group**, if necessary click the **Size** button. By clicking the spin box arrows, change the **Shape Height** to **2.6″** and the **Shape Width** to **6.5″**.

e. With the SmartArt graphic still selected, on the **Design tab**, in the **SmartArt Styles group**, click the **Change Colors** button. Scroll down, and then under **Accent 5**, click the second style—**Colored Fill - Accent 5**.

f. On the **Design tab**, in the **SmartArt Styles group**, click the **More** button. Under **3-D**, click the second style—**Inset**. Click anywhere in the document to deselect the graphic. Press Ctrl + Home to move the insertion point to the beginning of the document.

g. Display **Backstage** view, on the right, under the screen thumbnail, click **Properties**, and then click **Show Document Panel**. In the **Author** box, type your firstname and lastname. In the **Subject** box type your course name and section number, and in the **Keywords** box type **student constitution**

h. **Close** the Document Panel. Click **Save**. Display **Backstage** view and click the **Print tab**. Examine the **Print Preview**. Print or submit electronically as directed. **Close** Word.

End **You have completed Project 1D** ———————————————

Apply 1A skills from these Objectives:

1 Create a New Document and Insert Text

2 Insert and Format Graphics

3 Insert and Modify Text Boxes and Shapes

4 Preview and Print a Document

Mastering Word | Project 1E Retreat

In the following Mastering Word project, you will create a flyer announcing a retreat for the Associated Students of Laurel College Board. Your completed document will look similar to Figure 1.52.

Project Files

For Project 1E, you will need the following files:

New blank Word document
w01E_Retreat_Text
w01E_Retreat_Picture

You will save your document as:

Lastname_Firstname_1E_Retreat

Project Results

ASLC Board Retreat

College President Diane Gilmore is pleased to announce a retreat for the Board of the Associated Students of Laurel College.

Invitees include the ASLC Board, consisting of the Executive Officers and their appointed directors, Student Senators, Club Presidents, and members of the Judicial Review Committee. The retreat will be held at the Fogelsville campus of Penn State University on Friday, November 12.

The morning session will begin with a continental breakfast at 8:30 a.m., and will include presentations on effective ways to set and achieve goals. Lunch will be served at noon. The afternoon session will begin at 1:30 p.m., and will include small breakout sessions for the sharing and development of goals and a series of exercises to facilitate group interaction.

In addition to goal setting, the retreat is organized to provide a means for Board members to get to know one another. Students are so busy with courses, student government duties, and personal responsibilities that they rarely get to interact with other Board members outside of their immediate circles. The afternoon will be devoted to a series of exercises specially designed for this retreat. It will enable all participants to meet every other person in attendance and to exchange ideas. We have hired the well-known group, Mountain Retreat Planners, to conduct this portion of the program. They have some entertaining activities planned that will help break down barriers to becoming acquainted with other participants.

Prize drawings at lunch include concert tickets, college football jerseys, coffee mugs, and restaurant gift cards.

Lastname_Firstname_1E_Retreat

Figure 1.52

(Project 1E Retreat continues on the next page)

Content-Based Assessments

Mastering Word | Project 1E Retreat (continued)

1 **Start** Word and display a new blank document. **Save** the document in your **Word Chapter 1** folder as **Lastname_Firstname_1E_Retreat** and then add the file name to the footer. Be sure the formatting marks and rulers display.

2 Type **ASLC Board Retreat** and press Enter two times. Type **College President Diane Gilmore is pleased to announce a retreat for the Board of the Associated Students of Laurel College**. Press Enter one time. **Insert** the file **w01E_Retreat_Text**.

3 Select the title *ASLC Board Retreat*. On the **Home tab**, in the **Font group**, display the **Text Effects** gallery, and then in the third row, apply the first effect—**Fill - White, Gradient Outline - Accent 1**. Change the **Font Size** to **56** pt. Apply a **Shadow** text effect using the first effect under **Outer—Offset Diagonal Bottom Right**. Change the **Font Color** to **Olive Green, Accent 3, Darker 25%**—in the seventh column, the fifth color.

4 Click to position the insertion point at the beginning of the paragraph that begins *College President*, and then from your student files, **Insert** the picture **w01E_Retreat_Picture**. Change the **Shape Height** of the picture to **2″**, and then set the **Wrap Text** to **Square**. Move the picture so that the right edge aligns with the right margin, and the top edge aligns with the top edge of the text that begins *College President*. Apply a **Film Grain Artistic Effect**—the third effect in the third row. From **Picture Effects**, add a **5 Point Soft Edge**.

5 Scroll to view the lower portion of the page. **Insert** a **Text Box** beginning at the left margin and at approximately **7 inches on the vertical ruler** that is approximately 1″ high and 4.5″ wide. Then, in the **Size group**, make the measurements exact by setting the **Height** to 1″ and the **Width** to **4.6″**. Type the following text in the text box:

> **Prize drawings at lunch include concert tickets, college football jerseys, coffee mugs, and restaurant gift cards.**

6 Select the text in the text box. Change the **Font Size** to **16** pt, apply **Bold**, and **Center** the text. Add a **Shape Fill** to the text box using the theme color **Olive Green, Accent 3, Lighter 40%**. Then apply a **Gradient** fill using the **Linear Right** gradient. Change the **Shape Outline** color to **White, Background 1**. Drag the text box as necessary to center it horizontally between the left and right margins, and vertically between the last line of text and the footer.

7 Display the **Document Panel**. Type your firstname and lastname in the **Author** box, your course name and section number in the **Subject** box, and then in the **Keywords** box type **retreat, ASLC**

8 **Close** the Document Panel. **Save** and preview your document, make any necessary adjustments, and then print your document or submit it electronically as directed. **Close** Word.

End **You have completed Project 1E**

Apply 1B skills from these Objectives:

- ▣ Change Document and Paragraph Layout
- ▣ Create and Modify Lists
- ▣ Set and Modify Tab Stops
- ▣ Insert a SmartArt Graphic

Mastering Word | Project **1F** Cycling Trip

In the following Mastering Word project, you will create an informational handout about a planned trip by the Laurel College Cycling Club. Your completed document will look similar to Figure 1.53.

Project Files

For Project 1F, you will need the following file:

w01F_Cycling_Trip

You will save your document as:

Lastname_Firstname_1F_Cycling_Trip

Project Results

Figure 1.53

(Project 1F Cycling Trip continues on the next page)

Content-Based Assessments

Mastering Word | Project **1F** Cycling Trip (continued)

1 **Start** Word. From your student files open the document **w01F_Cycling_Trip**. **Save** the document in your **Word Chapter 1** folder as **Lastname_Firstname_1F_Cycling_Trip** Add the file name to the footer. Display formatting marks.

2 Display the **Page Setup** dialog box. Set the **Top** margin to **1.25"** and the other three margins to **1"**. Select all of the text in the document, including the title. Add **6 pt** spacing after all paragraphs. Change the **Line Spacing** to **1.15**. Change the alignment to **Align Text Left**. **Center** the document title—*Cycling Club Trip*.

3 Locate the paragraph that begins *Bicycle in good*. Select that paragraph and the three paragraphs that follow it. Create a bulleted list from the selected text. Use the shortcut menu to display bullet options, and change the bullet character to a **check mark** or another symbol if the check mark is unavailable.

4 Position the insertion point in the blank paragraph at the end of the document. Add a **Right** tab stop at **3.5"**. Display the **Tabs** dialog box and add a dot leader. **Set** the tab stop, and then add and **Set** another **Right** tab stop with a dot leader at **6.5"**.

5 Type the text shown in **Table 1**, pressing Tab between columns and Enter at the end of each line. Refer to Figure 1.53.

6 Select the first two lines in the tabbed list and change the **Space After** to **0 pt**. Near the top of the document, position the insertion point in the blank line below the title. Display the **Choose a SmartArt Graphic** dialog box, select the **Cycle** category, and then in the second row, select the first style—**Continuous Cycle**.

7 Display the **Text Pane**. Add the following cities in this order: **Allentown** and **Cemerton** and **Palmerton** and **Berlinsville** and **Pennsville**

8 **Close** the Text Pane. Click the SmartArt border. On the **Format tab**, set the **Shape Width** of the SmartArt graphic to **6.5"** and the **Shape Height** to **3"**. On the **Design tab**, from the **SmartArt Styles** gallery, apply the **Cartoon 3-D** style, and change the colors to the first color under **Colorful—Colorful – Accent Colors**.

9 Display the **Document Panel**, type your firstname and lastname in the **Author** box, your course name and section number in the **Subject** box, and then in the **Keywords** box type **cycling, cycling club**

10 **Close** the Document Panel. **Save** your document. Preview your document, check for and make any adjustments, and then print your document or submit it electronically as directed. **Close** Word.

Table 1

Thursday, October 7	3:00 p.m.	Field House Room B
Thursday, November 11	7:30 p.m.	Student Activities Center L-7
Thursday, December 9	5:00 p.m.	Little Theater

- - - ▶ (Return to Step 6)

End You have completed Project 1F ————————————

Content-Based Assessments

1. Create a New Document and Insert Text
2. Insert and Format Graphics
3. Insert and Modify Text Boxes and Shapes
4. Preview and Print a Document
5. Change Document and Paragraph Layout
6. Create and Modify Lists
7. Set and Modify Tab Stops
8. Insert a SmartArt Graphic

Mastering Word | Project **1G** Web Sites

In the following Mastering Word project, you will edit guidelines for club Web sites at Laurel College. Your completed document will look similar to Figure 1.54.

Project Files

For Project 1G, you will need the following files:

New blank Word document
w01G_Chess_Club_Picture
w01G_Web_Sites_Text

You will save your document as:

Lastname_Firstname_1G_Web_Sites

Project Results

Club Web Sites

Published by Student Computing Services

The Web site that your club develops will represent your club and its membership. The site can promote interest in your club and attract new members—think of it as advertising. The site is also a main source of information for current members. Always consider how others will view or interpret the content of your site. Use the guidelines listed below as you develop and update the information you publish.

The college Student Computing Services office is available to assist clubs with Web site development and maintenance. Consult the contact information, listed at the end of these guidelines, to set up a meeting with one of our staff members.

General Information Guidelines

Be sure that:

- All information on the Web site is club related.
- No personal information or links to personal information is on the Web site unless the content has a specific relationship to the club.
- Updates to the Web site are frequent enough to eliminate outdated content and to add new content.
- Instruction is available to club members regarding proper use of bulletin boards, including general etiquette rules.
- Protected information on the Web site is available only to club members who have been issued user names and passwords.
- The club's faculty advisor approves all Web site content and updates to the site.

General information about the club should include:

1. Purpose and goals of the club
2. Names of club officers and their campus email addresses
3. Dates and locations of club meetings
4. Dates and locations of special events
5. Applications for club membership
6. Information about election of officers and nomination forms

Lastname_Firstname_1G_Web_Sites

Figure 1.54

(Project 1G Web Sites continues on the next page)

Content-Based Assessments

Mastering Word | Project **1G** Web Sites (continued)

1 **Start** Word and display a new blank document. Display formatting marks and rulers. **Save** the document in your **Word Chapter 1** folder as **Lastname_Firstname_ 1G_Web_Sites** Add the file name to the footer.

Type **Club Web Sites** and then press [Enter]. Select the title you just typed. From the **Text Effects** gallery, in the fourth row, apply the second effect—**Gradient Fill - Orange, Accent 6, Inner Shadow**, change the **Font Size** to **72** pt, and **Center** the title.

2 Click in the blank line below the title. Locate and insert the file **w01G_Web_Sites_Text**. *Except* for the document title, select all of the document text. **Align Text Left**, change the **Line Spacing** to **1.15**, and change the **Spacing After** to **6 pt**. Locate and **Center** the document subtitle that begins *Published by*.

3 In the middle of **Page 1**, under the subheading *Be sure that*, select the six paragraphs down to, but not including, the *General information* subheading. Format the selected text as a bulleted list. Near the bottom of **Page 1** and the top of **Page 2**, under the *Web Site Design Guidelines* subheading, select all of the paragraphs to the end of the document—not including the blank paragraph mark—and create another bulleted list.

4 Under the subheading that begins *General information*, select the six paragraphs and apply **Numbering** to create a numbered list.

Near the top of the document, position the insertion point to the left of the paragraph that begins The Web site. **Insert** the picture **w01G_Chess_Club_Picture**. Set the **Wrap Text** to **Square**. Decrease the picture **Width** to **2.7″**. From the **Picture Effects** gallery, apply the **Soft Edges** effect using **5 Point**.

5 Press [Ctrl] + [End] to move to the blank line at the end of the document. Type **For assistance, Student Computing Services hours are:** and then press [Enter]. Set a **Left** tab stop at **1.5″**. Display the **Tabs** dialog box. At **5″** add a **Right** tab stop with a **dot leader** and click **Set**. Click **OK** to close the dialog box, press [Tab] to begin, and then type the following information; be sure to press [Tab] to

begin each line and press [Tab] between the days and the times and press [Enter] at the end of each line:

Monday–Thursday	8 a.m. to 10 p.m.
Friday	8 a.m. to 5 p.m.
Saturday	8 a.m. to 12 noon

6 At the top of **Page 2**, position the insertion point to the left of the subheading *Web Site Design Guidelines*. Press [Enter] one time, and then click in the blank paragraph you just created. **Insert** a **SmartArt** graphic, and then from the **Process** group, select the **Basic Chevron Process**—in the fourth row, the third graphic. Click the border of the graphic, and then on the **Format tab**, set the **Shape Height** of the graphic to **1″** and the **Shape Width** of the graphic to **6.5″**. From the **Design tab**, display the **Text Pane**, and then type **Club** and **Web Site** and **New Members Close** the **Text Pane**. Change style to **3-D Inset** and the colors to **Colored Fill – Accent 6**, which is in the last set of colors.

7 At the bottom of **Page 2**, **Insert** a **Text Box** and set the height to **0.7″** and the width to **5″**. In the text box, type: **The Student Computing Services office is located in the Cedar Building, Room 114, call (215) 555-0932.**

Select the text in the text box. From the Mini toolbar, change the **Font Size** to **16** pt, apply **Bold**, and **Center** the text. Change the **Shape Fill** to **Orange, Accent 6, Darker 25%**. From the **Shape Effects** gallery, apply a **Circle Bevel**. By using the pointer, visually center the text box horizontally between the left and right margins and vertically between the tabbed list and the footer.

8 As the document properties, type your firstname and lastname in the **Author** box, your course name and section number in the **Subject** box, and then in the **Keywords** box type **Web sites, guidelines, Student Computing Services Save** your document, examine the Print Preview, check for and make any adjustments, and then print your document or submit it electronically as directed. **Close** Word.

End You have completed Project 1G ————————

Content-Based Assessments

GO! Fix It | Project **1H** Guidelines

Project Files

For Project 1H, you will need the following file:

w01H_Guidelines

You will save your document as:

Lastname_Firstname_1H_Guidelines

From the student files that accompany this textbook, locate and open the file w01H_More_Guidelines, and then save the file in your Word Chapter 1 folder as **Lastname_Firstname_1H_Guidelines**

This document contains errors that you must find and correct. Read and examine the document, and then edit to correct any errors that you find and to improve the overall document format. Types of errors could include, but are not restricted to:

- Wasted space due to text not wrapping around pictures
- Inconsistent line spacing in paragraphs
- Inconsistent spacing between paragraphs
- Inconsistent paragraph indents
- Inconsistent indenting of lists
- Titles that do not extend across the page
- Text boxes that are too small
- Tabbed lists with wide spaces that do not contain leaders
- Spaces between paragraphs created using empty paragraphs rather than space after paragraphs

Things you should know to complete this project:

- Displaying formatting marks will assist in locating spacing errors.
- There are no errors in the fonts, although the title font size is too small.
- The final flyer should fit on one page.

Save your document and add the file name to the footer. In the Document Panel, type your firstname and lastname in the Author box and your course name and section number in the Subject box. In the Keywords box type **Web site guidelines** and then save your document and submit as directed.

End **You have completed Project 1H** ———————————————

Content-Based Assessments

Apply a combination of the 1A and 1B skills.

GO! Make It | Project 1I Flyer

Project Files

For Project 1I, you will need the following files:

w01I_Team_Building   w01I_Park_Picture

You will save your document as:

Lastname_Firstname_1I_Team_Building

From the student files that accompany this textbook, locate and open the file w01I_Team_Building, and then save the file in your chapter folder as **Lastname_Firstname_1I_Team_Building**

Use the skills you have practiced, create the document shown in Figure 1.55. The title uses Gradient Fill – Blue, Accent 1, 48 pt. The SmartArt graphic uses the Radial Cycle with an Intense Effect style, is 3″ high and 6.5″ wide, has the Colorful Range – Accent Colors 2 to 3 applied. The w01I_Park_Picture picture has a 2.5 pt soft edge, and is 2.5″ wide. The page border uses Dark Blue, Text 2.

Add the file name to the footer; in the Document Panel, add your name and course information and the Keywords **team building**; save your document; and then submit as directed.

Project Results

Figure 1.55

Team Building Session

The administration at Laurel College is organizing a retreat for the ASLC Board, consisting of the Executive Officers and their appointed directors, Student Senators, Club Presidents, and members of the Judicial Review Committee. The retreat will be held at the Fogelsville campus of Penn State University on Friday, November 12.

The afternoon session will begin at 1:30 p.m. When the retreat was first organized, the afternoon session was to include small group work sessions for the sharing and development of goals and a series of exercises to facilitate group interaction. However, we have been fortunate to secure the services of F. B Lewis, the nationally-renowned team-building expert. Therefore, the afternoon session will consist of an outdoor team-building exercise.

The exercise will be held in Westfield Park, which is shown in the picture, and will enable each participant to:

- Decide when teams are appropriate, and when they are not
- Devise new conflict resolution strategies
- Strengthen leadership skills
- Strengthen interpersonal skills
- Value and understand diversity

Lastname_Firstname_1I_Team_Building

End You have completed Project 1I

Content-Based Assessments

GO! Solve It | Project **1J** Food Drive

Project Files

For Project 1J, you will need the following file:

New blank Word document
w01J_Food_Drive

You will save your document as:

Lastname_Firstname_1J_Food_Drive

Create a new document and save it in your Word Chapter 1 folder as **Lastname_Firstname_1J_Food_Drive** Use the following information to create a flyer that includes a title that uses Text Effects, introductory text, two lists of an appropriate type, one text box, and a picture with appropriate formatting and text wrapping. Use your own picture or w01J_Food_Drive.

This Thanksgiving, the Associated Students of Laurel College is sponsoring a food drive for the local community. All college clubs are invited to participate. Results will be adjusted for club membership by measuring the results in pounds of food per member. Three kinds of food are acceptable: canned goods, non-perishable dry goods, and boxed or canned dry drink mixes, such as coffee, tea, or lemonade.

To participate, a club must follow this procedure: fill out a competition form, collect the goods, and then turn the food in on November 13. The address and telephone number for the ASLC is the Cedar Building, Room 222, Laurelton, PA 19100, (215) 555-0902.

Add the file name to the footer. To the Properties area, add your name, your course name and section number, and the keywords **food drive, clubs**

	Performance Level		
	Exemplary: You consistently applied the relevant skills	**Proficient:** You sometimes, but not always, applied the relevant skills	**Developing:** You rarely or never applied the relevant skills
Create and format lists	Both lists use the proper list type and are formatted correctly.	One of the lists is formatted correctly.	Neither of the lists are formatted correctly.
Insert and format a picture	The picture is inserted and positioned correctly, and text is wrapped around the picture.	The picture is inserted but not formatted properly.	No picture is inserted.
Insert a text box	A text box with appropriate information is inserted and formatted.	A text box is adequately formatted but is difficult to read or unattractive.	No text box is inserted.
Insert introductory text	Introductory text explains the reason for the flyer, with no spelling or grammar errors.	Some introductory text is included, but does not contain sufficient information and/or includes spelling or grammar errors.	No introductory text, or insufficient introductory text.
Insert title using Text Effects	Text Effects title inserted and centered on the page.	Text Effects title is inserted, but not centered or formatted attractively on the page.	No Text Effects title is included.

Performance Criteria (vertical label on left side of table)

End You have completed Project 1J

Content-Based Assessments

Apply a combination of the 1A and 1B skills..

GO! Solve It | Project **1K** Fitness Services

Project Files

For Project 1K, you will need the following files:

New blank Word document
w01K_Volleyball

You will save your document as:

Lastname_Firstname_1K_Fitness_Services

Create a new file and save it as **Lastname_Firstname_1K_Fitness Services** Use the following information to create a flyer that includes introductory text, a SmartArt graphic, a title that uses Text Effects, and a picture that has an artistic effect applied and uses text wrapping. Use your own picture or w01K_Volleyball.

The Associated Students of Laurel College sponsors fitness activities. These take place both on campus and off campus. The activities fall into two categories: Fitness Services and Intramural Sports. Fitness Services are noncompetitive activities, with the most popular being Kickboxing, Jogging, and Aerobics. The most popular Intramural Sports activities—which include competitive team and club sports—are Field Hockey, Volleyball, and Basketball.

Add the file name to the footer, and add your name, your course name and section number, and the keywords **fitness, sports** to the Properties area.

	Performance Level		
	Exemplary: You consistently applied the relevant skills	**Proficient:** You sometimes, but not always, applied the relevant skills	**Developing:** You rarely or never applied the relevant skills
Insert title using Text Effects	Text Effects title inserted and centered on the page.	Text Effects title is inserted, but not centered on the page.	No Text Effects title is included.
Insert introductory text	Introductory text explains the reason for the flyer, with no spelling or grammar errors.	Some introductory text is included, but does not sufficiently explain the topic and/or includes spelling or grammar errors.	No or insufficient introductory text is included.
Insert and format a picture	The picture is inserted and positioned correctly, an artistic effect is applied, and text is wrapped around the picture.	The picture is inserted but not formatted properly.	No picture is inserted in the document.
Insert and format SmartArt	The SmartArt graphic displays both categories of fitness activities and examples of each type.	The SmartArt graphic does not display fitness activities by category.	No SmartArt graphic inserted.

Performance Criteria

End You have completed Project 1K

Outcomes-Based Assessments

Rubric

The following outcomes-based assessments are *open-ended assessments*. That is, there is no specific correct result; your result will depend on your approach to the information provided. Make *Professional Quality* your goal. Use the following scoring rubric to guide you in *how* to approach the problem and then to evaluate *how well* your approach solves the problem.

The *criteria*—Software Mastery, Content, Format and Layout, and Process—represent the knowledge and skills you have gained that you can apply to solving the problem. The *levels of performance*—Professional Quality, Approaching Professional Quality, or Needs Quality Improvements—help you and your instructor evaluate your result.

	Your completed project is of Professional Quality if you:	Your completed project is Approaching Professional Quality if you:	Your completed project Needs Quality Improvements if you:
1-Software Mastery	Choose and apply the most appropriate skills, tools, and features and identify efficient methods to solve the problem.	Choose and apply some appropriate skills, tools, and features, but not in the most efficient manner.	Choose inappropriate skills, tools, or features, or are inefficient in solving the problem.
2-Content	Construct a solution that is clear and well organized, contains content that is accurate, appropriate to the audience and purpose, and is complete. Provide a solution that contains no errors in spelling, grammar, or style.	Construct a solution in which some components are unclear, poorly organized, inconsistent, or incomplete. Misjudge the needs of the audience. Have some errors in spelling, grammar, or style, but the errors do not detract from comprehension.	Construct a solution that is unclear, incomplete, or poorly organized; contains some inaccurate or inappropriate content; and contains many errors in spelling, grammar, or style. Do not solve the problem.
3-Format and Layout	Format and arrange all elements to communicate information and ideas, clarify function, illustrate relationships, and indicate relative importance.	Apply appropriate format and layout features to some elements, but not others. Overuses features, causing minor distraction.	Apply format and layout that does not communicate information or ideas clearly. Do not use format and layout features to clarify function, illustrate relationships, or indicate relative importance. Use available features excessively, causing distraction.
4-Process	Use an organized approach that integrates planning, development, self-assessment, revision, and reflection.	Demonstrate an organized approach in some areas, but not others; or, uses an insufficient process of organization throughout.	Do not use an organized approach to solve the problem.

Outcomes-Based Assessments

Apply a combination of the 1A and 1B skills..

GO! Think | Project **1L** Academic Services

Project Files

For Project 1L, you will need the following file:

New blank Word document

You will save your document as:

Lastname_Firstname_1L_Academic_Services

The Services Coordinator of the Associated Students of Laurel College needs to create a flyer to inform students of academic services available at the ASLC office. Referrals are available for medical, legal, and counseling services, as well as tutoring and volunteer organizations. Among the services offered at the ASLC office are free printing (up to 250 pages per semester), help with minor legal issues, housing information, bicycle repair, minor computer repair, and help placing students with volunteer organizations.

Create a flyer with basic information about the services provided. Be sure the flyer is easy to read and understand and has an attractive design. If you need more information about student services available at other colleges, search the Web for **student government** and add whatever services you think might be (or should be) available at your college. Add appropriate information to the Document Panel. Save the document as **Lastname_Firstname_1L_Academic_Services** and submit it as directed.

End **You have completed Project 1L** —————————————————

Apply a combination of the 1A and 1B skills.

GO! Think | Project **1M** Campus Bookstore

Project Files

For Project 1M, you will need the following files:

New blank Word document
w01L_Campus_Bookstore

You will save your document as:

Lastname_Firstname_1M_Campus_Bookstore

The manager of the Laurel College Bookstore needs to create a flyer that can be handed out by the ASLC to students during Welcome Week. The bookstore gives students attending Welcome Week a discount of 20% on special items such as sweatshirts and other college-related clothing, coffee mugs, calendars, and similar items. Door prizes will also be awarded. The bookstore is open Monday and Thursday from 8 a.m. to 10 p.m., Tuesday and Wednesday from 8 a.m. to 8 p.m., and Friday from 8 a.m. to 5 p.m.

Using your own campus bookstore as an example, create a flyer that gives general information about the bookstore, provides one or more lists of items that are on sale, displays the picture w01M_ Campus_Bookstore, and has a highlighted area that gives the store hours.

Add appropriate information to the Document Panel. Save the document as **Lastname_Firstname_1M_Campus_Bookstore** and submit it as directed.

End **You have completed Project 1M** —————————————————

Outcomes-Based Assessments

Apply a combination of the 1A and 1B skills.

You and GO! | Project **1N** Family Flyer

Project Files

For Project 1N, you will need the following file:

New blank Word document

You will save your document as

Lastname_Firstname_1N_Family_Flyer

In this project, you will create a one-page flyer that you can send to your family. Include any information that may interest your family members, such as work-related news, school events, vacation plans, and the activities and accomplishments of you, your spouse, your friends, or other family members. Choose any writing style that suits you—chatty, newsy, entertaining, or humorous.

To complete the assignment, be sure to include a title, at least one list, a picture, and either a SmartArt graphic or a text box or shape. Before you submit the flyer, be sure to check it for grammar and spelling errors, and also be sure to format the document in an attractive manner, using the skills you practiced in this chapter.

Save the file as **Lastname_Firstname_1N_Family_Flyer** Add the file name to the footer, and add your name, your course name and section number, and the keywords **flyer** and **family** to the Properties area. Submit your file as directed.

End **You have completed Project 1N** ——————————————————————

Using Tables and Templates to Create Resumes and Cover Letters

OUTCOMES

At the end of this chapter you will be able to:

OBJECTIVES

Mastering these objectives will enable you to:

PROJECT 2A

Create a resume by using a Word table.

1. Create a Table (p. 107)
2. Add Text to a Table (p. 108)
3. Format a Table (p. 111)

PROJECT 2B

Create a cover letter and resume by using a template.

4. Create a New Document from an Existing Document (p. 120)
5. Change and Reorganize Text (p. 123)
6. Use the Proofing Options (p. 130)
7. Create a Document Using a Template (p. 134)

James Thew/Shutterstock

In This Chapter

Tables are useful for organizing and presenting data. Because a table is so easy to use, many individuals prefer to arrange tabular information in a Word table rather than setting a series of tabs. Use a table when you want to present rows and columns of information or to create a structure for a document such as a resume.

When using Word to write business or personal letters, use a commonly approved letter format. You will make a good impression on prospective employers if you use a standard business letter style when you are writing a cover letter for a resume. You can create a resume using one of the Microsoft resume templates included with Microsoft Office or available online.

The projects in this chapter relate to **Madison Staffing Services**. Many companies prefer to hire employees through a staffing service, so that both the employer and the employee can determine if the match is a good fit. Madison Staffing Services takes care of the details of recruiting, testing, hiring, and paying the employee. At the end of the employment assignment, neither the employer nor the employee is required to make a permanent commitment. Many individuals find full-time jobs with an employer for whom they initially worked through a staffing agency.

Project 2A Resume

Project Activities

In Activities 2.01 through 2.09, you will create a table to use as the structure for a resume for one of Madison Staffing Services' clients. Your completed document will look similar to Figure 2.1.

Project Files

For Project 2A, you will need the following file:

w02A_Experience

You will save your document as:

Lastname_Firstname_2A_Resume

Project Results

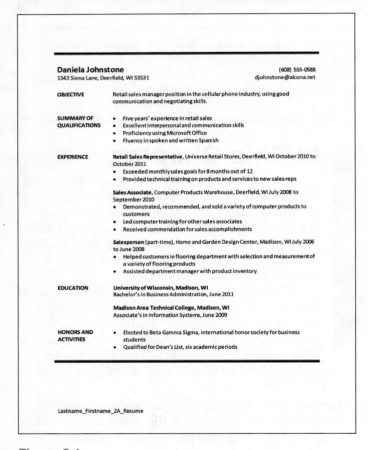

Figure 2.1
Project 2A Resume

Objective 1 | Create a Table

A *table* is an arrangement of information organized into rows and columns. The intersection of a row and a column in a table creates a box called a *cell* into which you can type. Tables are useful to present information in a logical and orderly manner.

Activity 2.01 | Creating a Table

1 Start **Word**, and in the new blank document, display formatting marks and rulers.

2 Click the **File tab**, and then in **Backstage** view, click **Save As**. In the **Save As** dialog box, navigate to the location where you are storing your projects for this chapter. Create a new folder named **Word Chapter 2**

3 **Save** the file in the **Word Chapter 2** folder as **Lastname_Firstname_2A_Resume**

4 Scroll to the end of the document, right-click near the bottom of the page, and then click **Edit Footer**. On the **Design tab**, in the **Insert group**, click the **Quick Parts** button, and then click **Field**.

5 Under **Field names**, scroll down, click **FileName**, and then click **OK**. **Close** the footer area.

6 On the **Insert tab**, in the **Tables group**, click the **Table** button. In the **Table** grid, in the fourth row, point to the second square, and notice that the cells display in orange and *2 × 4 Table* displays at the top of the grid. Compare your screen with Figure 2.2.

Figure 2.2

Table button
Table size
Pointer indicates table size
Preview of table

7 Click one time to create the table. Notice that formatting marks in each cell indicate the end of the contents of each cell and the mark to the right of each *row* indicates the row end. **Save** your document, and then compare your screen with Figure 2.3.

A table with four rows and two columns displays at the insertion point location, and the insertion point displays in the upper left cell. The table fills the width of the page, from the left margin to the right margin. On the Ribbon, Table Tools display and add two tabs—*Design* and *Layout*. Borders display around each cell in the table.

Figure 2.3

Table Tools
Indicates the end of a row
Indicates the end of cell contents

Objective 2 | Add Text to a Table

In a Word table, each cell behaves similarly to a document. For example, as you type in a cell, when you reach the right border of the cell, wordwrap moves the text to the next line. When you press Enter, the insertion point moves down to a new paragraph in the same cell. You can also insert text from another document into a table cell.

Activity 2.02 | Adding Text to a Table

There are numerous acceptable formats for resumes, many of which can be found in Business Communications textbooks. The layout used in this project is suitable for a recent college graduate and places topics in the left column and details in the right column.

1 Scroll up to view the top of the document. With the insertion point blinking in the first cell in the first row, type **OBJECTIVE** and then press Tab.

> Pressing Tab moves the insertion point to the next cell in the row, or, if the insertion point is already in the last cell in the row, pressing Tab moves the insertion point to the first cell in the following row.

2 Type **Retail sales manager position in the cellular phone industry, using good communication and negotiating skills.** Notice that the text wraps in the cell and the height of the row adjusts to fit the text.

3 Press Tab to move to the first cell in the second row. Type **SUMMARY OF QUALIFICATIONS** and then press Tab. Type the following, pressing Enter at the end of each line *except* the last line:

Five years' experience in retail sales

Excellent interpersonal and communication skills

Proficiency using Microsoft Office

Fluency in spoken and written Spanish

> The default font and font size in a table are the same as for a document—Calibri 11 pt. The default line spacing in a table is single spacing with no space before or after paragraphs, which differs from the defaults for a document.

4 **Save** 💾 your document, and then compare your screen with Figure 2.4.

Figure 2.4

Text typed in cells

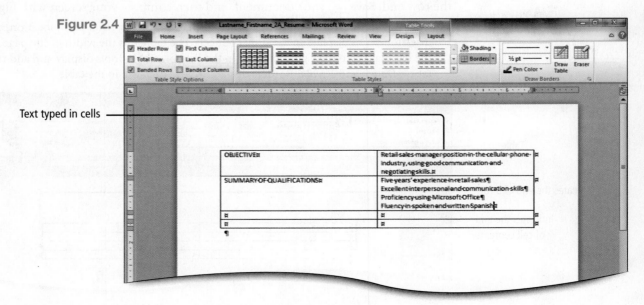

Activity 2.03 | Inserting Existing Text into a Table Cell

1 Press `Tab` to move to the first cell in the third row. Type **EXPERIENCE** and then press `Tab`.

2 Type the following, pressing `Enter` after each line:

Retail Sales Representative, Universe Retail Stores, Deerfield, WI October 2010 to October 2011

Exceeded monthly sales goals for 8 months out of 12

Provided technical training on products and services to new sales reps

3 Be sure your insertion point is positioned in the second column to the left of the cell marker below *sales reps*. Compare your screen with Figure 2.5.

Figure 2.5

Insertion point in blank line at bottom of cell

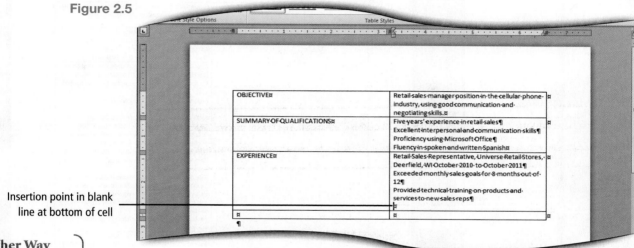

Another Way

Open the second document and select the text you want. Copy the text, and then paste at the desired location.

4 On the **Insert tab**, in the **Text group**, click the **Object button arrow**, and then click **Text from File**. Navigate to your student files, select **w02A_Experience**, and then click **Insert**.

5 Press `Backspace` one time to remove the blank line at the end of the inserted text, and then compare your screen with Figure 2.6.

Figure 2.6

Text inserted from file

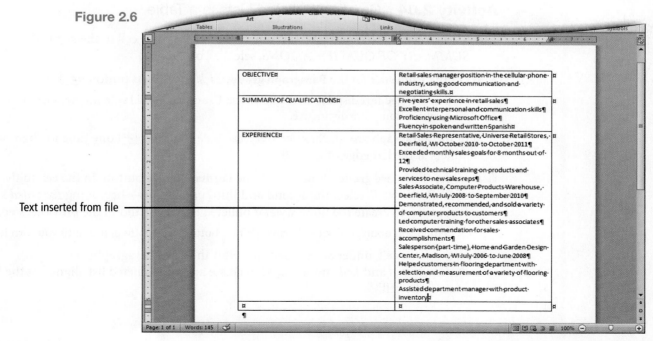

6 Press `Tab` to move to the first cell in the fourth row. Type **EDUCATION** and then press `Tab`.

7 Type the following, pressing `Enter` at the end of each item *except* the last one:

> **University of Wisconsin, Madison, WI**
>
> **Bachelor's in Business Administration, June 2011**
>
> **Madison Area Technical College, Madison, WI**
>
> **Associate's in Information Systems, June 2009**

8 Compare your screen with Figure 2.7.

Figure 2.7

Text entered in new cell

9 **Save** your document.

Activity 2.04 | Creating Bulleted Lists in a Table

1 Scroll to view the top of your document, and then in the cell to the right of *SUMMARY OF QUALIFICATIONS*, select all of the text.

2 On the **Home tab**, in the **Paragraph group**, click the **Bullets** button.

The selected text displays as a bulleted list. Using a bulleted list in this manner makes each qualification more distinctive.

3 In the **Paragraph group**, click the **Decrease Indent** button one time to align the bullets at the left edge of the cell.

4 In the **Clipboard group**, double-click the **Format Painter** button. In the cell to the right of *EXPERIENCE*, select the second and third paragraphs—beginning *Exceeded* and *Provided*—to create the same style of bulleted list as you did in the previous step.

When you double-click the Format Painter button, it remains active until you turn it off.

5 In the same cell, under *Sales Associate*, select the three paragraphs that begin *Demonstrated* and *Led* and *Received* to create another bulleted list aligned at the left edge of the cell.

Another Way

Click the Format Painter again.

6 With the Format Painter pointer still active, in the same cell, select the paragraphs that begin *Helped* and *Assisted* to create the same type of bulleted list.

7 Press (Esc) to turn off the Format Painter. Click anywhere in the table to deselect the text, and then compare your screen with Figure 2.8.

Figure 2.8

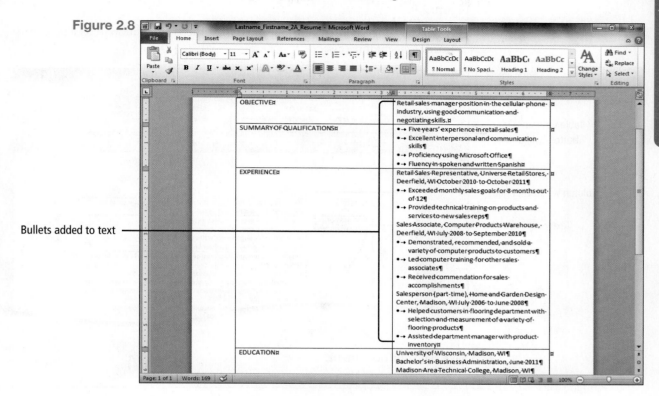

Bullets added to text

8 Save your document.

Objective 3 | Format a Table

Use Word's formatting tools to make your tables attractive and easy to read. Types of formatting you can add to a table include changing the row height and the column width, removing or adding borders, increasing or decreasing the paragraph or line spacing, or enhancing the text.

Activity 2.05 | Changing the Width of Table Columns

When you create a table, all of the columns are of equal width. In this activity, you will change the width of the columns.

1 In any row, point to the vertical border between the two columns to display the pointer.

2 Drag the column border to the left to approximately **1.25 inches on the horizontal ruler**.

3 Scroll to the top of the document. Notice that in the second row, the text *SUMMARY OF QUALIFICATIONS* wraps to two lines to accommodate the new column width.

4 If necessary, in the left column, click in any cell. On the Ribbon, under **Table Tools**, click the **Layout tab**.

5 In the **Cell Size group**, click the **Table Column Width button spin arrows** ⊞ 1.37″ ↕ as necessary to change the width of the first column to **1.4″**. Compare your screen with Figure 2.9.

> After dragging a border with your mouse, use the Width button to set a precise measurement if necessary.

Figure 2.9

Table Column Width button spin arrows

Column width changed

Text wraps in cell

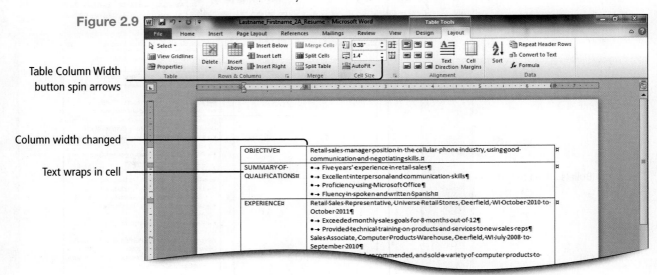

6 **Save** 🖫 your document.

More Knowledge | Changing Column Widths

You will typically get the best results if you change the column widths starting at the left side of the table, especially in tables with three or more columns. Word can also calculate the best column widths for you. To do this, select the table. Then, on the Layout tab, in the Cell Size group, click the AutoFit button and click AutoFit Contents.

Activity 2.06 | Adding Rows to a Table

You can add rows or columns anywhere in a table.

1 Scroll to view the lower portion of the table. In the last row of the table, click anywhere in the *second* cell that contains the educational information, and then press Tab.

> A new row displays at the bottom of the table. When the insertion point is in the last cell in the bottom row of a table, you can add a row by pressing the Tab key; the insertion point will display in the first cell of the new row.

2 Type **HONORS AND ACTIVITIES** and then press Tab.

3 Type the following, pressing Enter after the first item but not the second item:

Elected to Beta Gamma Sigma, international honor society for business students

Qualified for Dean's List, six academic periods

4 Select the text you typed in the last cell of the bottom row. On the **Home tab**, in the **Paragraph group**, click the **Bullets** button ⊞▾, and then click the **Decrease Indent** button ⊞ one time to align the bullets at the left edge of the cell.

5 Scroll up to view the entire table, click anywhere in the table to deselect the text, and then compare your screen with Figure 2.10.

Figure 2.10

Row added to table

Bullets added to text

6 Click anywhere in the top row of the table.

Another Way

Right-click in the top row, point to Insert, and then click Insert Rows Above.

7 On the **Layout tab**, in the **Rows & Columns group**, click the **Insert Above** button. Compare your screen with Figure 2.11.

> A new row displays above the row that contained the insertion point, and the new row is selected.

Figure 2.11

Row inserted at top of table

8 **Save** 🖫 your document.

Activity 2.07 | Merging Cells

The title of a table typically spans all of the columns. In this activity, you will merge cells so that you can position the personal information across both columns.

1 Be sure the two cells in the top row are selected; if necessary, drag across both cells to select them.

2 On the **Layout tab**, in the **Merge group**, click the **Merge Cells** button.

The cell border between the two cells no longer displays.

3 With the merged cell still selected, on the **Home tab**, in the **Paragraph group**, click the **Dialog Box Launcher** ⌐ to display the **Paragraph** dialog box.

4 In the **Paragraph** dialog box, on the **Indents and Spacing tab**, in the lower left corner, click the **Tabs** button to display the **Tabs** dialog box.

5 In the **Tabs** dialog box, under **Tab stop position**, type **6.5** and then under **Alignment**, click the **Right** option button. Click **Set**, and then click **OK** to close the dialog box.

6 Type **Daniela Johnstone** Hold down Ctrl and then press Tab. Notice that the insertion point moves to the right-aligned tab stop at 6.5″.

In a Word table, you must use Ctrl + Tab to move to a tab stop, because pressing Tab is reserved for moving the insertion point from cell to cell.

7 Type **(608) 555-0588** and then press Enter.

8 Type **1343 Siena Lane, Deerfield, WI 53531** Hold down Ctrl and then press Tab.

9 Type **djohnstone@alcona.net** and then compare your screen with Figure 2.12.

Figure 2.12

Right tab stop added to ruler

Cells merged in top row

10 **Save** 🖫 your document.

Activity 2.08 | Formatting Text in Cells

1 In the first row of the table, select the name *Daniela Johnstone*, and then on the Mini toolbar, apply **Bold** **B** and change the **Font Size** to **16**.

2 Under *Daniela Johnstone*, click anywhere in the second line of text, which contains the address and e-mail address.

3 On the **Page Layout tab**, in the **Paragraph group**, click the **Spacing After up spin arrow** three times to add **18 pt** spacing between the first row of the table and the second row. Compare your screen with Figure 2.13.

> These actions separate the personal information from the body of the resume and adds focus to the applicant's name.

Figure 2.13

Text formatted

18 pt space added after paragraph

4 Using the technique you just practiced, in the second column, click in the last paragraph of every cell and add **18 pt Spacing After** the last paragraph of all rows including the last row; a border will be added to the bottom of the table, and spacing will be needed between the last row and the border.

5 In the second row, point to the word *OBJECTIVE*, hold down the left mouse button, and then drag downward in the first column only to select all the headings in uppercase letters. On the Mini toolbar, click the **Bold** button ⒝.

Note | Selecting Only One Column

When you drag downward to select the first column, a fast mouse might also begin to select the second column when you reach the bottom. If this happens, drag upward slightly to deselect the second column and select only the first column.

---

6 In the cell to the right of *EXPERIENCE*, without selecting the following comma, select *Retail Sales Representative* and then on the Mini toolbar, click the **Bold** button ⒝.

7 In the same cell, apply **Bold** ⒝ to the other job titles—*Sales Associate* and *Salesperson*—but do not bold *(part time)*.

8 In the cell to the right of *EDUCATION*, apply **Bold** ⒝ to *University of Wisconsin, Madison, WI* and *Madison Area Technical College, Madison, WI*.

9 In the same cell, click anywhere in the line beginning *Bachelor's*. On the **Page Layout tab**, in the **Paragraph group**, click the **Spacing After up spin arrow** two times to add **12 pt** spacing after the paragraph.

10 In the cell to the right of *EXPERIENCE*, under *Retail Sales Representative*, click anywhere in the second bulleted item, and then add **12 pt Spacing After** the item.

11 In the same cell, repeat this process for the last bulleted item under *Sales Associate*.

12 Scroll to the top of the screen, and then compare your screen with Figure 2.14.

Figure 2.14

Bold emphasis added to first column

Space added after paragraphs in second column

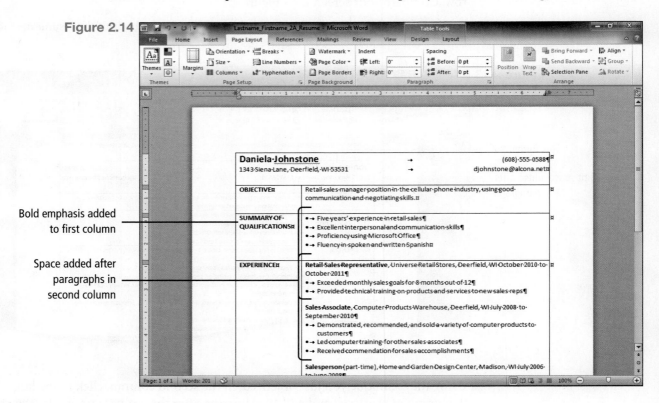

13 Save your document.

Activity 2.09 | Changing the Table Borders

When you create a table, all of the cells have black borders. Most resumes do not display any cell borders. A border at the top and bottom of the resume, however, is attractive and adds a professional look to the document.

1 If necessary, press Ctrl + Home to move the insertion point to the top of the table, and then point slightly outside of the upper left corner of the table to display the **table move handle** ⊞.

2 With the ⊠ pointer, click one time to select the entire table, and notice that the row markers at the end of each row are also selected.

Shaded row markers indicate that the entire row is selected.

3 Click the **Design tab**. In the **Table Styles group**, click the **Borders button arrow**, and then click **No Border**.

The black borders no longer display; instead, depending on your setup, either no borders—the default setting—or nonprinting blue dashed borders display.

4 Click the **File tab** to display **Backstage** view, and then click the **Print tab** to preview the table. Notice that no borders display in the preview, as shown in Figure 2.15.

Figure 2.15

Document preview

All table borders removed

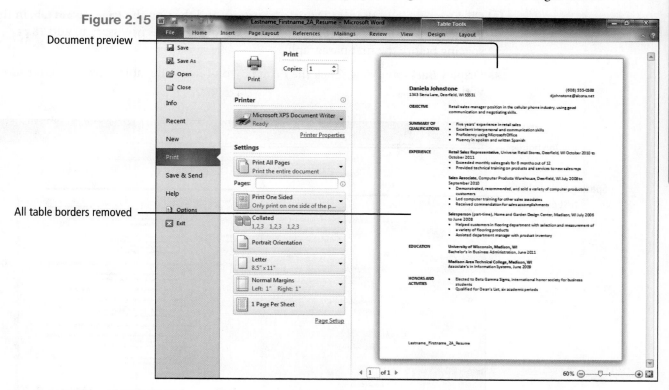

Another Way

Right-click the selected table, click Borders and Shading, and then click the Borders tab.

5 Click the **Design tab**; be sure the table is still selected. In the **Table Styles group**, click the **Borders button arrow**, and then at the bottom of the **Borders** gallery, click **Borders and Shading**.

6 Under **Setting**, click the **Custom** button. Under **Style**, scroll down about a third of the way and click the style with the thick upper line and the thin lower line.

Another Way

Click the top border button, which is one of the buttons that surround the Preview.

7 In the **Preview** box at the right, point to the *top* border of the small preview and click one time.

8 Under **Style**, click the style with the thin upper line and the thick lower line, and then in the **Preview** box, click the *bottom* border of the preview. Compare your screen with Figure 2.16.

Figure 2.16

Borders applied to table

Borders display in Preview

9 Click **OK**, click anywhere to cancel the selection, and then notice that there is only a small amount of space between the upper border and the first line of text.

10 Click anywhere in the text *Daniela Johnstone*, and then on the **Page Layout tab**, in the **Paragraph group**, click the **Spacing Before up spin arrow** as necessary to add **18 pt** spacing before the first paragraph.

11 Display **Backstage** view. Click the **Print tab** to preview the table. Compare your screen with Figure 2.17.

Figure 2.17

Top border

Spacing added above first paragraph

Bottom border

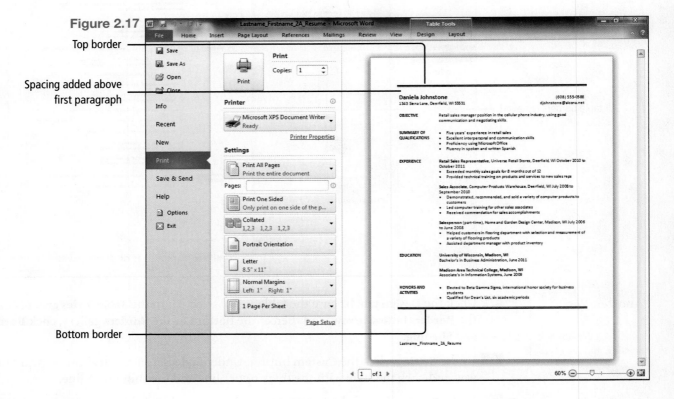

12 In **Backstage** view, click the **Info tab**. On the right, under the document thumbnail, click **Properties**, and then click **Show Document Panel**. In the **Author** box, delete any text and then type your firstname and lastname. In the **Subject** box, type your course name and section number, and in the **Keywords** box type **resume, Word table**

13 **Close** ☒ the **Document Panel**. **Save** 🔲 and then print your document, or submit it electronically, as directed by your instructor. **Exit** Word.

End You have completed Project 2A ——————————

Project 2B Cover Letter and Resume

Project Activities

In Activities 2.10 through 2.22, you will create a letterhead, and then use the letterhead to create a cover letter. You will also create a short resume using a Microsoft template and save it as a Web page. Your completed documents will look similar to Figure 2.18.

Project Files

For Project 2B, you will need the following file:

w02B_Cover_Letter_Text

You will save your documents as:

Lastname_Firstname_2B_Letterhead
Lastname_Firstname_2B_Cover_Letter
Lastname_Firstname_2B_Brief_Resume
Lastname_Firstname_2B_HTML_Resume

Project Results

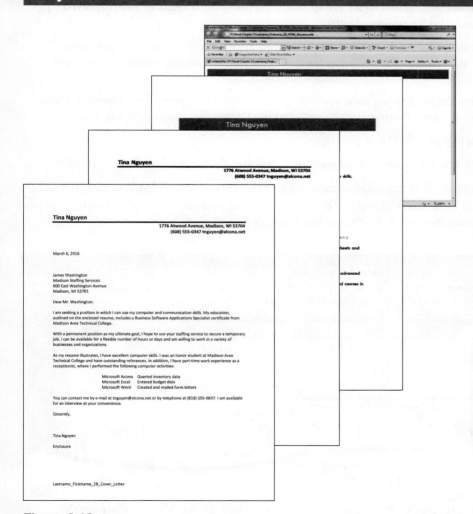

Figure 2.18
Project 2B Cover Letter and Resume

Objective 4 | Create a New Document from an Existing Document

A **template** is an *existing* document that you use as a starting point for a *new* document. The template document opens a copy of itself, unnamed, and then you use the structure—and possibly some content, such as headings—as the starting point for a new document.

All documents are based on a template. When you create a new blank document, it is based on Word's **Normal template**, which serves as the starting point for all new Word documents.

Activity 2.10 | Creating a Letterhead

A **letterhead** is the personal or company information that displays at the top of a letter, and which commonly includes a name, address, and contact information. The term also refers to a piece of paper imprinted with such information at the top.

1 **Start** Word, and in the new blank document, be sure that formatting marks and rulers display.

2 On the **Home tab**, in the **Styles group**, click the **More** button ⊡. In the displayed gallery, click the **No Spacing** button.

> Recall that the default spacing for a new Word document is 10 points of blank space following a paragraph and line spacing of 1.15. The **No Spacing style** inserts *no* extra space following a paragraph and uses single spacing.

> By using the No Spacing style, you will be able to follow the prescribed format of a letter, which Business Communications texts commonly describe in terms of single spacing.

3 Type **Tina Nguyen** and then press Enter.

4 Type **1776 Atwood Avenue, Madison, WI 53704** and then press Enter.

5 Type **(608) 555-0347 tnguyen@alcona.net** and then press Enter. If the e-mail address changes to blue text, right-click the e-mail address, and then from the shortcut menu, click **Remove Hyperlink**. Compare your screen with Figure 2.19.

Figure 2.19

No Spacing style button

No Spacing style applied

6 Select the first paragraph—*Tina Nguyen*—and then on the Mini toolbar, apply **Bold** B and change the **Font Size** to **16**.

Another Way

Press Ctrl + R to align text to the right.

7 Select the second and third paragraphs. On the Mini toolbar, apply **Bold** B and change the **Font Size** to **12**.

8 With the two paragraphs still selected, on the **Home tab**, in the **Paragraph group**, click the **Align Text Right** button ⊟.

9 Click anywhere in the first paragraph—*Tina Nguyen*. In the **Paragraph group**, click the **Borders button arrow** ⊞▾, and then at the bottom, click **Borders and Shading**.

10 In the **Borders and Shading** dialog box, under **Style**, be sure the first style—a single solid line—is selected.

Another Way

Alternatively, click the bottom border button ⊟.

11 Click the **Width arrow**, and then click **3 pt**. To the right, under **Preview**, click the bottom border of the diagram. Under **Apply to**, be sure *Paragraph* displays. Compare your screen with Figure 2.20.

Figure 2.20

Borders button arrow

3 pt line applied to bottom border

Width arrow

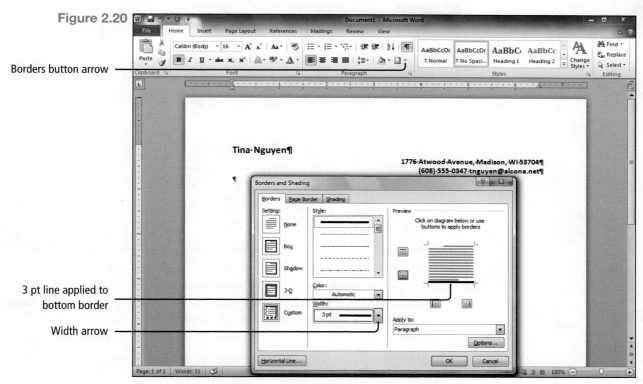

12 Click **OK** to display a 3 pt line below *Tina Nguyen*, which extends from the left margin to the right margin.

13 Display **Save As** dialog box, **Save** the document in your **Word Chapter 2** folder as **Lastname_Firstname_2B_Letterhead** and then add the file name to the footer.

14 Display **Backstage** view, click the **Info tab**, and then on the right, under the document thumbnail, click **Properties**. Click **Show Document Panel**. In the **Author** box, delete any text and then type your firstname and lastname. In the **Subject** box, type your course name and section number, and in the **Keywords** box type **personal letterhead**

15 Close ☒ the **Document Panel**.

16 Save 🖫 your document. Display **Backstage** view, and then click **Close** to close the document but leave Word open. Hold this file until you complete this project.

Activity 2.11 | Creating a Document from an Existing Document

To use an existing document as the starting point for a new document, Word provides the ***New from existing*** command.

1 Click the **File tab** to display **Backstage** view, and then click **New** to display the new document options. Compare your screen with Figure 2.21.

> Here you can create a new document in a variety of ways, including from an existing document.

New from Existing template —

Figure 2.21

2 Under **Available Templates**, click the **New from existing** button. In the displayed **New from Existing Document** dialog box, if necessary, navigate to your **Word Chapter 2** folder, click your **Lastname_Firstname_2B_Letterhead** document to select it, and then in the lower right corner, click **Create New**. Compare your screen with Figure 2.22.

> Word opens a copy of your 2B_Letterhead document in the form of a new Word document—the title bar indicates *Document* followed by a number. You are not opening the original document, and changes that you make to this new document will not affect the contents of your 2B_Letterhead document.

Figure 2.22

Document opens unnamed —

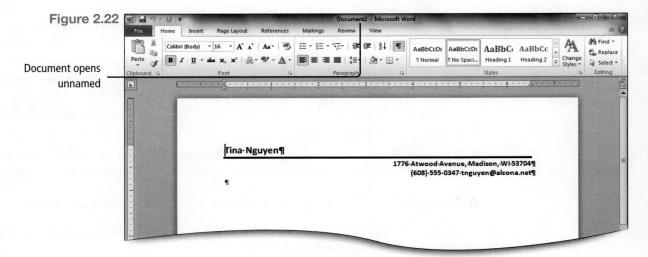

3 Display the **Save As** dialog box, and then navigate to your **Word Chapter 2** folder. **Save** the file as **Lastname_Firstname_2B_Cover_Letter**

> The personal information that you typed in the 2B_Letterhead Document Panel remains in the new document.

4 Scroll down to view the footer area, and notice that a footer displays.

> The footer displays because it was included in the document that you saved as a template. The *FileName* field does not automatically update to the new file name.

5 Point to the footer and right-click, and then click **Edit Footer**. Point to the highlighted footer text, right-click, and then from the shortcut menu, click **Update Field**. At the far right end of the Ribbon, click the **Close Header and Footer** button.

6 Save 🖫 your document.

More Knowledge | Creating a Template File

You can also identify an original document so that your Windows operating system always knows that you want to create a new unnamed copy. To do so, save your document as a template file instead of a document. Word will then attach the dotx extension to the file, instead of the docx extension that is applied for a document, and will store the template file in a special location with other templates. Then, you can open the template from the New Document dialog box by clicking *My templates*.

Objective 5 | Change and Reorganize Text

Business letters follow a standard format and contain the following parts: the current date, referred to as the *date line*; the name and address of the person receiving the letter, referred to as the *inside address*; a greeting, referred to as the *salutation*; the text of the letter, usually referred to as the *body* of the letter; a closing line, referred to as the *complimentary closing*; and the *writer's identification*, which includes the name or job title (or both) of the writer, and which is also referred to as the *writer's signature block*.

Some letters also include the initials of the person who prepared the letter, an optional *subject line* that describes the purpose of the letter, or a list of *enclosures*—documents included with the letter.

Activity 2.12 | Recording AutoCorrect Entries

You can correct commonly misspelled words automatically by using Word's *AutoCorrect* feature. Commonly misspelled words—such as *teh* instead of *the*—are corrected using a built-in list that is installed with Office. If you have words that you frequently misspell, you can add them to the list for automatic correction.

1 Click the **File tab** to display **Backstage** view. On the **Help tab**, click **Options** to display the **Word Options** dialog box.

2 On the left side of the **Word Options** dialog box, click **Proofing**, and then under **AutoCorrect options**, click the **AutoCorrect Options** button.

3 In the **AutoCorrect** dialog box, click the **AutoCorrect tab**. Under **Replace**, type **resumee** and under **With**, type **resume**

> If another student has already added this AutoCorrect entry, a Replace button will display.

4 Click **Add**. If the entry already exists, click Replace instead, and then click Yes.

5 In the **AutoCorrect** dialog box, under **Replace**, type **computr** and under **With**, type **computer** and then compare your screen with Figure 2.23.

Figure 2.23

Replace box

With box

Add (or Replace) button

6 Click **Add** (or Replace) and then click **OK** two times to close the dialog boxes.

Activity 2.13 | Creating a Cover Letter

There are a variety of accepted letter formats that you will see in reference manuals and Business Communication texts. The one used in this chapter is a block style cover letter taken from *Business Communication Today*.

1 Press Ctrl + End to move the insertion point to the blank line below the letterhead. Press Enter three times, and then type **March 16, 2016** to create the dateline.

> Most Business Communication texts recommend that the dateline be positioned at least 0.5 inch (3 blank lines) below the letterhead; or, position the dateline approximately 2 inches from the top edge of the paper.

2 Press Enter four times, which leaves three blank lines. Type the following inside address on four lines, but do not press Enter following the last line:

James Washington

Madison Staffing Services

600 East Washington Avenue

Madison, WI 53701

> The recommended space between the dateline and inside address varies slightly among Business Communication texts and office reference manuals. However, all indicate that the space can be from one to 10 blank lines depending on the length of your letter.

3 Press [Enter] two times to leave one blank line. Compare your screen with Figure 2.24.

Figure 2.24

Three blank lines between letterhead and dateline

Dateline

Three blank lines between dateline and inside address

Inside address

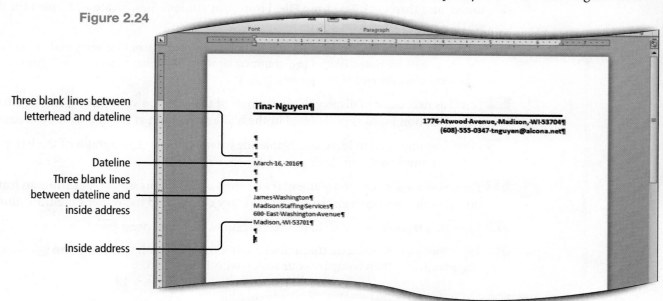

4 Type the salutation **Dear Mr. Washington:** and then press [Enter] two times.

Always leave one blank line above and below the salutation.

5 Type, exactly as shown, the following opening paragraph that includes an intentional word usage error: **I am seeking a position in witch I can use my** and press [Spacebar]. Type, exactly as shown, **computr** and then watch *computr* as you press [Spacebar].

The AutoCorrect feature recognizes the misspelled word, and then changes *computr* to *computer* when you press [Spacebar], [Enter], or a punctuation mark.

6 Type the following, including the misspelled last word: **and communication skills. My education, outlined on the enclosed resumee** and then type **,** (a comma). Notice that when you type the comma, AutoCorrect replaces *resumee* with *resume*.

7 Press [Spacebar]. Complete the paragraph by typing **includes a Business Software Applications Specialist certificate from MATC.** Compare your screen with Figure 2.25.

Figure 2.25

Paragraphs are single spaced

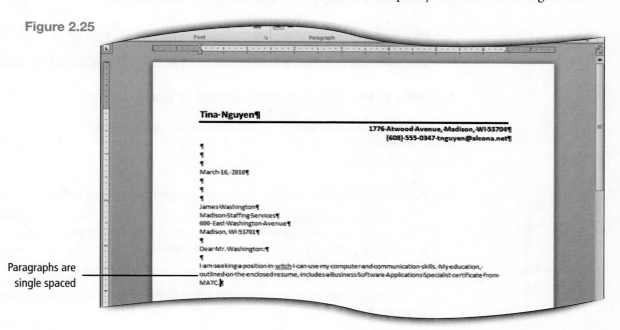

8 Press [Enter] two times. On the **Insert tab**, in the **Text group**, click the **Object button arrow**, and then click **Text from File**. From your student files, locate and **Insert** the file **w02B_Cover_Letter_Text**.

Some of the words in the cover letter text display red, green, or blue wavy underlines. These indicate potential spelling, grammar, or word usage errors, and you will correct them before the end of this project.

9 Scroll as necessary to display the lower half of the letter on your screen, and be sure your insertion point is positioned in the blank paragraph at the end of the document.

10 Press [Enter] one time to leave one blank line between the last paragraph of the letter and the complimentary closing.

11 Type **Sincerely,** as the complimentary closing, and then press [Enter] four times to leave three blank lines between the complimentary closing and the writer's identification.

12 Type **Tina Nguyen** as the writer's identification, and then press [Enter] two times.

13 Type **Enclosure** to indicate that a document is included with the letter. **Save** 🖫 your document, and then compare your screen with Figure 2.26.

Figure 2.26

Wavy underlines indicate potential errors

Text inserted from another document

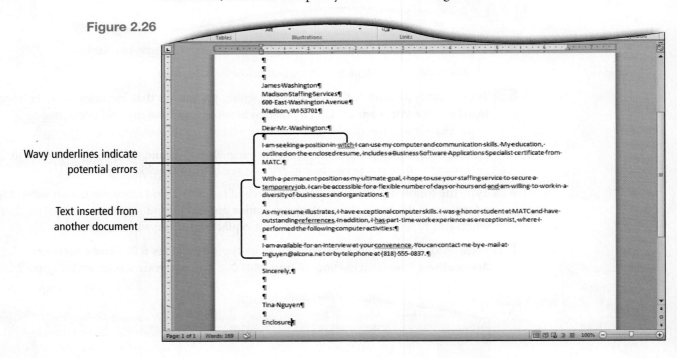

Activity 2.14 | Finding and Replacing Text

Use the Find command to locate text in a document quickly. Use the Find and Replace command to make the same change, or to make more than one change at a time, in a document.

1 Press [Ctrl] + [Home] to position the insertion point at the beginning of the document.

Because a find operation—or a find and replace operation—begins from the location of the insertion point and proceeds to the end of the document, it is good practice to position the insertion point at the beginning of the document before initiating the command.

Another Way

Hold down [Ctrl] and press [F].

2 On the **Home tab**, in the **Editing group**, click the **Find** button.

The Navigation Pane displays on the left side of the screen, with a search box at the top of the pane.

3 In the search box, type **ac** If necessary, scroll down slightly in your document to view the entire body text of the letter, and then compare your screen with Figure 2.27.

> In the document, the search letters *ac* are selected and highlighted in yellow for all three words that contain the letters *ac* together. In the Navigation Pane, the three instances are shown in context—*ac* displays in bold.

Figure 2.27

Find button

Search term

Matches found in the document

4 In the search box, complete the word **accessible**.

> One match for the search term displays in context in the Navigation Pane and is highlighted in the document.

5 In the document, point to the yellow highlighted word *accessible*, double-click, and then type **available** to replace the word. Notice that the list of results is now empty.

6 **Close** ✕ the **Navigation Pane**, and then on the **Home tab**, in the **Editing group**, click the **Replace** button.

7 In the **Find and Replace** dialog box, in the **Find what** box, replace the existing text by typing **MATC** In the **Replace with** box, type **Madison Area Technical College** and then compare your screen with Figure 2.28

Figure 2.28

Search term

Replacement text

8 In the lower left corner of the dialog box, click the **More** button to expand the dialog box, and then under **Search Options**, select the **Match case** check box.

> The acronym *MATC* appears in the document two times. In a formal letter, the reader may not know what the acronym means, so you should include the full text instead of an acronym. In this instance, you must select the *Match case* check box so that the replaced text will match the case you typed in the Replace with box, and *not* display in all uppercase letters in the manner of *MATC*.

9 In the **Find and Replace** dialog box, click the **Replace All** button to replace both instances of *MATC*. Click **OK** to close the message box.

10 In the **Find and Replace** dialog box, clear the **Match case** check box, click the **Less** button, and then **Close** the dialog box.

> The Find and Replace dialog box opens with the settings used the last time it was open. Thus, it is good practice to reset this dialog box to its default settings each time you use it.

11 Save 💾 your document.

Activity 2.15 | Selecting and Moving Text to a New Location

By using Word's *drag-and-drop* feature, you can use the mouse to drag selected text from one location to another. Drag-and-drop is most effective when the text to be moved and the destination are on the same screen.

1 Take a moment to study the table in Figure 2.29 to become familiar with the techniques you can use to select text in a document quickly.

Selecting Text in a Document

To Select	Do This
A portion of text	Click to position the insertion point at the beginning of the text you want to select, hold down Shift, and then click at the end of the text you want to select. Alternatively, hold down the left mouse button and drag from the beginning to the end of the text you want to select.
A word	Double-click the word.
A sentence	Hold down Ctrl and click anywhere in the sentence.
A paragraph	Triple-click anywhere in the paragraph; or, move the pointer to the left of the line, into the margin area. When the ⟰ pointer displays, double-click.
A line	Move the pointer to the left of the line. When the ⟰ pointer displays, click one time.
One character at a time	Position the insertion point to the left of the first character, hold down Shift, and press ← or → as many times as desired.
A string of words	Position the insertion point to the left of the first word, hold down Shift and Ctrl, and then press ← or → as many times as desired.
Consecutive lines	Position the insertion point to the left of the first word, hold down Shift and press ↑ or ↓.
Consecutive paragraphs	Position the insertion point to the left of the first word, hold down Shift and Ctrl and press ↑ or ↓.
The entire document	Hold down Ctrl and press A. Alternatively, move the pointer to the left of any line in the document. When the ⟰ pointer displays, triple-click.

Figure 2.29

2 Be sure you can view the entire body of the letter on your screen. In the paragraph that begins *With a permanent position*, in the second line, locate and double-click *days*.

3 Point to the selected word to display the ▷ pointer.

4 Drag to the right until the dotted vertical line that floats next to the pointer is positioned to the right of the word *hours* in the same line, as shown in Figure 2.30.

Figure 2.30

Word will be dragged to new location

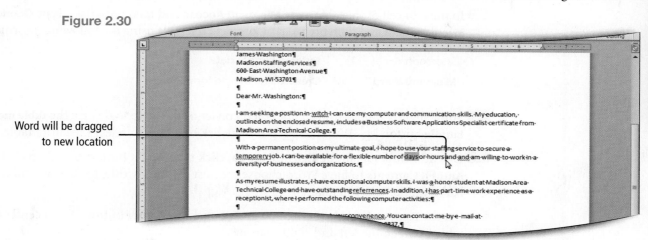

5 Release the mouse button to move the text. Select the word *hours* and drag it to the left of the word *or*—the previous location of the word *days*. Click anywhere in the document to deselect the text.

6 Examine the text that you moved, and add or remove spaces as necessary.

7 Hold down Ctrl, and then in the paragraph that begins *I am available*, click anywhere in the first sentence to select the entire sentence.

8 Drag the selected sentence to the end of the paragraph by positioning the small vertical line that floats with the pointer to the left of the paragraph mark. Compare your screen with Figure 2.31.

Figure 2.31

Sentence moved to end of paragraph

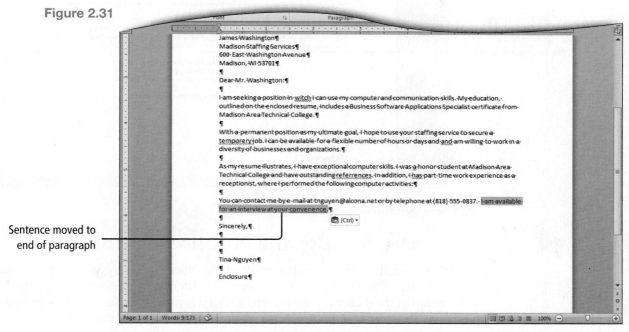

9 **Save** 🖫 your document.

Activity 2.16 | Inserting and Formatting a Table in a Document

1 Locate the paragraph that begins *As my resume*, and then click to position the insertion point in the blank line below that paragraph. Press Enter one time.

2 On the **Insert tab**, in the **Tables group**, click the **Table** button. In the **Table** grid, in the third row, click the second square to insert a 2 × 3 table.

3 In the first cell of the table, type **Microsoft Access** and then press Tab. Type **Queried inventory data** and then press Tab. Complete the table using the following information:

Microsoft Excel	**Entered budget data**
Microsoft Word	**Created and mailed form letters**

4 Point slightly outside of the upper left corner of the table to display the **table move handle** button ⊞. With the ⇱ pointer, click one time to select the entire table.

5 On the **Layout tab**, in the **Cell Size group**, click the **AutoFit** button, and then click **AutoFit Contents** to have Word choose the best column widths for the two columns based on the text you entered.

6 On the **Home tab**, in the **Paragraph group**, click the **Center** button ≣ to center the table between the left and right margins.

7 On the **Design tab**, in the **Table Styles group**, click the **Borders button arrow**, and then click **No Border**. Click anywhere to cancel the selection of the table, and then compare your screen with Figure 2.32.

> A light dashed line may display in place of the original table borders if your default settings have been changed.

Figure 2.32

Table inserted in letter ———

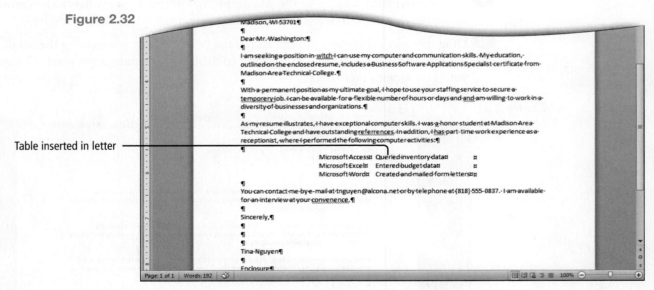

8 **Save** 🖫 your document.

Objective 6 | Use the Proofing Options

Word compares your typing to words in the Office dictionary and compares your phrases and punctuation to a list of grammar rules. This automatic proofing is set by default. Words that are not in the dictionary are marked with a wavy red underline. Phrases and punctuation that differ from the grammar rules are marked with a wavy green underline.

Word also compares commonly misused words with a set of word usage rules, and marks misused words with a wavy blue underline; for example the misuse of *their*, *there*, and *they're*. However, Word will not flag the word *sign* as misspelled even though you intended to type *sing a song* rather than *sign a song*, because both are words contained within Word's dictionary. Your own knowledge and proofreading skills are still required, even when using a sophisticated Word processing program like Word.

Activity 2.17 | Checking Spelling and Grammar Errors

There are two ways to respond to spelling and grammar errors flagged by Word. You can right-click a flagged word or phrase, and then from the shortcut menu choose a correction or action. Or, you can initiate the Spelling and Grammar command to display the Spelling and Grammar dialog box, which provides more options than the shortcut menus.

Alert! | Spelling and Grammar Checking

If you do not see any wavy red, green, or blue lines under words, the automatic spelling and/or grammar checking has been turned off on your system. To activate the spelling and grammar checking, display Backstage view, on the Help tab, click Options, click Proofing, and then under *When correcting spelling in Microsoft Office programs*, select the first four check boxes. Under *When correcting spelling and grammar in Word*, select the first four check boxes, and then click the Writing Style arrow and click Grammar Only. Under *Exceptions for*, clear both check boxes. To display the flagged spelling and grammar errors, click the Recheck Document button, and then close the dialog box.

---

1 Position the body of the letter on your screen, and then examine the text to locate green, red, and blue wavy underlines. Compare your screen with Figure 2.33.

> A list of grammar rules applied by a computer program like Word can never be exact, and a computer dictionary cannot contain all known words and proper names. Thus, you will need to check any words flagged by Word with wavy underlines, and you will also need to proofread for content errors.

Figure 2.33

Blue wavy underline indicates potential word usage problem

Red wavy underline indicates potential spelling problem

Green wavy underline indicates potential grammar problem

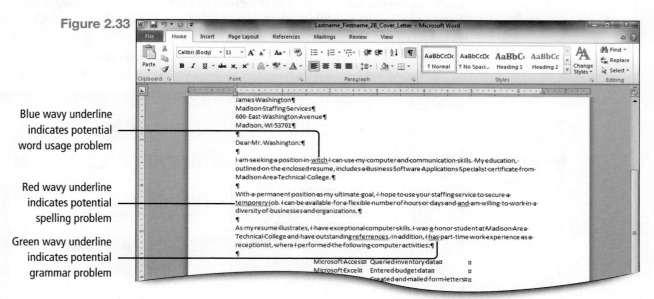

2 In the lower left corner of your screen, in the status bar, locate and point to the icon to display the ScreenTip *Proofing errors were found. Click to correct.*

> If this button displays, you know there are potential errors identified in the document.

3 In the paragraph that begins *With a permanent*, locate the word *temporery* with the wavy red underline. Point to the word and right-click to display the shortcut menu, and then compare your screen with Figure 2.34.

Figure 2.34

Suggested spelling correction

Misspelled word

Shortcut menu

4 On the shortcut menu, click **temporary** to correct the spelling error.

5 In the next line, locate the word *and* that displays with a wavy red underline, point to word and right-click, and then from the shortcut menu, click **Delete Repeated Word** to delete the duplicate word.

Another Way
Press F7 to start the Spelling & Grammar command.

6 Press Ctrl + Home to move the insertion point to the beginning of the document. Click the **Review tab**, and then in the **Proofing group**, click the **Spelling & Grammar** button to check the spelling and grammar of the text in the document. Compare your screen with Figure 2.35.

The word *witch* is highlighted—a *Possible Word Choice Error*—and the sentence containing the potential error displays in the dialog box. A suggested change also displays.

Figure 2.35

Word usage error

Suggested correction

7 In the **Spelling and Grammar** dialog box, click the **Change** button to change to the correct usage *which*.

> The next marked word—a possible spelling error—displays.

8 Click the **Change** button to change *refferences* to *references*. Notice that the next error is a possible grammar error.

9 Click the **Change** button to change *a* to *an*. Continue the spelling and grammar check and change *has* to *have* and correct the spelling of *convenence*.

10 When Word indicates *The spelling and grammar check is complete*, click **OK**.

11 Save 🖫 your document.

Activity 2.18 | Using the Thesaurus

A ***thesaurus*** is a research tool that lists ***synonyms***—words that have the same or similar meaning to the word you selected.

1 Scroll so that you can view the body of the letter. In the paragraph that begins *With a permanent*, at the end of the second line, locate and right-click the word *diversity*.

2 On the shortcut menu, point to **Synonyms**, and then compare your screen with Figure 2.36.

> A list of synonyms displays; the list will vary in length depending on the selected word.

Figure 2.36

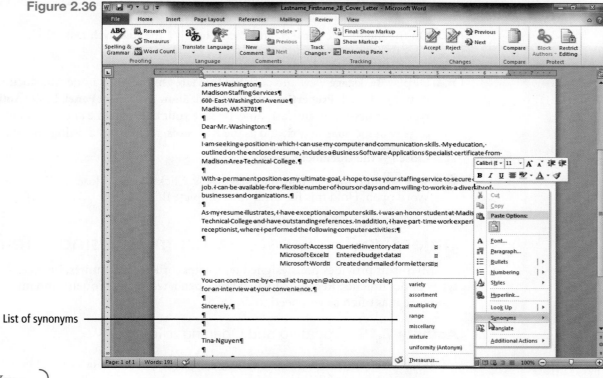

List of synonyms

Another Way

Click the word, and then on the Review tab, in the Proofing group, click the Thesaurus button.

3 From the list of synonyms, click **variety** to replace *diversity* with *variety*.

4 In the paragraph that begins *As my resume*, point to the word *exceptional*, right-click, point to **Synonyms**, and then at the bottom of the shortcut menu, click **Thesaurus** to display the **Research** task pane.

5 In the **Research** task pane, under **Thesaurus**, point to the non-bold word *excellent*, and then click the **arrow**. Compare your screen with Figure 2.37.

Figure 2.37

Synonym

Selected word

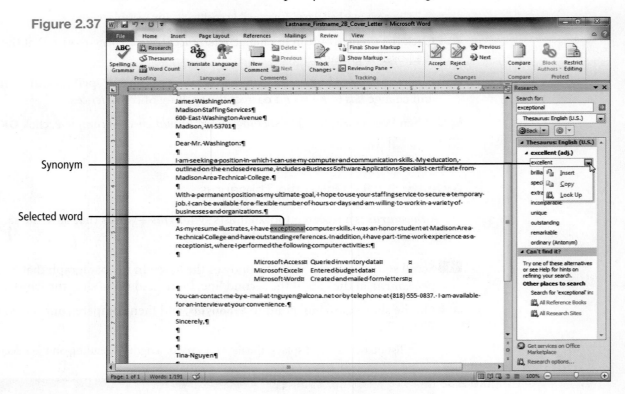

6 On the menu, click **Insert**, and then **Close** ✖ the **Research** task pane.

excellent replaces the word *exceptional*.

7 Display **Backstage** view and click the **Info tab**. On the right, under the document thumbnail, click **Properties**, and then click **Show Document Panel**. In the **Author** box, type your firstname and lastname. Be sure your course name and section number display in the **Subject** box, and as the **Keywords**, replace any existing text with **cover letter**

8 **Close** ✖ the **Document Panel**.

9 **Save** 💾, and then display **Backstage** view. Click **Close** to close the document but leave Word open. Hold this file until you complete this project.

Objective 7 | Create a Document Using a Template

Microsoft provides pre-designed templates for letters, resumes, invoices, and other types of documents. Recall that when you open a template, it opens unnamed so that you can reuse it as often as you need to do so.

Activity 2.19 | Locating and Opening a Template

If you need to create a short resume quickly, or if you need ideas about how to format your resume, Microsoft Word provides pre-designed resume templates. Some templates are available on your computer; many more are available online. After opening a template, you can add text as indicated, modify the layout and design, and add or remove resume elements.

1 Close any open documents, and then from **Backstage** view, click **New**.

2 Under **Available Templates**, click **Sample templates**.

3 Under **Available Templates**, scroll toward the bottom of the window, and then click **Median Resume**. Notice that a preview of the *Median Resume* template displays on the right. Compare your screen with Figure 2.38.

Figure 2.38

Preview of template

Selected template

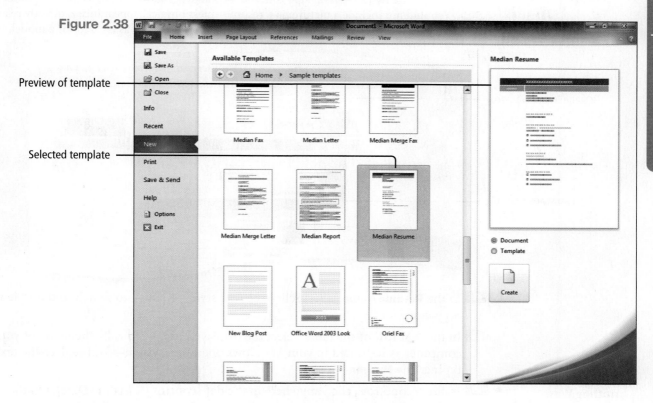

4 In the lower right corner, click the **Create** button.

The template opens a copy of itself in the form of a new Word document—the title bar indicates *Document* followed by a number. Recall that you are not opening the template itself, and that changes you make to this new document will not affect the contents of the template file.

5 Display the **Save As** dialog box. **Save** the document in your **Word Chapter 2** folder as **Lastname_Firstname_2B_Brief_Resume** and then add the file name to the footer—called the *First Page Footer* in this template.

6 **Save** your document.

Activity 2.20 │ Replacing Template Placeholder Text

After you save the template file as a Word document, you can begin to substitute your own information in the indicated locations. You can also remove unneeded resume elements that are included with the template.

1 Click on the picture, and notice that a Picture Tool tab is added to the Ribbon.

2 Click the **Layout tab**, and then in the **Table group**, click the **View Gridlines** button to display non-printing table borders.

This template consists of two Word tables, and the name in the first row of the upper table displays either the user name or the text *[Type your name]* in square brackets.

3 At the top of the upper table, click the **Resume Name tab arrow**, and then compare your screen with Figure 2.39.

> There are two styles available with the Median template—with or without a photo. You should not include a picture on a resume unless physical appearance is directly related to the job for which you are applying—for example, for a job as an actor or a model.

Figure 2.39

Resume Name tab arrow

Two styles available

4 In the **Resume Name** gallery, click the first style—**Name**—to switch to the style with no picture.

5 In the first row of the table, select the displayed text—typically the name of your computer as indicated in your Windows operating system—and replace the text by typing **Tina Nguyen**

Another Way

Select the entire row, right-click, and then from the shortcut menu, click Delete Rows.

6 In the second row, click anywhere in the date control *[Select the Date]*. On the Ribbon, click the **Layout tab**. In the **Rows & Columns group**, click the **Delete** button, and then click **Delete Rows**.

> Text surrounded by brackets is called a ***content control***. There are several different types of content controls, including date, picture, and ***text controls***. Most of the controls in this template are text controls. Because resumes do not typically include a date, you can delete this row.

7 Click anywhere in the content control *[Type your address]*. Compare your screen with Figure 2.40.

> For the name and address at the top of the document, all of the text controls are grouped together. Each control has ***placeholder text***, text that indicates the type of information to be entered. The name in the first row may also be a content control with placeholder text.

Figure 2.40

Placeholder text replaced

Date removed

Picture removed

8 Complete the personal information by using the following information:

[Type your address]	**1776 Atwood Avenue, Madison, WI 53704**
[Type your phone number]	**(608) 555-0347**
[Type your e-mail address]	**tnguyen@alcona.net**
[Type your website address]	(leave this blank)

9 In the lower table, click in the *[Type your objectives]* control, and then type **To obtain a position using my computer and communications skills.**

10 Complete the **Education** section by using the following information:

[Type the school name]	**Madison Area Technical College**
[Type the completion date]	**June 2015**
[Type list of degrees, awards and accomplishments] *(type three separate lines)*	**Business Computing Specialist certificate** **Dean's List, four semesters** **President, Community Service Club**

11 Complete the **Experience** section by using the following information:

[Type the job title]	**Office Assistant (part-time)**
[Type the company name]	**The Robinson Company**
[Type the start date]	**September 2014**
[Type the end date]	**present**
[Type list of job responsibilities]	**Data entry and report generation using company spreadsheets and databases.**

12 Click in the *[Type list of skills]* control, type **Proficiency using Word, Excel, and Access (completed advanced courses in Microsoft Office programs)** and then press Enter.

13 As the second bulleted point, type **Excellent written and verbal communications (completed courses in Business Communications, PowerPoint, and Speech)** and then compare your screen with Figure 2.41. **Save** 🖫 your document.

Figure 2.41

Placeholder text replaced ———

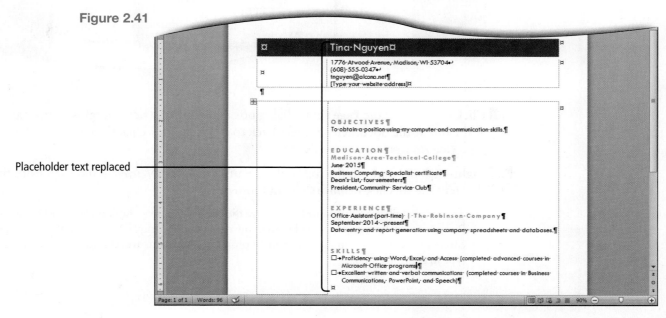

Activity 2.21 | Removing Template Controls and Formatting the Resume

1 Near the top of the document, point to the text control that you did not use—*[Type your website address]*. Right-click the control, and then from the shortcut menu, click **Remove Content Control**. Press ⌷Backspace⌷ as necessary to position the insertion point at the end of the e-mail address. Select the three lines with the address, phone, and e-mail information. On the Mini toolbar, notice that the text size is *11.5*. Click the **Font Size button arrow**, and then click **12**.

2 Click anywhere in lower table—the table with the *Objectives* row at the top—and then point to the upper left corner of the active table to display the **move table handle**. Click one time to select the lower table.

3 On the Mini toolbar, change the **Font Size** to **12** to match the table above.

4 Click anywhere to cancel the selection. On the **Page Layout tab**, in the **Page Setup group**, click the **Margins** button, and then click **Custom Margins**. Change the **Top** margin to **1.5** and the **Left** and **Right** margins to **1** to make this short resume better fill the page. Compare your screen with Figure 2.42.

Figure 2.42

New margins

5 Click **OK** to close the **Page Setup** dialog box and apply the new margins. If the name at the top of the document changes back to a placeholder, click the control and type **Tina Nguyen**

6 Right-click the name at the top of the document—*Tina Nguyen*—and then from the shortcut menu, click **Remove Content Control**.

This action will leave the name but remove the control. Remove the control if the Document Properties will have an author other than the name in this control. If you do *not* remove the content control, when you add document properties, the name will change to the name you type in the Author box.

7 Press `Ctrl` + `F2` to display the Print Preview in **Backstage** view. Click the **Info tab**. On the right, under the document thumbnail, click **Properties**, and then click **Show Document Panel**. In the **Author** box, delete any text and then type your firstname and lastname. In the **Subject** box, type your course name and section number, and in the **Keywords** box, type **short resume, template**

8 Close `X` the **Document Panel**. Save `💾` your document, and then hold this file until you complete this project. Leave the resume displayed on your screen.

Activity 2.22 | Saving a Resume as a Web Page

You can save your resume as a Web page. This enables you to post the Web page on your own Web site or on Web space provided by your college. It also enables you to send the resume as an e-mail attachment that can be opened using any Web browser.

1 With your **2B_Brief_Resume** still open on your screen, click **Save** `💾` to be sure the current version of the document is saved.

2 Display the **Save As** dialog box. In the lower portion of the **Save As** dialog box, click the **Save as type arrow**, and then click **Single File Web Page**.

A *Single File Web Page* is a document saved using the *Hypertext Markup Language (HTML)*. HTML is the language used to format documents that can be opened using a Web browser such as Internet Explorer.

3 In the **Save As** dialog box, in the **File name** box, type **Lastname_Firstname_2B_HTML_Resume** Click **Save**, and then click **Yes** if a message box displays. Notice that the Web page displays in Word.

4 Display **Backstage** view. On the right, click **Properties**, and then click **Advanced Properties**. In the **Properties** dialog box, on the **Summary tab**, in the **Subject** box, be sure your course name and section number display. In the **Author** box, be sure your first and last names display. In the **Keywords** box, replace the existing text with **HTML** Click **OK**, and then click the **Home tab**. Save `💾` the document; print or submit electronically as directed.

5 **Exit** Word. From the **Start** menu `⊞`, click **Computer**. Navigate to your **Word Chapter 2** folder, and then double-click your **Lastname_Firstname_2B_HTML_Resume** file to open the resume in your Web browser. Compare your screen with Figure 2.43.

Figure 2.43

Resume displayed in a Web browser

6 Close `X` your Web browser. As directed by your instructor, print or submit electronically the four files from this project—2B_Letterhead, 2B_Cover_Letter, 2B_Brief_Resume, and 2B_HTML_Resume.

End **You have completed Project 2B** ——————————————

Content-Based Assessments

Summary

In this chapter, you created a table, and then used the table to create a resume. You created a letterhead template, and then created a document using a copy of the letterhead template. You created a cover letter for the resume, moved text, corrected spelling and grammar, and used the built-in thesaurus. Finally, you created a short resume using a template, and also saved the resume as a Web page.

Key Terms

AutoCorrect 123

Body...............................123

Cell................................107

Complimentary closing 123

Content control..............136

Date line 123

Drag and drop................128

Enclosures 123

HTML.............................139

Hypertext Markup Language (HTML) 139

Inside address 123

Letterhead......................120

New from existing 121

No Spacing style............120

Normal template.............120

Placeholder text 136

Salutation 123

Single File Web Page 139

Subject line 123

Synonyms 133

Table 107

Template 120

Text control 136

Thesaurus 133

Writer's identification 123

Writer's signature block 123

Matching

Match each term in the second column with its correct definition in the first column by writing the letter of the term on the blank line in front of the correct definition.

_____ 1. An arrangement of information organized into rows and columns.

_____ 2. The box at the intersection of a row and column in a table.

_____ 3. A document structure that opens a copy of itself, opens unnamed, and is used as the starting point for another document.

_____ 4. The template that serves as a basis for all new Word documents.

_____ 5. The personal or company information that displays at the top of a letter.

_____ 6. The Word style that inserts no extra space following a paragraph and uses single spacing.

_____ 7. The first line in a business letter that contains the current date and that is positioned just below the letterhead if a letterhead is used.

_____ 8. The name and address of the person receiving a letter and positioned below the date line.

_____ 9. The greeting line of a letter.

_____ 10. A parting farewell in a letter.

_____ 11. The name and title of the author of a letter, placed near the bottom of the letter under the complimentary closing.

_____ 12. The optional line following the inside address in a business letter that states the purpose of the letter.

A AutoCorrect

B Cell

C Complimentary closing

D Date line

E Drag and drop

F Enclosures

G Inside address

H Letterhead

I No Spacing

J Normal template

K Salutation

L Subject line

M Table

N Template

O Writer's identification

_____ 13.   Additional documents included with a business letter.

_____ 14.   A Word feature that corrects common spelling errors as you type, for example changing _teh_ to _the_.

_____ 15.   A technique by which you can move, by dragging, selected text from one location in a document to another.

Multiple Choice

Circle the correct answer.

1.   When you create a table, the width of all of cells in the table is:
   A. equal   **B.** proportional   **C.** 1 inch

2.   To indicate words that might be misspelled because they are not in Word's dictionary, Word flags text with:
   A. blue wavy underlines   **B.** green wavy underlines   **C.** red wavy underlines

3.   To indicate possible grammar errors, Word flags text with:
   A. blue wavy underlines   **B.** green wavy underlines   **C.** red wavy underlines

4.   To indicate possible errors in word usage, Word flags text with:
   A. blue wavy underlines   **B.** green wavy underlines   **C.** red wavy underlines

5.   A research tool that provides a list of words with similar meanings is:
   A. a thesaurus   **B.** a dictionary   **C.** an encyclopedia

6.   A word with the same or similar meaning as another word is:
   A. an acronym   **B.** a search term   **C.** a synonym

7.   In a template, an area indicated by placeholder text into which you can add text, pictures, dates, or lists is a:
   A. text control   **B.** content control   **C.** quick control

8.   A document saved in HTML, which can be opened using a Web browser, is a:
   A. Web page   **B.** template   **C.** resume

9.   Using drag-and-drop to move text is most useful when both the text and the destination are on the same:
   A. document   **B.** section   **C.** screen

10. To locate specific text in a document quickly, use the:
   A. Find command   **B.** Replace command   **C.** Locate command

Skills Review | Project **2C** Student Resume

In the following Skills Review, you will use a table to create a resume for Joshua Green. Your completed resume will look similar to Figure 2.44.

Project Files

For Project 2C, you will need the following files:

New blank Word document
w02C_Skills
w02C_Experience

You will save your document as:

Lastname_Firstname_2C_Student_Resume

Project Results

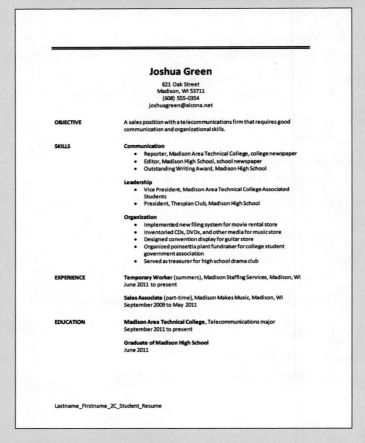

Figure 2.44

(Project 2C Student Resume continues on the next page)

Content-Based Assessments

1 **Start** Word. In the new blank document, be sure that formatting marks and rulers display. **Save** the document in your **Word Chapter 2** folder as **Lastname_Firstname_2C_Student_Resume**

a. Add the file name to the footer, and then close the footer area. Click the **Insert tab**, and then in the **Tables group**, click the **Table** button. In the **Table** grid, in the fourth row, click the second square to insert a **2 × 4** table.

b. In the first cell of the table, type **Joshua Green** and then press [Enter]. Type the following text, pressing [Enter] after each line *except* the last line:

   821 Oak Street

   Madison, WI 53711

   (608) 555-0354

   joshuagreen@alcona.net

c. Press [↓] to move to the first cell in the second row. Type **SKILLS** and then press [↓] to move to the first cell in the third row.

d. Type **EXPERIENCE** and then press [↓]. Type **EDUCATION**

e. In the first cell, if the e-mail address displays in blue, right-click the e-mail address, and then from the shortcut menu, click **Remove Hyperlink. Save** your document

2 Click in the cell to the right of *SKILLS*, and then type the following, pressing [Enter] after each item:

   Communication
   Reporter, Madison Area Technical College, college newspaper
   Editor, Madison High School, school newspaper
   Outstanding Writing Award, Madison High School

a. With the insertion point in the new line at the end of the cell, click the **Insert tab**. In the **Text group**, click the **Object button arrow**, and then click **Text from File**.

b. Navigate to your student files, select **w02C_Skills**, and then click **Insert**. Press [Backspace] one time to remove the blank line.

c. Click in the cell to the right of *EXPERIENCE*, and then insert the file **w02C_Experience**. Press [Backspace] one time to remove the blank line.

d. Click in the cell to the right of *EDUCATION*, and then type the following, pressing [Enter] after all *except* the last item:

Madison Area Technical College, Telecommunications major

September 2011 to present

Graduate of Madison High School

June 2011

3 Click anywhere in the top row of the table. Click the **Layout tab**, and then in the **Rows & Columns group**, click the **Insert Below** button. Type **OBJECTIVE** and then press [Tab].

a. Type **A sales position with a telecommunications firm that requires good communication and organizational skills.**

b. In any row, point to the vertical border between the two columns to display the [⊹] pointer. Drag the column border to the left to approximately **1.75 inches on the horizontal ruler**.

c. Click anywhere in the left column. Click the **Layout tab**. In the **Cell Size group**, in the **Table Column Width** box, if necessary, type **1.75** and press [Enter].

d. In the first row of the document, drag across both cells to select them. On the **Layout tab**, in the **Merge group**, click the **Merge Cells** button. Right-click the selected cell, and then from the Mini toolbar, click the **Center** button.

e. In the top row, select the first paragraph of text— *Joshua Green*. From the Mini toolbar, increase the **Font Size** to **20** and apply **Bold**.

f. In the second row, point to the word *OBJECTIVE*, hold down the left mouse button, and then drag down to select the row headings in uppercase letters. On the Mini toolbar, click the **Bold** button. **Save** your document.

4 Click in the cell to the right of *OBJECTIVE*. On the **Page Layout tab**, in the **Paragraph group**, click the **Spacing After up spin arrow** three times to change the spacing to **18 pt**.

a. In the cell to the right of *SKILLS*, apply **Bold** to the words *Communication*, *Leadership*, and *Organization*. Then, under each bold heading in the cell, select the lines of text, and create a bulleted list.

b. In the first two bulleted lists, click in the last bullet item, and then on the **Page Layout tab**, in the **Paragraph group**, set the **Spacing After** to **12 pt**.

(Project 2C Student Resume continues on the next page)

Skills Review | Project **2C** Student Resume (continued)

c. In the last bulleted list, click in the last bullet item, and then set the **Spacing After** to **18 pt**.

d. In the cell to the right of *EXPERIENCE*, apply **Bold** to *Temporary Worker* and *Sales Associate*. Click in the line *June 2011 to present* and apply **Spacing After** of **12 pt**. Click in the line *September 2009 to May 2011* and apply **Spacing After** of **18 pt**.

e. In the cell to the right of *EDUCATION*, apply **Bold** to *Madison Area Technical College* and *Graduate of Madison High School*.

f. In the same cell, click in the line *September 2011 to present* and apply **Spacing After** of **12 pt**.

g. In the first row, click in the last line—*joshuagreen@alcona.net*—and then change the **Spacing After** to **18 pt**. Click in the first line—*Joshua Green*—and set the **Spacing Before** to **30 pt** and the **Spacing After** to **6 pt**.

5 Point to the upper left corner of the table, and then click the displayed **table move handle** button ⊞, to select the entire table. On the **Design tab**, in the **Table Styles group**, click the **Borders button arrow**, and then click **No Border**.

a. On the **Design tab**, in the **Table Styles group**, click the **Borders button arrow** again, and then at the bottom of the gallery, click **Borders and Shading**. In the **Borders and Shading** dialog box, under **Setting**, click **Custom**. Under **Style**, scroll down slightly, and then click the style with two equal lines.

b. Click the **Width arrow**, and then click **1 1/2 pt**. Under **Preview**, click the top border of the preview box, and then click **OK**.

c. Click the **File tab** to display **Backstage** view, and then click the **Print tab** to display the Print Preview.

d. Click the **Info tab**. On the right side, under the document thumbnail, click **Properties**, and then click **Show Document Panel**.

e. In the **Author** box, delete any text and then type your firstname and lastname. In the **Subject** box, type your course name and section number, and in the **Keywords** box type **resume, table**

f. **Close** the Document Panel. **Save** 🔲 and then, as directed by your instructor, print your document or submit it electronically. **Exit** Word.

End **You have completed Project 2C** ⎯⎯⎯⎯⎯⎯⎯⎯⎯⎯⎯⎯⎯⎯⎯⎯⎯⎯⎯⎯⎯⎯⎯⎯⎯⎯⎯⎯

Content-Based Assessments

Apply 2B skills from these Objectives:

4. Create a New Document from an Existing Document
5. Change and Reorganize Text
6. Use the Proofing Options
7. Create a Document Using a Template

Skills Review | Project **2D** Ross Letter

In the following Skills Review, you will create a letterhead, and then create a new document from the letterhead to create a resume cover letter. You will also create a short resume using a Microsoft template and save it as a Web page. Your completed documents will look similar to Figure 2.45.

Project Files

For Project 2D, you will need the following files:

New blank Word document
w02D_Letter_Text
Equity Resume Template from Word's installed templates

You will save your documents as:

Lastname_Firstname_2D_Ross_Letterhead
Lastname_Firstname_2D_Ross_Letter
Lastname_Firstname_2D_Resume
Lastname_Firstname_2D_Web_Resume

Project Results

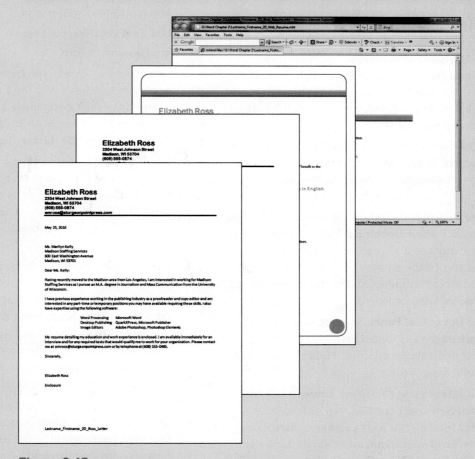

Figure 2.45

(Project 2D Ross Letter continues on the next page)

Content-Based Assessments

Skills Review | Project 2D Ross Letter (continued)

1 **Start** Word. In the new blank document, be sure that formatting marks and rulers display. On the **Home tab**, in the **Styles group**, click the **No Spacing** button.

a. Type **Elizabeth Ross** and then press Enter. Type **2304 West Johnson Street** and press Enter. Type **Madison, WI 53704** and then press Enter.

b. Type **(608) 555-0874** and then press Enter. Type **emross@sturgeonpointpress.com** and then press Enter three times. If the e-mail address changes to blue text, right-click the e-mail address, and then click Remove Hyperlink.

c. Select all five lines of the personal information, but do not select the blank paragraphs. From the Mini toolbar, change the **Font** to **Arial Rounded MT Bold**. Select the first paragraph—*Elizabeth Ross*—and then on the Mini toolbar, apply **Bold** and change the **Font Size** to **20**.

d. Click anywhere in the fifth line of text—the e-mail address. On the **Home tab**, in the **Paragraph group**, click the **Borders button arrow**, and then click **Borders and Shading**. Under **Style**, click the first style—a single solid line. Click the **Width arrow**, and then click **3 pt**. In the **Preview** area, click the bottom border, and then click **OK**.

e. Display **Backstage** view, and then click **Save As**. Save the document in your **Word Chapter 2** folder as **Lastname_Firstname_2D_Ross_Letterhead**

f. Add the file name to the footer, and then close the footer area. Display **Backstage** view, click **Properties**, and then click **Show Document Panel**. In the **Author** box, delete any text and then type your firstname and lastname. In the **Subject** box, type your course name and section number, and in the **Keywords** box, type **personal letterhead**

g. **Close** the **Document Panel**. **Save** your document. From **Backstage** view, click **Close** to close the document but leave Word open. Hold this file until you complete the project.

2 From **Backstage** view, click **New**. Under **Available Templates**, click **New from existing**. Navigate to your **Word Chapter 2** folder, click your **Lastname_Firstname_2D_Ross_Letterhead** document, and then in the lower right corner, click **Create New**. From **Backstage** view, click **Save As**. Navigate to your **Word Chapter 2** folder, and **Save** the file as **Lastname_Firstname_2D_Ross_Letter**

Double-click the footer, right-click the file name, and then click **Update Field**. Close the footer area.

a. From **Backstage** view, display the **Word Options** dialog box. In the **Word Options** list, click **Proofing**, and then under **AutoCorrect options**, click the **AutoCorrect Options** button.

b. In the **AutoCorrect** dialog box, click the **AutoCorrect tab**. Under **Replace**, type **expereince** and under **With**, type **experience** Click **Add**. If the entry already exists, click Replace instead, and then click Yes. Click **OK** two times to close the dialog boxes.

c. Press Ctrl + End, type **May 25, 2016** and then press Enter four times. Type the following inside address using four lines:

Ms. Marilyn Kelly

Madison Staffing Services

600 East Washington Avenue

Madison, WI 53701

d. Press Enter two times, type **Dear Ms. Kelly:** and then press Enter two times. On the **Insert tab**, in the **Text group**, click the **Object button arrow**, and then click **Text from File**. From your student files, locate and insert the file **w02D_Letter_Text**.

e. Scroll to view the lower portion of the page, and be sure your insertion point is in the empty paragraph mark at the end. Press Enter, type **Sincerely,** and then press Enter four times. Type **Elizabeth Ross** and press Enter two times. Type **Enclosure** and then **Save** your document.

f. Near the bottom of the document, locate the paragraph that begins *I am available* and click to position the insertion point at the beginning of the paragraph. Type **My resume detailing my education and work** Press Spacebar and then type the misspelled word **expereince** Press Spacebar and notice that AutoCorrect corrects the misspelling. Type **is enclosed.** and then press Spacebar.

g. Press Ctrl + Home. On the **Home tab**, in the **Editing group**, click the **Replace** button. In the **Find what** box, type **association** In the **Replace with** box, type **organization** and then click **Replace All**. Click **OK** to close the message box, and then **Close** the **Find and Replace** dialog box.

(Project 2D Ross Letter continues on the next page)

Content-Based Assessments

h. In the paragraph that begins *I have previous*, double-click *experience*. Point to the selected word to display the ⬚ pointer, and then drag the word to the left of *working*. Adjust spacing as necessary.

i. Below the paragraph that begins *I have previous*, position the insertion point in the second blank line. On the **Insert tab**, in the **Tables group**, click the **Table** button. In the **Table** grid, in the third row, click the second square to insert a 2 × 3 table. Type the following information in the table:

Word Processing	Microsoft Word
Desktop Publishing	QuarkXPress, Microsoft Publisher
Image Editors	Adobe Photoshop, Photoshop Elements

j. Point outside of the upper left corner and click the **table move handle** button to select the entire table. On the **Layout tab**, in the **Cell Size group**, click the **AutoFit** button, and then click **AutoFit Contents**. On the **Home tab**, in the **Paragraph group**, click the **Center** button. On the **Design tab**, in the **Table Styles group**, click the **Borders button arrow**, and then click **No Border**. **Save** your document.

3 If you do not see any wavy red and green lines under words, refer to the Alert in Activity 2.17 to enable the default settings for automatic proofing.

a. In the paragraph that begins *Having lately*, in the second line, locate and right-click the phrase *an M.A. degrees*, and then from the shortcut menu, click *an M.A. degree*. In the same paragraph, locate and right-click *Journlism*. From the shortcut menu, click *Journalism*.

b. Press Ctrl + Home. On the **Review tab**, in the **Proofing group**, click the **Spelling & Grammar** button. In the **Spelling and Grammar** dialog box, click the **Change** button to change *are* to *am*. For the misspelled word *expertis*, under **Suggestions**, be sure *expertise* is selected, and then click **Change**.

c. **Change** *qualifie* to *qualify*, and then click **OK** to close the message box.

d. Near the top of the document, in the paragraph that begins *Having lately*, right-click *lately*. In the shortcut menu, point to **Synonyms**, and then click *recently*. In the same line, right-

click *region*, and replace it with the synonym *area*.

e. Display **Backstage** view, click **Properties**, and then click **Show Document Panel**. Type your firstname and lastname as the **Author** and your course number and section as the **Subject**. In the **Keywords** box, replace any existing text with **cover letter Close** the **Document Panel**. **Save** your document. From **Backstage** view, **Close** the document but leave Word open. Hold this file until you complete the project.

4 Display **Backstage** view, and then click **New**. Under **Available Templates**, click **Sample templates**. Locate and click **Equity Resume**. In the lower right corner, click **Create**.

a. **Save** the document in your **Word Chapter 2** folder as **Lastname_Firstname_2D_Resume** and then add the file name to the footer—called *First Page Footer* in this template. At the top of the resume, select the text in the first control, which displays the name of the computer at which you are working. Replace this text by typing **Elizabeth Ross** Right-click the name, and then from the shortcut menu, click **Remove Content Control**.

b. Click the *[Type your phone number]* control, and then type **(608) 555-0874** Click the *[Type your address]* control, type **2304 West Johnson Street** and press Enter. Type **Madison, WI 53703**

c. Click the *[Type your e-mail address]* control, and then type **emross@sturgeonpointpress.com** Right-click the *[Type your website]* control, and then from the shortcut menu, click **Remove Content Control**. Press Backspace to remove the *website* line.

d. Click the *[Type the objectives]* control, and then type **A copy editing or proofreading position where my editing and advanced computer skills will be of benefit to the organization.**

e. Under *Education*, click the *[Type the completion date]* control, and then type **University of Wisconsin-Milwaukee, May 2015** Click the *[Type the degree]* control, and then type **Bachelor of Arts in English** For the *[Type list of accomplishments]* bulleted list, type:

Dean's list, six terms

Harriet McArthur Creative Writing Award

(Project 2D Ross Letter continues on the next page)

Skills Review | Project **2D** Ross Letter (continued)

Assistant Editor of college newspaper

3.8 GPA

f. Under *Experience*, enter the text shown in **Table 1** below.

g. Click the *[Type list of skills]* control and type **Word** Press Enter, and then type two additional bullet points with **QuarkXPress** and **Adobe Photoshop**

h. Display **Backstage** view, click **Properties**, and then click **Show Document Panel**. Type your firstname and lastname as the **Author**. In the **Subject** box, type your course and section number. In the **Keywords** box, **resume, template Close** the **Document Panel**.

i. **Save** your document.

j. Display **Backstage** view, click **Save As**, and then in the **Save as type** box, click **Single File Web Page**. Navigate to your **Word Chapter 2** folder. In the **File name** box,

type **Lastname_Firstname_2D_Web_Resume** Click **Save**.

k. Display **Backstage** view, click **Properties**, and then click **Advanced Properties**. In the **Properties** dialog box, be sure your name displays in the *Author* box, and then in the **Keywords** box, add **HTML** to the list of keywords. Click **OK** and **Save** your document.

l. **Exit** Word. From the **Start** menu, click **Computer** (or My Computer). Navigate to your **Word Chapter 2** folder, and then double-click your **2D_Web_Resume** file to open the resume in your Web browser. **Close** the Web browser. As directed by your instructor, print or submit electronically the four files that are the results of this project—2D_Ross_Letterhead, 2D_Ross_Letter, 2D_Resume, and 2D_Web_Resume.

Table 1

[Type the start date]	**May 2012**
[Type the end date]	**Present-**
[Type the job title]	**Senior Copy Editor**
[Type the company name]	**Sturgeon Point Press**
[Type the company address]	**Milwaukee, WI**
[Type job responsibilities]	**Produced final edited copy of books, technical manuals, and pamphlets; supervised three copy editors.**

(**Return to Step 4-g**)

End **You have completed Project 2D** ——————————————

Content-Based Assessments

Apply 2A skills from these Objectives:

1. Create a Table
2. Add Text to a Table
3. Format a Table

Mastering Word | Project 2E Job Listings

In the following Mastering Word project, you will create an announcement for new job postings at Madison Staffing Services. Your completed document will look similar to Figure 2.46.

Project Files

For Project 2E, you will need the following files:

New blank Word document
w02E_New_Jobs

You will save your document as:

Lastname_Firstname_2E_Job_Listings

Project Results

Madison Staffing Services

Job Alert! New Health Care Listings Just Added!

January 7

Madison Staffing Services has just added several new jobs in the Health Care industry for the week of January 7. These listings are just in, so apply now to be one of the first candidates considered!

For further information about any of these new jobs, or a complete listing of jobs that are available through Madison Staffing Services, please call Marilyn Kelly at (608) 555-0386 or visit our Web site at www.madisonstaffing.com.

New Health Care Listings for the Week of January 7		
Job Title	**Type**	**Location**
Computer Developer	Radiology Office	Dane County
Executive Assistant	Medical Records	Deerfield
Insurance Biller	Dental Office	Madison
Office Assistant	Health Clinic	Madison

To help prepare yourself before applying for these jobs, we recommend that you review the following articles on our Web site at www.madisonstaffing.com.

Topic	Article Title
Research	Working in Health Care
Interviewing	Interviewing in Health Care

Lastname_Firstname_2E_Job_Listings

Figure 2.46

(Project 2E Job Listings continues on the next page)

Content-Based Assessments

Mastering Word | Project 2E Job Listings (continued)

1 **Start** Word and display a new blank document; display formatting marks and rulers. **Save** the document in your **Word Chapter 2** folder as **Lastname_Firstname_ 2E_Job_Listings** and then add the file name to the footer.

2 Type **Madison Staffing Services** and press Enter. Type **Job Alert! New Health Care Listings Just Added!** and press Enter. Type **January 7** and press Enter two times. **Insert** the file **w02E_New_Jobs**.

3 At the top of the document, select and **Center** the three title lines. Select the title *Madison Staffing Services* and change the **Font Size** to **20** pt and apply **Bold**. Apply **Bold** to the second and third title lines. Locate the paragraph that begins *For further information*, and then below that paragraph, click to position the insertion point in the second blank paragraph. **Insert** a **3 × 4** table. Enter the following:

Job Title	Type	Location
Executive Assistant	Medical Records	Deerfield
Insurance Biller	Dental Office	Madison
Office Assistant	Health Clinic	Madison

4 In the table, click anywhere in the second row, and then insert a row above. Add the following information so that the job titles remain in alphabetic order:

Computer Developer	Radiology Office	Dane County

5 Select the entire table. On the **Layout tab**, in the **Cell Size group**, use the **AutoFit** button to **AutoFit Contents**. With the table still selected, **Center** the table. With the table still selected, on the **Page Layout tab**, add **6 pt Spacing Before** and **6 pt Spacing After**.

6 With the table still selected, remove all table borders, and then add a **Custom 1 pt** solid line top border and bottom border. Select all three cells in the first row, apply **Bold**, and then **Center** the text. Click anywhere in the first row, and then insert a new row above. Merge the three cells in the new top row, and then type **New Health Care Listings for the Week of January 7** Notice that the new row keeps the formatting of the row from which it was created.

7 At the bottom of the document, **Insert** a **2 × 3** table. Enter the following:

Topic	Article Title
Research	Working in Health Care
Interviewing	Interviewing in Health Care

8 Select the entire table. On the **Layout tab**, in the **Cell Size group**, use the **AutoFit** button to **AutoFit Contents**. On the **Home tab**, **Center** the table. On the **Page Layout tab**, add **6 pt Spacing Before** and **6 pt Spacing After**.

9 With the table still selected, remove all table borders, and then add a **Custom 1 pt** solid line top border and bottom border. Select the cells in the first row, apply **Bold**, and then **Center** the text.

10 In the **Document Panel**, add your name and course information and the **Keywords new listings, health care Save** and then print or submit the document electronically as directed. **Exit** Word.

End You have completed Project 2E

Content-Based Assessments

Apply **2B** skills from
these Objectives:

- **4** Create a New
  Document from an
  Existing Document
- **5** Change and
  Reorganize Text
- **6** Use the Proofing
  Options
- **7** Create a Document
  Using a Template

Mastering Word | Project **2F** Job Tips

In the following Mastering Word project, you will create a fax and a memo that includes job tips for Madison Staffing Services employees. Your completed documents will look similar to Figure 2.47.

Project Files

For Project 2F, you will need the following files:

> w02F_Memo_Heading
> w02F_Memo_Text
> Origin Fax template from Word's installed templates

You will save your documents as:

> Lastname_Firstname_2F_Job_Tips
> Lastname_Firstname_2F_Fax

Project Results

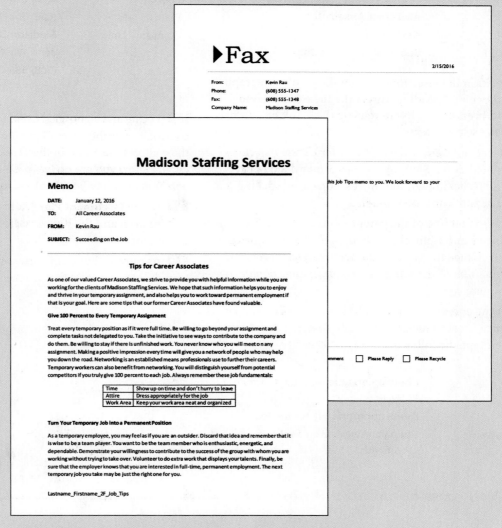

Figure 2.47

(Project 2F Job Tips continues on the next page)

Mastering Word | Project **2F** Job Tips (continued)

1 **Start** Word; display rulers and formatting marks. In **Backstage** view, create a **New** document using the **New from existing** template. In the **New from Existing Document** dialog box, navigate to your student files, click **w02F_Memo_Heading**, and then click **Create New**.

2 Display the **Document Panel**, add your name and course information and the **Keywords memo, associates**

3 **Save** the document in your **Word Chapter 2** folder as **Lastname_Firstname_2F_Job_Tips** Add the file name to the footer.

4 At the top of your document, in the *DATE* paragraph, click to the right of the tab formatting mark, and then type **January 12, 2016** Use a similar technique to add the following information:

TO:	**All Career Associates**
FROM:	**Kevin Rau**
SUBJECT:	**Succeeding on the Job**

5 Position the insertion point in the blank paragraph below the memo heading. **Insert** the file **w02F_Memo_Text** and press ⟨Backspace⟩ to remove the blank line at the end of the selected text.

6 Select and **Center** the title *Tips for Career Associates*. By using either the **Spelling and Grammar** dialog box, or by right-clicking selected words, correct all spelling, grammar, and word usage errors.

7 In the first line of the paragraph that begins *Treat every*, locate and right-click *provisional*. Use the shortcut menu to change the word to the synonym *temporary*. In the second line of the same paragraph, change *donate* to the synonym *contribute*.

8 At the end of the paragraph that begins *Treat every temporary*, create a blank paragraph. **Insert** at **2 × 3** table, and then type the following information:

Time	Show up on time and don't hurry to leave
Attire	Dress appropriately for the job
Work Area	Keep your work area neat and organized

9 Select the entire table. **AutoFit Contents**, **Center** the table, and remove the table borders. Display **Backstage** view and preview the document. **Save** and **Close** the document but leave Word open. Hold this file until you complete this project.

10 From **Sample templates**, create a document based on the **Origin Fax** template. Save the document in your **Word Chapter 2** folder as **Lastname_Firstname_2F_Fax** and then add the file name to the footer—called the *First Page Footer* in this template.

11 Click the *Pick a date* placeholder, type **2/15/2016** and then type the following for the remaining controls:

From:	**Kevin Rau**
Phone:	**(608) 555-1347**
Fax:	**(608) 555-1348**
Company Name:	**Madison Staffing Services**
To:	**Jane Westerfield**
Phone:	**(608) 555-0034**
Fax:	**(608) 555-0035**

12 Locate and right-click *Kevin Rau*; remove the content control. Delete the lower *Company Name* text and remove the control to its right. In the *Type comments* control, type **Jane: I know you are on leave, so I thought I would fax this Job Tips memo to you. We look forward to your return.**

13 In the **Document Panel**, add your name and course information and the **Keywords job tips, fax Save** the document.

14 As directed by your instructor, print or submit electronically the two files that are the results of this project. **Exit** Word.

End **You have completed Project 2F** ———————————

Content-Based Assessments

Apply **2A** and **2B** skills from these Objectives:

- ◾ Create a Table
- ◾ Add Text to a Table
- ◾ Format a Table
- ◾ Create a New Document from an Existing Document
- ◾ Change and Reorganize Text
- ◾ Use the Proofing Options
- ◾ Create a Document Using a Template

Mastering Word | Project **2G** Job Letter

In the following Mastering Word project, you will create a new document from an existing document, format a table, and then create a fax cover using a template. Your completed documents will look similar to Figure 2.48.

Project Files

For Project 2G, you will need the following files:

w02G_Letter_Text
w02G_Letterhead
w02G_Resume
Equity Fax template from Word's installed templates

You will save your documents as:

Lastname_Firstname_2G_Job_Letter
Lastname_Firstname_2G_Resume
Lastname_Firstname_2G_Fax

Project Results

Figure 2.48

(Project 2G Job Letter continues on the next page)

Content-Based Assessments

1 **Start** Word and display rulers and formatting marks. By using the **New from existing** template, create a document from the file **w02G_Letterhead**. **Save** the document in your **Word Chapter 2** folder as **Lastname_Firstname_2G_Job_Letter** Add the file name to the footer. Move to the end of the document, and then on the **Home tab**, apply the **No Spacing** style. Type **March 6, 2016** and then press [Enter] four times. Type the following:

> **James Washington**
> **Madison Staffing Services**
> **600 East Washington Avenue**
> **Madison, WI 53701**

2 Press [Enter] two times, type **Dear Mr. Washington:** and press [Enter] two times. **Insert** the text from the file **w02G_Letter_Text** and remove the blank line at the bottom of the selected text.

3 Move to the top of the document, and then by using either the **Spelling and Grammar** dialog box, or by right-clicking selected words, correct spelling, grammar, and word usage errors. In the paragraph that begins *I was looking*, in the third line, locate and right-click *corporation*. Use the shortcut menu to open the **Thesaurus** and change the word to the synonym *company*. In the same line, change *correct* to the synonym *right*.

4 In the paragraph that begins *I currently*, select the first sentence of the paragraph and drag it to the end of the same paragraph. In the second blank line below the paragraph that begins *The job description*, **Insert** a **2 × 3** table, and then type the text shown in **Table 1** below.

5 Select the entire table. **AutoFit Contents**, **Center** the table, remove the table borders, and then add **3 pt** spacing before and after by typing **3** in the **Spacing** boxes and pressing [Enter].

6 In the **Document Panel**, add your name and course information and the **Keywords job letter** Preview the document. **Save** and **Close** the document but leave Word open. Hold the file until you complete this project.

7 From your student files, open **w02G_Resume**. **Save** the document in your **Word Chapter 2** folder as **Lastname_Firstname_2G_Resume** Add the file name to the footer.

8 **Insert** a new second row in the table. In the first cell of the new row, type **OBJECTIVE** and then press [Tab]. Type **To obtain a Help Desk Technician position that will use my technical and communication skills and computer support experience.** In the same cell, add **12 pt Spacing After**.

9 Select the entire table. On the **Layout tab**, **AutoFit Contents**. Remove the table borders, and then display the **Borders and Shading** dialog box. With the table selected, create a **Custom** single solid line **1 1/2 pt** top border.

10 In the first row of the table, select both cells and then **Merge Cells**. **Center** the five lines and apply **Bold**. In the first row, select *Marilynn Long* and change the **Font Size** to **20 pt** and add **36 pt Spacing Before**. In the e-mail address at the bottom of the first row, add **24 pt Spacing After**.

11 In the first column, apply **Bold** to the four headings. In the cell to the right of *EDUCATION*, **Bold** the names of the two schools, and add **12 pt Spacing After** the two lines that begin *September*. In the cell to the right of *RELEVANT EXPERIENCE*, bold the names of the two jobs—*IT Help Desk Specialist* and *Computer Technician*. In the same cell, below the line that begins *January 2014*, apply bullets to the four lines that comprise the job duties. Create a similar bulleted list for the duties as a Computer Technician. Add **12 pt Spacing After** to the last line of each of the bulleted lists.

12 In the cell to the right of *CERTIFICATIONS*, select all four lines and create a bulleted list. In the **Document Panel**, add your name and course information and the **Keywords help desk resume** and then submit your document as directed. **Save** and **Close** the document but leave Word open.

13 From **Sample templates**, create a document based on the **Origin Fax** template. **Save** the document in your **Word**

Table 1

Education	Bachelor of Science, Information Technology, Marquette University
Experience	Two years of help desk experience at a major university
Required Certifications	MCITP, MCDST

(Return to Step 5)

(Project 2G Job Letter continues on the next page)

Content-Based Assessments

Chapter 2 folder as **Lastname_Firstname_2G_Fax** and then add the file name to the footer—called a *First Page Footer* in this template.

14 Type the text shown in **Table 2** for the content controls.

15 Locate and right-click *Marilynn Long*; remove the content control. In the **Document Panel**, add your name and course information and the **Keywords fax cover page** As directed by your instructor, print or submit electronically the three files from this project. **Exit** Word.

Table 2

Pick a date	3/6/2016
From:	**Marilynn Long**
Phone:	**(608) 555-0967**
Fax:	**(608) 555-0966**
Company Name:	Remove this content control and row heading
To:	**James Washington, Recruiter**
Phone:	**(608) 555-0034**
Fax:	**(608) 555-0035**
Company Name	**Madison Staffing Services**
Comments:	**Two pages to follow that include my resume and a cover letter for the position of Help Desk Technician.**

(Return to Step 15)

End **You have completed Project 2G** ——————————————————

GO! Fix It | Project **2H** New Jobs

In this project, you will construct a solution by applying any combination of the skills you practiced from the Objectives in Projects 2A and 2B.

Project Files

For Project 2H, you will need the following file:

> w02H_New_Jobs

You will save your document as:

> Lastname_Firstname_2H_New_Jobs

From the student files that accompany this textbook, locate and open the file w02H_New_Jobs, and then save the file in your Word Chapter 2 folder as **Lastname_Firstname_2H_New_Jobs**

This document contains errors that you must find and correct. Read and examine the document, and then edit to correct the errors that you find and to improve the overall document format. Types of errors could include, but are not restricted to:

- Spelling errors
- Grammar errors
- Word choice errors
- Duplicate words
- Unattractive table column widths
- Title not merged across the top row of the table
- Inconsistent spacing before and after paragraphs in the table

Things you should know to complete this project:

- Viewing the document in Print Preview will help identify some of the problems
- The Spelling and Grammar checker will be useful
- Adjust the column widths *before* merging the title

Save your document and add the file name to the footer. In the Document Panel, type your firstname and lastname in the Author box and your course name and section number in the Subject box. In the Keywords box type **job listings** and then save your document and submit as directed.

End You have completed Project 2H _____

Content-Based Assessments

Apply a combination of the **2A** and **2B** skills.

GO! Make It | Project 2I Training

Project Files

For Project 2I, you will need the following file:

New blank Word document

You will save your document as:

Lastname_Firstname_2I_Training

Start Word, and then save the file in your Word Chapter 2 folder as **Lastname_Firstname_2I_Training**

Use the skills you practiced in this chapter to create the table shown in Figure 2.49. The first row font is Cambria 16 pt, the remainder is Cambria 14 pt. The spacing after the first row is 36 pt, the spacing at the bottom of the rows is 12 pt.

Add the file name to the footer; in the Document Panel, add your name and course information and the Keywords **online training** Save your document, and then submit as directed.

Project Results

Selected Training Programs Available Online

Software	Program Title
Microsoft Word	• Create your first Word document I • Getting started with Word 2010 • Use the Navigation Pane to search and move around in your document • Create your first Word document II
Microsoft Excel	• Get to know Excel 2010: Create your first workbook • Charts I: How to create a chart in Excel • Get to know Excel 2010: Enter formulas • Sort data in a range or table

Lastname_Firstname_2I_Training

Figure 2.49

End You have completed Project 2I

Content-Based Assessments

GO! Solve It | Project **2J** Job Postings

Project Files

For Project 2J, you will need the following files:

New blank Word document
w02J_Job_Postings

You will save your documents as:

Lastname_Firstname_2J_Letterhead
Lastname_Firstname_2J_Job_Postings

Print the w02J_Job_Postings document, and use the information to complete this project. Create a new company letterhead and save it in your Word Chapter 2 folder as **Lastname_Firstname_2J_Letterhead** Add the file name to the footer. Add your name, your course name and section number, and the keyword **letterhead** to the Properties area.

Create a new document based on the existing document you just created. The new document will be a list of new jobs posted by Madison Staffing Services. The job posting should include the letterhead, introductory text, and a table that includes the information about the new jobs that are currently available. The job list should be in table format. Use either two or three columns, and label the columns appropriately. Format the table, the table borders, and the text in an attractive, readable manner.

Save the document as **Lastname_Firstname_2J_Job_Postings** Add the file name to the footer, and add your name, your course name and section number, and the keywords **new jobs** to the Properties area. Submit your two files as directed.

Performance Level			
Performance Element	**Exemplary:** You consistently applied the relevant skills	**Proficient:** You sometimes, but not always, applied the relevant skills	**Developing:** You rarely or never applied the relevant skills
Create and format a letterhead template	The text in the letterhead is appropriately formatted, the company name stands out, and the spacing between paragraphs is attractive.	The letterhead is complete, but the line spacing or text formatting is not appropriate for a letterhead.	The spacing and formatting is not appropriate for a letterhead.
Insert a table	The inserted table has the appropriate number of columns and rows to display the information.	The table is not structured to effectively display the information.	No table is inserted in the document.
Format the table structure	Table column widths fit the information, extra space is added between the rows, and borders are attractively formatted.	The column widths do not reflect the amount of information in the column, and the spacing between the cells is insufficient.	Table displays only default column widths and spacing.
Format the text in the table	Important text is highlighted and formatted appropriately, making the text easy to read and interpret.	Some text formatting is added, but the formatting does not highlight the important information.	No text formatting is included.

End You have completed Project 2J

Content-Based Assessments

Apply a combination of the **2A** and **2B** skills.

GO! Solve It | Project **2K** Agenda

Project Files

For Project 2K, you will need the following file:

Agenda template from Word's Online templates

You will save your document as:

Lastname_Firstname_2K_Agenda

Create a new document based on an agenda template—such as the *Formal meeting agenda* template—from the Agenda templates at Microsoft Office Online. Save the agenda as **Lastname_Firstname_2K_Agenda** Use the following information to prepare an agenda for a Madison Staffing Services meeting.

The meeting will be chaired by Marilyn Kelly and will be the monthly meeting of the company administrators—Kevin Rau, Marilyn Kelly, Andre Randolph, Susan Nguyen, and Charles James. The meeting will be held on March 15, 2016, at 3:00 p.m. The old business (open issues) include 1) expanding services into the printing and food service industries; 2) recruitment at the UW-Madison and MATC campuses; and 3) the addition of a part-time trainer. The new business will include 1) recruitment at the University of Wisconsin, Milwaukee; 2) rental of office space in or around Milwaukee; 3) purchase of new computers for the training room; and 4) renewal of snow removal service contract.

Add the file name to the footer, and add your name, your course name and section number, and the keywords **agenda, monthly administrative meeting** to the Properties area. Submit as directed.

		Performance Level	
	Exemplary: You consistently applied the relevant skills	**Proficient:** You sometimes, but not always, applied the relevant skills	**Developing:** You rarely or never applied the relevant skills
Select an agenda template	Agenda template is appropriate for the information provided for the meeting.	Agenda template is used, but does not fit the information provided.	No template is used for the agenda.
Add appropriate information to the template	All information is inserted in the appropriate places. All unused controls are removed.	All information is included, but not in the appropriate places, and not all of the unused controls are removed.	Information is missing and unused placeholders are not removed.
Format template information	All text in the template is properly aligned and formatted.	All text is included, but alignment or formatting is inconsistent.	No additional formatting has been added.

Performance Element (left side label)

End You have completed Project 2K

Outcomes-Based Assessments

Rubric

The following outcomes-based assessments are *open-ended assessments*. That is, there is no specific correct result; your result will depend on your approach to the information provided. Make *Professional Quality* your goal. Use the following scoring rubric to guide you in *how* to approach the problem and then to evaluate *how well* your approach solves the problem.

The *criteria*—Software Mastery, Content, Format and Layout, and Process—represent the knowledge and skills you have gained that you can apply to solving the problem. The *levels of performance*—Professional Quality, Approaching Professional Quality, or Needs Quality Improvements—help you and your instructor evaluate your result.

	Your completed project is of Professional Quality if you:	Your completed project is Approaching Professional Quality if you:	Your completed project Needs Quality Improvements if you:
1-Software Mastery	Choose and apply the most appropriate skills, tools, and features and identify efficient methods to solve the problem.	Choose and apply some appropriate skills, tools, and features, but not in the most efficient manner.	Choose inappropriate skills, tools, or features, or are inefficient in solving the problem.
2-Content	Construct a solution that is clear and well organized, contains content that is accurate, appropriate to the audience and purpose, and is complete. Provide a solution that contains no errors in spelling, grammar, or style.	Construct a solution in which some components are unclear, poorly organized, inconsistent, or incomplete. Misjudge the needs of the audience. Have some errors in spelling, grammar, or style, but the errors do not detract from comprehension.	Construct a solution that is unclear, incomplete, or poorly organized; contains some inaccurate or inappropriate content; and contains many errors in spelling, grammar, or style. Do not solve the problem.
3-Format and Layout	Format and arrange all elements to communicate information and ideas, clarify function, illustrate relationships, and indicate relative importance.	Apply appropriate format and layout features to some elements, but not others. Overuse features, causing minor distraction.	Apply format and layout that does not communicate information or ideas clearly. Do not use format and layout features to clarify function, illustrate relationships, or indicate relative importance. Use available features excessively, causing distraction.
4-Process	Use an organized approach that integrates planning, development, self-assessment, revision, and reflection.	Demonstrate an organized approach in some areas, but not others; or, use an insufficient process of organization throughout.	Do not use an organized approach to solve the problem.

Outcomes-Based Assessments

Apply a combination of the 2A and 2B skills.

GO! Think | Project 2L Workshops

Project Files

For Project 2L, you will need the following files:

New blank Word document
w02L_Workshop_Information

You will save your document as:

Lastname_Firstname_2L_Workshops

Madison Staffing Services offers a series of workshops for its employee-clients. Any temporary employee who is available during the workshop hours can attend the workshops and there is no fee. Currently, the company offers three-session workshops covering Excel and Word, a two-session workshop covering Business Communication, and a one-session workshop covering *Creating a Resume*.

Print the w02L_Workshop_Information file and use the information to complete this project. Create an announcement with a title, an introductory paragraph, and a table listing the workshops and the topics covered in each workshop. Use the file w02L_Workshop_Information for help with the topics covered in each workshop. Format the table cells appropriately. Add an appropriate footer and information to the Document Panel. Save the document as **Lastname_Firstname_2L_Workshops** and submit it as directed.

 End You have completed Project 2L ─────────────────────

Apply a combination of the 2A and 2B skills.

GO! Think | Project 2M Planner

Project Files

For Project 2M, you will need the following files:

Weekly appointment sheet template from Word's Online templates
w02M_Workshop_Information

You will save your document as:

Lastname_Firstname_2M_Planner

To keep track of workshops provided to employees, the trainer fills out a weekly schedule. Each workshop lasts two hours. Print the w02M_Workshop_Information file and use part or all of the information to complete this project.

Create a new document using a template, for example the *Weekly appointment sheet* template found in the Planners category in the online template list. Create a template for a week, and include the first part of each workshop series, along with the Creating a Resume workshop. Customize the template as necessary to include *Room* and *Workshop* titles for each day of the week. The computer skills workshops are held in the Lab, the others are held in Room 104. The trainer always schedules the hour before each workshop for preparation. Fill out the workshop schedule and use your choice of formatting to indicate that the workshops cover a two-hour period. Add appropriate information to the Document Panel. Save the document as **Lastname_Firstname_2M_Planner** and submit it as directed.

End You have completed Project 2M ─────────────────────

Outcomes-Based Assessments

You and GO! | Project **2N** Personal Resume

Project Files

For Project 2N, you will need the following file:

New blank Word document

You will save your documents as

Lastname_Firstname_2N_Personal_Resume
Lastname_Firstname_2N_Cover_Letter

Locate and print the information for a job for which you would like to apply, and then create your own personal resume using a table and a cover letter. Include any information that is appropriate, including your objective for a specific job, your experience, skills, education, honors, or awards. Create your own letterhead and cover letter, using the cover letter you created in Project 2B as a guide.

To complete the assignment, be sure to format the text appropriately, resize the table columns in the resume to best display the information, and check both documents for spelling and grammar errors.

Save the resume as **Lastname_Firstname_2N_Personal_Resume** and the cover letter as **Lastname_Firstname_2N_Personal_Cover_Letter** Add the file name to the footer, and add your name, your course name and section number, and the keywords **my resume** and **cover letter** to the Properties area. Submit your file as directed.

End **You have completed Project 2N** —————————————————

Creating Research Papers, Newsletters, and Merged Mailing Labels

OUTCOMES

At the end of this chapter you will be able to:

OBJECTIVES

Mastering these objectives will enable you to:

PROJECT 3A

Create a research paper that includes citations and a bibliography.

1. Create a Research Paper (p. 165)
2. Insert Footnotes in a Research Paper (p. 167)
3. Create Citations and a Bibliography in a Research Paper (p. 172)

PROJECT 3B

Create a multiple-column newsletter and merged mailing labels.

4. Format a Multiple-Column Newsletter (p. 181)
5. Use Special Character and Paragraph Formatting (p. 186)
6. Create Mailing Labels Using Mail Merge (p. 189)

prism68/Shutterstock

In This Chapter

Microsoft Word provides many tools for creating complex documents. For example, Word has tools that enable you to create a research paper that includes citations, footnotes, and a bibliography. You can also create multiple-column newsletters, format the nameplate at the top of the newsletter, use special character formatting to create distinctive title text, and add borders and shading to paragraphs to highlight important information.

In this chapter, you will edit and format a research paper, create a two-column newsletter, and then create a set of mailing labels to mail the newsletter to multiple recipients.

The projects in this chapter relate to **Memphis Primary Materials** located in the Memphis area. In addition to collecting common recyclable materials, the company collects and recycles computers, monitors, copiers and fax machines, cell phones, wood pallets, and compostable materials. The company's name comes from the process of capturing the "primary materials" of used items for reuse. Memphis Primary Materials ensures that its clients comply with all state and local regulations. They also provide training to clients on the process and benefits of recycling.

Project 3A Research Paper

Project Activities

In Activities 3.01 through 3.07, you will edit and format a research paper that contains an overview of recycling activities in which businesses can engage. This paper was created by Elizabeth Freeman, a student intern working for Memphis Primary Metals, and will be included in a customer information packet. Your completed document will look similar to Figure 3.1.

Project Files

For Project 3A, you will need the following file:

> w03A_Green_Business

You will save your document as:

> Lastname_Firstname_3A_Green_Business

Project Results

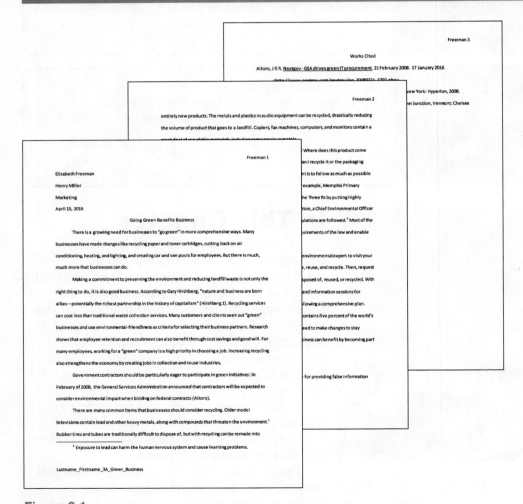

Figure 3.1
Project 3A Green Business

Objective 1 | Create a Research Paper

When you write a research paper or a report for college or business, follow a format prescribed by one of the standard *style guides*—a manual that contains standards for the design and writing of documents. The two most commonly used styles for research papers are those created by the *Modern Language Association (MLA)* and the *American Psychological Association (APA)*; there are several others.

Activity 3.01 | Formatting Text and Page Numbers in a Research Paper

When formatting the text for your research paper, refer to the standards for the style guide that you have chosen. In this activity, you will create a research paper using the MLA style. The MLA style uses 1-inch margins, a 0.5″ first line indent, and double spacing throughout the body of the document, with no extra space above or below paragraphs.

1 **Start** Word. From your student files, locate and open the document **w03A_Green_Business**. If necessary, display the formatting marks and rulers. In the location where you are storing your projects for this chapter, create a new folder named **Word Chapter 3** and then save the file in the folder as **Lastname_Firstname_3A_Green_Business**

2 Press Ctrl + A to select the entire document. On the **Home tab**, in the **Paragraph group**, click the **Line and Paragraph Spacing** button, and then change the line spacing to **2.0**. On the **Page Layout tab**, in the **Paragraph group**, change the **Spacing After** to **0 pt**.

3 Press Ctrl + Home to deselect and move to the top of the document. Press Enter one time to create a blank line at the top of the document, and then click to position the insertion point in the blank line. Type **Elizabeth Freeman** and press Enter.

4 Type **Henry Miller** and press Enter. Type **Marketing** and press Enter. Type **April 15, 2016** and press Enter. Type **Going Green Benefits Business** Right-click anywhere in the line you just typed, and then on the Mini toolbar, click the **Center** button. Compare your screen with Figure 3.2.

Figure 3.2

Title centered

Text double-spaced

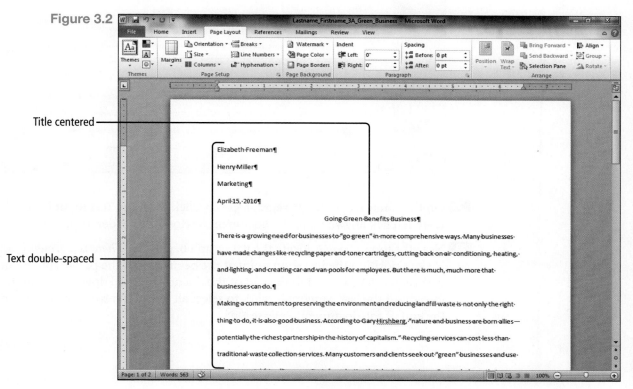

5 At the top of the **Page 1**, point anywhere in the white top margin area, right-click, and then click **Edit Header**. In the header area, type **Freeman** and then press ⎵Spacebar.

> Recall that the text you insert into a header or footer displays on every page of a document. Within a header or footer, you can insert many different types of information; for example, automatic page numbers, the date, the time, the file name, or pictures.

6 On the **Design tab**, in the **Header & Footer group**, click the **Page Number** button, and then point to **Current Position**. In the displayed gallery, under **Simple**, click **Plain Number**. Compare your screen with Figure 3.3.

> Word will automatically number the pages using this number format.

Figure 3.3

Page number field added to header

Last name in header

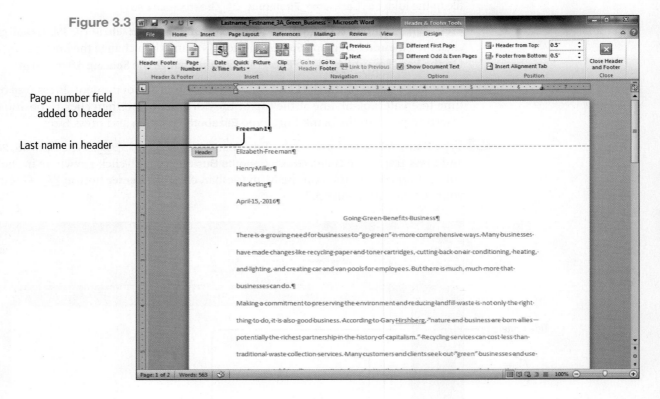

7 On the **Home tab**, in the **Paragraph group**, click the **Align Text Right** button ▤. Double-click anywhere in the document to close the header area.

8 Near the top of **Page 1**, locate the paragraph beginning *There is a growing*, and then click to position the insertion point at the beginning of the paragraph. By moving the vertical scroll bar, scroll to the end of the document, hold down ⇧Shift, and then click to right of the last paragraph mark to select all of the text from the insertion point to the end of the document. Release ⇧Shift.

Another Way

Right-click the selected text, click Paragraph, on the Indents and Spacing tab, under Indentation, click the Special arrow, and then click First line. Under Indentation, in the By box, be sure 0.5" displays.

9 With the text selected, on the ruler, point to the **First Line Indent** button, and then drag the button to **0.5" on the horizontal ruler**. Compare your screen with Figure 3.4.

The MLA style uses 0.5-inch indents at the beginning of the first line of every paragraph. Indenting—moving the beginning of the first line of a paragraph to the right or left of the rest of the paragraph—provides visual cues to the reader to help divide the document text and make it easier to read.

Figure 3.4

First Line Indent button moved to 0.5" on the ruler

First line indented 0.5 inch

10 Click anywhere to deselect the text. Scroll to view the bottom of **Page 1**, point anywhere in the bottom white margin area, right-click, and then click **Edit Footer**. On the **Design tab**, in the **Insert group**, click the **Quick Parts** button, and then click **Field**. In the **Field** dialog box, under **Field names**, locate and click **FileName**, and then click **OK**.

The file name in the footer is *not* part of the research report format, but it is included in projects in this textbook so that you and your instructor can identify your work.

11 Double-click anywhere in the document to close the Footer area, and then **Save** your document.

More Knowledge | Suppressing the Page Number on the First Page

Some style guidelines require that the page number and other header and footer information on the first page be hidden from view—*suppressed*. To hide the information contained in the header and footer areas on Page 1 of a document, double-click in the header or footer area. Then, on the Design tab, in the Options group, select the Different First Page check box.

Objective 2 | Insert Footnotes in a Research Paper

Reports and research papers typically include information that you find in other sources, and these must be credited. Within report text, numbers mark the location of *notes*—information that expands on the topic being discussed but that does not fit well in the document text. The numbers refer to *footnotes*—notes placed at the bottom of the page containing the note, or to *endnotes*—notes placed at the end of a document or chapter.

Activity 3.02 | Inserting Footnotes

Footnotes can be added as you type the document or after the document is complete. Word renumbers the footnotes automatically, so footnotes do not need to be entered in order, and if one footnote is removed, the remaining footnotes renumber automatically.

1 Scroll to view the top of **Page 2**. Locate the paragraph that begins *Consumers and businesses*. In the seventh line of text, toward the end of the line, click to position the insertion point to the right of the period after *followed*.

2 On the **References tab**, in the **Footnotes group**, click the **Insert Footnote** button.

> Word creates space for a footnote in the footnote area at the bottom of the page and adds a footnote number to the text at the insertion point location. Footnote *1* displays in the footnote area, and the insertion point moves to the right of the number. A short black line is added just above the footnote area. You do not need to type the footnote number.

3 Type **Tennessee, for example, imposes penalties of up to $10,000 for providing false information regarding the recycling of hazardous waste.**

> This is an explanatory footnote; the footnote provides additional information that does not fit well in the body of the report.

4 Click the **Home tab**, and then in the **Font group**, notice that the font size of the footer is *10 pt*. In the **Paragraph group**, click the **Line and Paragraph Spacing** button, and notice that the line spacing is *1.0*—single-spaced—even though the font size of the document text is 11 pt and the text is double-spaced, as shown in Figure 3.5.

Figure 3.5

Footnote text, single-spaced and 10 pt. font size

5 Scroll to view the bottom of **Page 1**, and then locate the paragraph that begins *There are many common*. At the end of the second line of text, click to position the insertion point to the right of the period following *environment*.

6 On the **References tab**, in the **Footnotes group**, click the **Insert Footnote** button. Type **Exposure to lead can harm the human nervous system and cause learning problems.** Notice that the footnote you just added becomes the new footnote *1*, as shown in Figure 3.6.

> The first footnote is renumbered as footnote *2*.

Figure 3.6

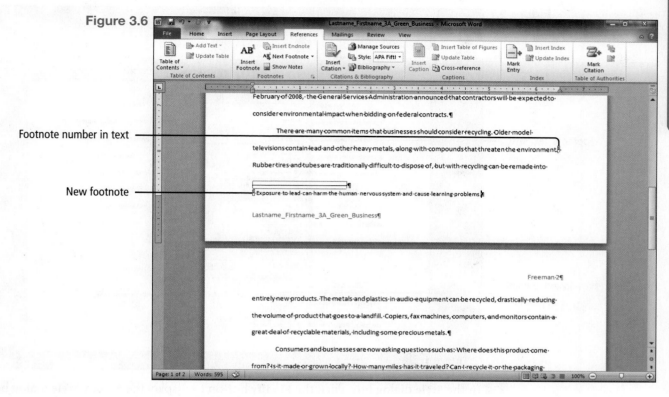

Footnote number in text

New footnote

7 **Save** your document.

More Knowledge | **Using Symbols Rather Than Numbers for Notes**

Instead of using numbers to designate footnotes, you can use standard footnote symbols. The seven traditional symbols, available from the Footnote and Endnote dialog box, in order, are * (asterisk), † (dagger), ‡ (double dagger), § (section mark), ‖ (parallels), ¶ (paragraph mark), and # (number or pound sign). This sequence can be continuous (this is the default setting), or can begin anew with each page.

Activity 3.03 | Modifying a Footnote Style

Microsoft Word contains built-in paragraph formats called *styles*—groups of formatting commands, such as font, font size, font color, paragraph alignment, and line spacing—which can be applied to a paragraph with one command.

The default style for footnote text is a single-spaced paragraph that uses a 10-point Calibri font and no paragraph indents. MLA style specifies double-spaced text in all areas of a research paper—including footnotes. According to the MLA style, first lines of footnotes must also be indented 0.5 inch and use the same font size as the report text.

1 Scroll to view the bottom of **Page 2**. Point anywhere in the footnote text and right-click, and then from the shortcut menu, click **Style**. Compare your screen with Figure 3.7.

The Style dialog box displays, listing the styles currently in use in the document, in addition to some of the word processing elements that come with special built-in styles. Because you right-clicked on the footnote text, the selected style is the Footnote Text style.

Figure 3.7

Style dialog box

Footnote Text style

Insertion point in footnote

2 In the **Style** dialog box, click the **Modify** button to display the **Modify Style** dialog box.

3 In the **Modify Style** dialog box, locate the small **Formatting** toolbar in the center of the dialog box, click the **Font Size button arrow**, click **11**, and then compare your screen with Figure 3.8.

Figure 3.8

Style name

Font Size button

Formatting toolbar

4 In the lower left corner of the dialog box, click the **Format** button, and then click **Paragraph**. In the **Paragraph** dialog box, under **Indentation**, click the **Special arrow**, and then click **First line**.

5 Under **Spacing**, click the **Line spacing** button arrow, and then click **Double**. Compare your dialog box with Figure 3.9.

Figure 3.9

First line indent selected ——

Line spacing set to *Double* ——

6 Click **OK** to close the **Paragraph** dialog box, click **OK** to close the **Modify Style** dialog box, and then click **Apply** to apply the new style. Notice that when you click Apply, the Style dialog box closes. Compare your screen with Figure 3.10.

Your inserted footnotes are formatted with the new Footnote Text paragraph style; any new footnotes that you insert will also use this format.

Figure 3.10

First line indented ——

Footnote text double-spaced ——

7 Scroll to view the bottom of **Page 1** to confirm that the new format was also applied to the first footnote, and then **Save** 🔲 your document.

Objective 3 | Create Citations and a Bibliography in a Research Paper

When you use quotations from, or detailed summaries of, other people's work, you must specify the source of the information. A *citation* is a note inserted into the text of a report or research paper that refers the reader to a source in the bibliography. Create a *bibliography* at the end of a document to list the sources referred to in the document. Such a list is typically titled *Works Cited* (in MLA style), *Bibliography*, *Sources*, or *References*.

Activity 3.04 | Adding Citations

When writing a long research paper, you will likely reference numerous books, articles, and Web sites. Some of your research sources may be referenced many times, others only one time. References to sources within the text of your research paper are indicated in an *abbreviated* manner. However, as you enter a citation for the first time, you can also enter the *complete* information about the source. Then, when you have finished your paper, you will be able to automatically generate the list of sources that must be included at the end of your research paper.

1 Press [Ctrl] + [Home], and then locate the paragraph that begins *Making a commitment*. In the third line, following the word *capitalism*, click to position the insertion point to the right of the quotation mark.

> The citation in the document points to the full source information in the bibliography, which typically includes the name of the author, the full title of the work, the year of publication, and other publication information.

2 On the **References tab**, in the **Citations & Bibliography group**, click the **Style button arrow**, and then click **MLA Sixth Edition** (or the latest edition) to insert a reference using MLA style.

3 Click the **Insert Citation** button, and then click **Add New Source**. Be sure *Book* is selected as the **Type of Source**. Add the following information, and then compare your screen with Figure 3.11:

Author:	**Hirshberg, Gary**
Title:	**Stirring it Up: How to Make Money and Save the World**
Year:	**2008**
City:	**New York**
Publisher:	**Hyperion**

In the MLA style, citations that refer to items on the *Works Cited* page are placed in parentheses and are referred to as *parenthetical references*—references that include the last name of the author or authors and the page number in the referenced source, which you add to the reference. No year is indicated, and there is no comma between the name and the page number.

Figure 3.11

MLA style selected

Source type

Citation information

> **Note** | Citing Corporate Authors
>
> If the author of a document is identified as the name of an organization only, select the Corporate Author check box and type the name of the organization in the Corporate Author box.

4 Click **OK** to insert the citation. In the paragraph, point to *(Hirshberg)* and click one time to select the citation.

5 In the lower right corner of the box that surrounds the reference, point to the small arrow to display the ScreenTip *Citation Options*. Click this **Citation Options arrow**, and then from the list of options, click **Edit Citation**.

6 In the **Edit Citation** dialog box, under **Add**, in the **Pages** box, type **1** to indicate that you are citing from page 1 of this source. Compare your screen with Figure 3.12.

Figure 3.12

Page number

Parenthetical reference

7 Click **OK** to display the page number of the citation. Click outside of the citation box to deselect it. Then type a period to the right of the citation, and delete the period to the left of the quotation mark.

> In the MLA style, if the reference occurs at the end of a sentence, the parenthetical reference always displays to the left of the punctuation mark that ends the sentence.

8 In the next paragraph, which begins *Government contractors*, click to position the insertion point at the end of the paragraph, but before the period.

9 In the **Citations & Bibliography group**, click the **Insert Citation** button, and then click **Add New Source**. Click the **Type of Source arrow**, scroll down as necessary, and then click **Web site**. Add the following information:

Author:	**Aitoro, Jill R.**
Name of Web Page:	**Nextgov - GSA drives green IT procurement**
Year:	**2008**
Month:	**February**
Day:	**21**
Year Accessed:	**2016**
Month Accessed:	**January**
Day Accessed:	**17**
URL:	**http://www.nextgov.com/nextgov/ng_20080221_8792.php**

10 Compare your screen with Figure 3.13, and then click **OK** to close the **Create Source** dialog box and add the citation.

> A parenthetical reference is added. Because the cited Web page has no page numbers, only the author name is used in the parenthetical reference.

Figure 3.13

Web site citation

Insertion point indicates location of parenthetical reference

11 Near the top of **Page 2**, in the paragraph that begins *Consumers and businesses*, in the third line, click to position the insertion point following the word *toxic* to the left of the question mark.

12 In the **Citations & Bibliography group**, click the **Insert Citation** button, and then click **Add New Source**. Click the **Type of Source arrow**, if necessary scroll to the top of the list, click **Book**, and then add the following information:

Author:	**Scott, Nicky**
Title:	**Reduce, Reuse, Recycle: An Easy Household Guide**
Year:	**2007**
City:	**White River Junction, Vermont**
Publisher:	**Chelsea Green Publishing**

13 Click **OK**. Click the inserted citation to select it, click the **Citation Options arrow**, and then click **Edit Citation**.

14 In the **Edit Citation** dialog box, under **Add**, in the **Pages** box, type **7** to indicate that you are citing from page 7 of this source. Click **OK**.

15 On the **References tab**, in the **Citations & Bibliography group**, click the **Manage Sources** button. In the **Source Manager** dialog box, under **Current List**, click the third source and then compare your screen with Figure 3.14.

> The Source Manager dialog box displays. Other citations on your computer display in the Master List box. The citations for the current document display in the Current List box. Word maintains the Master List so that if you use the same sources regularly, you can copy sources from your Master List to the current document. A preview of the selected bibliography entry also displays at the bottom of the dialog box.

Figure 3.14

Sources used in this document

Other available sources (yours will vary)

Preview of selected citation

16 At the bottom of the **Source Manager** dialog box, click **Close**. Click anywhere in the document to deselect the parenthetical reference, and then **Save** your document.

Activity 3.05 | Inserting Page Breaks

In this activity you will insert a manual page break so that you can begin your bibliography on a new page.

1 Press [Ctrl] + [End] to move the insertion point to the end of the document. Notice that the insertion point displays at the end of the final paragraph, but above the footnote—the footnote is always associated with the page that contains the citation.

2 Press [Ctrl] + [Enter] to insert a manual page break.

> A ***manual page break*** forces a page to end at the insertion point location, and then places any subsequent text at the top of the next page. Recall that the new paragraph retains the formatting of the previous paragraph, so the first line is indented.

3 On the ruler, point to the **First Line Indent** button ⬇, and then drag the **First Line Indent** button to the left to **0 inches on the horizontal ruler**.

4 Scroll as necessary to position the bottom of **Page 2** and the top of **Page 3** on your screen.

5 Compare your screen with Figure 3.15, and then **Save** 🖫 your document.

> A ***page break indicator***, which shows where a manual page break was inserted, displays at the bottom of the Page 2, and the footnote remains on the page that contains the citation, even though it displays below the page break indicator.

Figure 3.15

First Line Indent button at 0 inches

Page Break indicator shows manual page break inserted

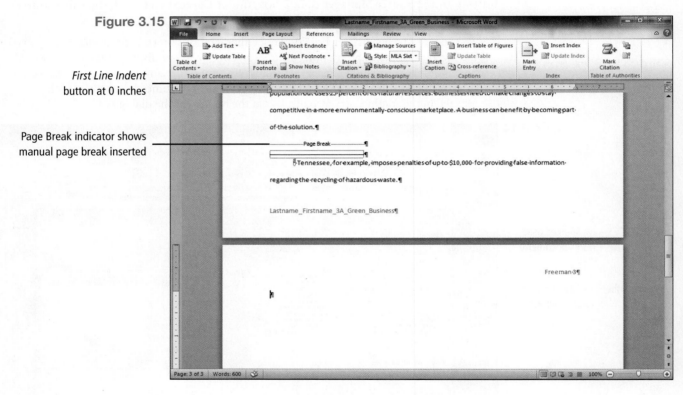

Activity 3.06 | Creating a Reference Page

At the end of a report or research paper, include a list of each source referenced. *Works Cited* is the reference page heading used in the MLA style guidelines. Other styles may refer to this page as a *Bibliography* (Business Style) or *References* (APA Style). This information is always displayed on a separate page.

1 With the insertion point blinking in the first line of **Page 3**, type **Works Cited** and then press [Enter]. On the **References tab**, in the **Citations & Bibliography group**, in the **Style** box, be sure *MLA* displays.

2 In the **Citations & Bibliography group**, click the **Bibliography** button, and then near the bottom of the list, click **Insert Bibliography**.

3 Scroll as necessary to view the entire list of three references, and then click anywhere in the inserted text.

The bibliography entries that you created display as a field, which is indicated by the gray shading when you click in the text. The field links to the Source Manager for the citations. The references display alphabetically by the author's last name.

4 In the bibliography, point to the left of the first entry—beginning *Aitoro, Jill*—to display the 🔏 pointer. Drag down to select all three references.

5 On the **Home tab**, in the **Paragraph group**, change the **Line spacing** to **2.0**, and then on the **Page Layout tab**, in the **Paragraph group**, change the **Spacing After** to **0 pt**.

The entries display according to MLA guidelines; the text is double-spaced, the extra space between paragraphs is removed, and each entry uses a *hanging indent*—the first line of each entry extends 0.5 inch to the left of the remaining lines of the entry.

6 At the top of **Page 3**, right-click the *Works Cited* title, and then click the **Center** button ☰. Compare your screen with Figure 3.16, and then **Save** 💾 your document.

In MLA style, the *Works Cited* title is centered.

Figure 3.16

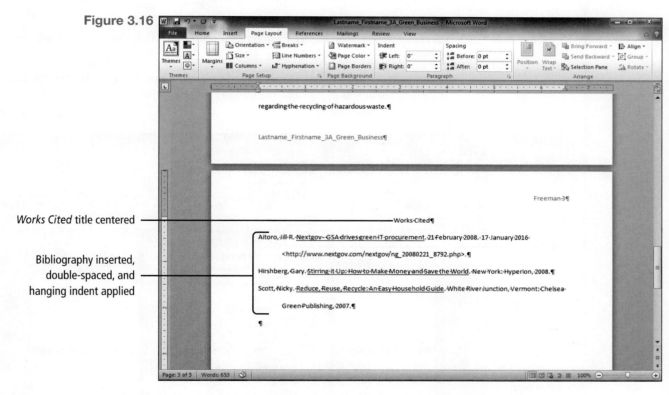

Works Cited title centered ——— Works Cited

Bibliography inserted, double-spaced, and hanging indent applied

Activity 3.07 | Managing Document Properties

Recall that document property information is stored in the Document Panel. An additional group of property categories is also available.

1 Display **Backstage** view. On the right, under the document thumbnail, click **Properties**, and then click **Show Document Panel** to display the **Document Panel**.

2 Type your name and course information, and then add the keywords **green business, research paper**

3 In the upper left corner of the **Document Panel**, click the **Document Properties** button, and then compare your screen with Figure 3.17.

Figure 3.17

Document Panel

Document Properties button

4 Click **Advanced Properties**. In the **Properties** dialog box, click the **Statistics tab**, and then compare your screen with Figure 3.18.

The document statistics show the number of revisions made to the document, the last time the document was edited, and the number of paragraphs, lines, words, and characters in the document.

Figure 3.18

Statistics tab

Document statistics
(yours may vary)

5 In the **Properties** dialog box, click the **Summary tab**. Notice that not all of the categories are filled in, and also notice that there are categories on this tab that are not found in the Document Panel.

Some of the boxes may contain information from your computer system.

6 In the **Properties** dialog box, click in the **Title** box and type **Going Green Benefits Business**

7 Click in the **Manager** box and type **Henry Miller**

8 In the **Company** box, select and delete any existing text, and then type **Memphis Primary Materials**

9 Click in the **Category** box and type **Marketing Documents**

10 Click in the **Comments** box and type **Draft copy of a research report that will be included in the marketing materials packet**

> Additional information categories are available by clicking the Custom tab.

11 Compare your screen with Figure 3.19, and then at the bottom of the **Properties** dialog box, click **OK**.

Figure 3.19

Summary tab

Properties not available on Document Information Panel

12 **Close** ☒ the **Document Panel**. Press ⌃Ctrl + F2, and then examine the three pages of your document in **Print Preview**. Redisplay your document.
If necessary, make any corrections or adjustments.

13 **Save** 🖫 your document, and then print or submit electronically as directed by your instructor. **Exit** Word.

End **You have completed Project 3A** ———————————————

Project 3B Newsletter with Mailing Labels

Project Activities

In Activities 3.08 through 3.17, you will edit a newsletter that Memphis Primary Materials sends to its list of customers and subscribers. Your completed documents will look similar to Figure 3.20.

Project Files

For Project 3B, you will need the following files:

New blank Word document
w03B_Memphis_Newsletter
w03B_Addresses

You will save your documents as:

Lastname_Firstname_3B_Memphis_Newsletter
Lastname_Firstname_3B_Mailing_Labels
Lastname_Firstname_3B_Addresses

Project Results

Figure 3.20
Project 3B Memphis Newsletter

Objective 4 | Format a Multiple-Column Newsletter

All newspapers and most magazines and newsletters use multiple columns for articles because text in narrower columns is easier to read than text that stretches across a page. Word has a tool with which you can change a single column of text into two or more columns, and then format the columns. If a column does not end where you want it to, you can end the column at a location of your choice by inserting a ***manual column break***.

Activity 3.08 | Changing One Column of Text to Two Columns

Newsletters are usually two or three columns wide. When using 8.5 × 11-inch paper in portrait orientation, avoid creating four or more columns because they are so narrow that word spacing looks awkward, often resulting in one long word on a line by itself.

1 **Start** Word. From your student files, locate and open the document **w03B_Memphis_Newsletter**. If necessary, display the formatting marks and rulers. **Save** the file in your **Word Chapter 3** folder as **Lastname_Firstname_3B_Memphis_Newsletter** and then add the file name to the footer.

2 Select the first paragraph of text—*Memphis Primary Materials*. From the Mini toolbar, change the **Font** to **Arial Black** and the **Font Size** to **24**.

3 Select the first two paragraphs—the title and the Volume information and date. From the Mini toolbar, click the **Font Color button arrow** A ·, and then under **Theme Colors**, in the fifth column, click the last color—**Blue, Accent 1, Darker 50%**.

4 With the text still selected, on the **Home tab**, in the **Paragraph group**, click the **Borders button arrow**, and then at the bottom, click **Borders and Shading**.

5 In the **Borders and Shading** dialog box, on the **Borders tab**, click the **Color arrow**, and then under **Theme Colors**, in the fifth column, click the last color—**Blue, Accent 1, Darker 50%**.

> **Another Way**
>
> In the Preview area, click the Bottom Border button.

6 Click the **Width arrow**, and then click **3 pt**. In the **Preview** box at the right, point to the *bottom* border of the small preview and click one time. Compare your screen with Figure 3.21.

Figure 3.21

Preview of border

Color set to *Blue, Accent 1, Darker 50%*

Line width set to 3 pt

7 In the **Borders and Shading** dialog box, click **OK**.

The line visually defines the newsletter *nameplate*—the banner on the front page of a newsletter that identifies the publication.

8 Below the nameplate, beginning with the paragraph *Memphis Primary Materials: An Introduction*, select all of the text to the end of the document, which extends to two pages.

9 On the **Page Layout tab**, in the **Page Setup group**, click the **Columns** button. From the **Columns** gallery, click **Two**.

10 Scroll up to view the top of **Page 1**, and then compare your screen with Figure 3.22, and then **Save** the document.

Word divides the text into two columns, and inserts a *section break* below the nameplate, dividing the one-column section of the document from the two-column section of the document. A *section* is a portion of a document that can be formatted differently from the rest of the document. A section break marks the end of one section and the beginning of another section. Do not be concerned if your columns do not break at the same line as shown in the figure.

Figure 3.22

Section break inserted

Text displays in two columns

Activity 3.09 | Formatting Multiple Columns

The uneven right margin of a single page-width column is easy to read. When you create narrow columns, justified text is sometimes preferable. Depending on the design and layout of your newsletter, you might decide to reduce extra space between paragraphs and between columns to improve the readability of the document.

1 With the two columns of text still selected, on the **Page Layout tab**, in the **Paragraph group**, click the **Spacing After down spin arrow** one time to change the spacing after to **6 pt**.

2 On the **Home tab**, in the **Paragraph group**, click the **Justify** button.

3 Click anywhere in the document to deselect the text, and then compare your screen with Figure 3.23. **Save** 🖫 the document.

Figure 3.23

Column text justified —————

More Knowledge | Justifying Column Text

Although many magazines and newspapers still justify text in columns, there are a variety of opinions about whether to justify the columns, or to use left alignment and leave the right edge uneven. Justified text tends to look more formal and cleaner, but in a word processing document, it also results in uneven spacing between words. It is the opinion of some authorities that justified text is more difficult to read, especially in a page-width document. Let the overall look and feel of your newsletter be your guide.

Activity 3.10 | Inserting a Column Break

1 Scroll down to view the lower portion of the page. In the first column, locate the company address that begins with the paragraph *Memphis Primary Materials*, and then select that paragraph and the three following paragraphs, ending with the telephone number.

2 On the **Page Layout tab**, in the **Paragraph group**, click the **Spacing After down spin arrow** one time to change the spacing after to **0 pt**.

3 Select the three paragraphs that begin with *CEO* and end with *CFO*, and then in the **Paragraph group**, change the **Spacing After** to **0 pt**.

4 Near the bottom of the first column, click to position the insertion point at the beginning of the line that begins *Make Recycling*.

5 On the **Page Layout tab**, in the **Page Setup group**, click the **Breaks** button to display the gallery of Page Breaks and Section Breaks. Compare your screen with Figure 3.24.

Figure 3.24

Column break command

6 Under **Page Breaks**, click **Column**. Scroll to view the bottom of the first column.

A column break displays at the insertion point; text to the right of the insertion point moves to the top of the next column.

7 Compare your screen with Figure 3.25, and then **Save** the document.

A *column break indicator*—a dotted line containing the words *Column Break*—displays at the bottom of the column.

Figure 3.25

with all state and local regulations regarding waste and equipment disposal. Our staff also provides training to clients on the process and benefits of recycling.¶

We strive to grow our business by advancing the ideas of reduce, reuse, and recycle among the business community.¶

Memphis Primary Materials¶
5360 Airways Blvd., Suite 10A¶
Memphis, TN 38114¶
(901) 555-0862¶
Memphismaterials.net¶

CEO: Harold Boyd III¶
President: Barbara Collins¶
CFO: Joe Hedgepeth¶
Chief Environmental Officer: Denisha Geater¶

··············Column Break··············

Manual column break inserted

various types of recycling bins around your workplace. Place paper recycle bins near copiers and printers where they are easily accessible. Place can and bottle bins in break rooms, near all trash cans, and near vending machines. Place battery bins around offices. For more very good ideas, visit the EPA Web site at www.epa.gov.¶

Activity 3.11 | Inserting a ClipArt Image

Clip art images—predefined graphics included with Microsoft Office or downloaded from the Web—can make your document visually appealing and more interesting.

1 Press [Ctrl] + [Home]. On the **Insert tab**, in the **Illustrations group**, click the **Clip Art** button to display the **Clip Art** task pane on the right of your screen.

2 In the **Clip Art** task pane, click in the **Search for** box, and then replace any existing text with **environmental awareness** so that Word can search for images that contain the keywords *environmental* and *awareness*.

3 In the **Clip Art** task pane, click the **Results should be arrow**. Be sure the **Illustrations** check box is selected, and then click as necessary to clear the *Photographs*, *Videos*, and *Audio* check boxes. Click the **Results should be** arrow again to collapse the list. Be sure the **Include Office.com content** check box is selected.

4 In the **Clip Art** task pane, click the **Go** button. Locate the image of the three white arrows in a blue circle. Click on the image to insert it, and then compare your screen with Figure 3.26.

> Recall that when you insert a graphic, it is inserted as an inline object; that is, it is treated as a character in a line of text. Here, the inserted clip art becomes the first character in the nameplate.

Figure 3.26

Clip Art task pane

Search term

Selected image

Image inserted in document

5 **Close** the **Clip Art** task pane. With the image still selected, on the **Format tab**, in the **Size group**, click in the **Shape Height** box, type **1** and then press Enter. In the **Arrange group**, click the **Wrap Text** button, and then click **Square**.

6 Point to the image to display the pointer, and then drag the image to the right so that the bottom edge aligns slightly above *January 2016*, and the right side aligns with the right margin. Recall that you can press the arrow keys as necessary to move the image in small, precise increments.

7 Compare your screen with Figure 3.27, and then **Save** the document.

Figure 3.27

Image resized

Text wrapping applied to image

Activity 3.12 | Inserting a Screenshot

A ***screenshot*** is an image of an active window on your computer that you can paste into a document. Screenshots are especially useful when you want to insert an image of a Web site into a document you are creating in Word. You can insert a screenshot of any open window on your computer.

1 In the second column, click to position the insertion point at the beginning of the paragraph that begins *You can make*. Open your Internet browser, and then in the address bar type **www.epa.gov/osw/conserve/rrr** and press Enter. Maximize ▣ the browser window, if necessary.

2 From the taskbar, redisplay your **3B_Memphis_Newletter** document.

3 On the **Insert tab**, in the **Illustrations group**, click the **Screenshot** button.

All of your open windows display in the Available Windows gallery and are available to paste into the document.

4 In the **Screenshot** gallery, click the browser window that contains the EPA site to insert the screenshot at the insertion point, and notice that the image resizes to fit between the column margins. Compare your screen with Figure 3.28. **Save** 🖫 the document.

Figure 3.28

Screenshot inserted in document

Objective 5 | Use Special Character and Paragraph Formatting

Special text and paragraph formatting is useful to emphasize text, and it makes your newsletter look more professional. For example, you can place a border around one or more paragraphs or add shading to a paragraph. When adding shading, use light colors; dark shading can make the text difficult to read.

Activity 3.13 | Applying the Small Caps Font Effect

For headlines and titles, ***small caps*** is an attractive font effect. The effect changes lowercase letters to uppercase letters, but with the height of lowercase letters.

1 At the top of the first column, select the paragraph *Memphis Primary Materials: An Introduction* including the paragraph mark.

2 Right-click the selected text, and then from the shortcut menu, click **Font**. In the **Font** dialog box, click the **Font color arrow**, and then under **Theme Colors**, in the fifth column, click the last color—**Blue, Accent 1, Darker 50%**.

3 Under **Font style**, click **Bold**. Under **Size**, click **18**. Under **Effects**, select the **Small caps** check box. Compare your screen with Figure 3.29.

> The Font dialog box provides more options than are available on the Ribbon and enables you to make several changes at the same time. In the Preview box, the text displays with the selected formatting options applied.

Figure 3.29

Small caps effect selected

Selected text

Preview of changes to text

4 Click **OK**. Right-click the selected text, and then on the Mini toolbar, click **Center** ≡.

5 With the text still selected, right-click, and then on the Mini toolbar, click the **Format Painter** button ✪. Then, with the ⒶI pointer, at the top of the second column, select the paragraph *Make Recycling Easy for Everyone!* to apply the same formats. Notice that the column title wraps placing a single word on the second line.

6 Position the insertion point to the right of the word *Recycling*, and then press Del to remove the space. Hold down Shift and then press Enter.

> Holding down Shift while pressing Enter inserts a ***manual line break***, which moves the text to the right of the insertion point to a new line while keeping the text in the same paragraph. A ***line break indicator***, in the shape of a bent arrow, indicates that a manual line break was inserted.

7 Compare your screen with Figure 3.30, and then **Save** 🖫 the document.

Figure 3.30

Manual line break inserted

Activity 3.14 | Adding a Border and Shading to a Paragraph

Paragraph borders provide strong visual cues to the reader. Paragraph shading can be used with or without borders. When used with a border, light shading can be very effective in drawing the reader's eye to the text.

1 In the first column, in the paragraph that begins *We strive to grow*, click to position the insertion point at the end of the paragraph, and then press Enter one time.

2 At the bottom of the column, select the nine lines of company information, beginning with *Memphis Primary Materials* and ending with the paragraph that begins *Chief Environmental*. On the Mini toolbar, apply **Bold** B and **Center** ≡.

3 With the text still selected, on the **Home tab**, in the **Paragraph group**, click the **Borders button arrow** ⊞▾, and then click **Borders and Shading**.

4 In the **Borders and Shading** dialog box, be sure the **Borders tab** is selected. Under **Setting**, click **Shadow**. If necessary, click the **Color arrow**, and then in the fifth column, click the last color—**Blue, Accent 1, Darker 50%**. Click the **Width arrow**, and then click **3 pt**. Compare your screen with Figure 3.31.

In the lower right portion of the Borders and Shading dialog box, the *Apply to* box displays *Paragraph*. The *Apply to* box directs where the border will be applied—in this instance, the border will be applied only to the selected paragraphs.

Figure 3.31

Preview of paragraph border

Shadow border selected

Note | Adding Simple Borders to Text

You can add simple borders from the Borders button gallery, located in the Paragraph group. This button offers less control over the border appearance, however, because the line thickness and color applied will match whatever was last used on this computer. The Borders and Shading dialog box enables you to make your own custom selections.

---

5 At the top of the **Borders and Shading** dialog box, click the **Shading tab**.

6 Click the **Fill arrow**, and then in the fifth column, click the second color—**Blue, Accent 1, Lighter 80%**. Notice that the shading change is reflected in the Preview area on the right side of the dialog box.

7 At the bottom of the **Borders and Shading** dialog box, click **OK**. Click anywhere in the document to deselect the text, and then compare your screen with Figure 3.32.

Figure 3.32

Shading applied to paragraph text

Shadowed border applied to selected paragraphs

8 From **Backstage** view, display the **Document Panel**.

9 In the **Author** box, delete any text and then type your firstname and lastname. In the **Subject** box, type your course name and section number, and in the **Keywords** box, type **newsletter, January Close** ☒ the **Document Panel**.

10 Press Ctrl + F2 to view the **Print Preview**. **Close** the preview, make any necessary corrections, and then click **Save** 🖫. **Exit** Word; hold this file until you complete this Project.

Objective 6 | Create Mailing Labels Using Mail Merge

Word's *mail merge* feature joins a *main document* and a *data source* to create customized letters or labels. The main document contains the text or formatting that remains constant. For labels, the main document contains the formatting for a specific label size. The data source contains information including the names and addresses of the individuals for whom the labels are being created. Names and addresses in a data source might come from a Word table, an Excel spreadsheet, or an Access database.

The easiest way to perform a mail merge is to use the Mail Merge Wizard, which asks you questions and, based on your answers, walks you step by step through the mail merge process.

Activity 3.15 | Opening the Mail Merge Wizard Template

In this activity, you will open the data source for the mail merge, which is a Word table containing names and addresses.

1 **Start** Word and display a new blank document. Display formatting marks and rulers. **Save** the document in your **Word Chapter 3** folder as **Lastname_Firstname_3B_Mailing_Labels**

2 With your new document open on the screen, **Open** the file **w03B_Addresses**. **Save** the address file in your **Word Chapter 3** folder as **Lastname_Firstname_3B_Addresses** and then add the file name to the footer.

> This document contains a table of addresses. The first row contains the column names. The remaining rows contain the names and addresses.

3 Click to position the insertion point in the last cell in the table, and then press Tab to create a new row. Enter the following information, and then compare your table with Figure 3.33:

First Name	**John**
Last Name	**Wisniewski**
Address 1	**1226 Snow Road**
Address 2	**#234**
City	**Lakeland**
State	**TN**
ZIP Code	**38002**

Figure 3.33

New record added to address list

4 **Save** 🖫, and then **Close** ❌ the table of addresses. Be sure your blank **Lastname_Firstname_3B_Mailing_Labels** document displays.

5 Click the **Mailings tab**. In the **Start Mail Merge group**, click the **Start Mail Merge** button, and then click **Step by Step Mail Merge Wizard** to display the **Mail Merge** task pane.

6 Under **Select document type**, click the **Labels** option button. At the bottom of the task pane, click **Next: Starting document** to display Step 2 of 6 of the Mail Merge Wizard.

7 Under **Select starting document**, be sure **Change document layout** is selected, and then under **Change document layout**, click **Label options**.

8 In the **Label Options** dialog box, under **Printer information**, click the **Tray arrow**, and then click **Default tray (Automatically Select)**—the exact wording may vary depending on your printer, but select the *Default* or *Automatic* option—to print the labels on regular paper rather than manually inserting labels in the printer.

9 Under **Label information**, click the **Label vendors arrow**, and then click **Avery US Letter**. Under **Product number**, scroll about halfway down the list, and then click **5160 Easy Peel Address Labels**. Compare your screen with Figure 3.34.

The Avery 5160 address label is a commonly used label. The precut sheets contain three columns of 10 labels each—for a total of 30 labels per sheet.

Figure 3.34

Label vendor

Product number

Label options

10 At the bottom of the **Label Options** dialog box, click **OK**. If a message box displays, click OK to set up the labels. At the bottom of the task pane, click **Next: Select recipients**.

The label page is set up with three columns and ten rows. The label borders may or may not display on your screen, depending on your settings. Here in Step 3 of the Mail Merge Wizard, you must identify the recipients—the data source. For your recipient data source, you can choose to use an existing list—for example, a list of names and addresses that you have in an Access database, an Excel worksheet, a Word table, or your Outlook contacts list. If you do not have an existing data source, you can type a new list at this point in the wizard.

11 If gridlines do not display, click the **Layout tab**. In the **Table group**, click the **View Gridlines** button, and then notice that each label is outlined with a dashed line. If you cannot see the right and left edges of the page, in the status bar, click the **Zoom Out** button ⊖ as necessary to see the right and left edges of the label sheet on your screen.

12 Under **Select recipients**, be sure the **Use an existing list** option button is selected. Under **Use an existing list**, click **Browse**.

13 Navigate to your **Word Chapter 3** folder, select your **Lastname_Firstname_3B_Addresses** file, and then click **Open** to display the **Mail Merge Recipients** dialog box.

In the Mail Merge Recipients dialog box, the column headings are formed from the text in the first row of your Word table of addresses. Each row of information that contains data for one person is referred to as a *record*. The column headings—for example, *Last_Name* and *First_Name*—are referred to as *fields*. An underscore replaces the spaces between words in the field name headings.

14 Compare your screen with Figure 3.35.

Figure 3.35

Mail Merge Recipients dialog box

Gridlines indicate label borders

Path containing your file name

Activity 3.16 | Completing the Mail Merge Wizard

You can add or edit names and addresses while completing the Mail Merge Wizard. You can also match your column names with preset names used in Mail Merge.

1 In the lower left portion of the **Mail Merge Recipients** dialog box, in the **Data Source** box, click the path that contains your file name. Then, at the bottom of the **Mail Merge Recipients** dialog box, click **Edit**.

2 In the upper right corner of the **Data Form** dialog box, click **Add New**. In the blank record, type the following, pressing Tab to move from field to field, and then compare your **Data Form** dialog box with Figure 3.36.

First_Name	**Susan**
Last_Name	**Ballard**
Address_1	**1251 Parker Road**
Unit:	
City	**Memphis**
State	**TN**
ZIP_Code	**38123**

Figure 3.36

New record

Edit button

3 In the lower right corner of the **Data Form** dialog box, click **Close**. Scroll to the end of the recipient list to confirm that the record for *Susan Ballard* that you just added is in the list. At the bottom of the **Mail Merge Recipients** dialog box, click **OK**.

4 At the bottom of the **Mail Merge** task pane, click **Next: Arrange your labels**.

5 Under **Arrange your labels**, click **Address block**. In the **Insert Address Block** dialog box, under **Specify address elements**, examine the various formats for names. If necessary, under *Insert recipient's name in this format*, select the *Joshua Randall Jr.* format. Compare your dialog box with Figure 3.37.

Figure 3.37

Format selected

Preview of address block

Match Fields button

6 In the lower right corner of the **Insert Address Block** dialog box, click **Match Fields**.

If your field names are descriptive, the Mail Merge program will identify them correctly, as is the case with most of the information in the *Required for Address Block* section. However, the Address 2 field is unmatched—in the source file, this column is named *Unit*.

7 Scroll down and examine the dialog box, and then compare your screen with Figure 3.38.

Figure 3.38

Address 2 unmatched

8 Click the **Address 2 arrow**, and then from the list of available fields, click **Unit** to match the Mail Merge field with the field in your data source.

9 At the bottom of the **Match Fields** dialog box, click **OK**. At the bottom of the **Insert Address Block** dialog box, click **OK**.

> Word inserts the Address block in the first label space surrounded by double angle brackets. The *AddressBlock* field name displays, which represents the address block you saw in the Preview area of the Insert Address Block dialog box.

10 In the task pane, under **Replicate labels**, click **Update all labels** to insert an address block in each label space for each subsequent record.

11 At the bottom of the task pane, click **Next: Preview your labels**. Notice that for addresses with four lines, the last line of the address is cut off.

12 Press [Ctrl] + [A] to select all of the label text, click the **Page Layout tab**, and then in the **Paragraph group**, click in the **Spacing Before** box. Type **3** and press [Enter].

13 Click in any label to deselect, and notice that 4-line addresses are no longer cut off. Compare your screen with Figure 3.39.

Figure 3.39

Preview of mailing labels —

14 At the bottom of the task pane, click **Next: Complete the merge**.

> Step 6 of the Mail Merge task pane displays. At this point you can print or edit your labels, although this is done more easily in the document window.

15 **Save** your labels, and then **Close** the **Mail Merge** task pane.

Activity 3.17 | Previewing and Printing the Mail Merge Document

If you discover that you need to make further changes to your labels, you can still make them even though the Mail Merge task pane is closed.

1 Add the file name to the footer, close the footer area, and then move to the top of Page 2. Click anywhere in the empty table row, click the **Layout tab**, in the **Rows & Columns group**, click the **Delete** button, and then click **Delete Rows**.

Adding footer text to a label sheet replaces the last row of labels on a page with the footer text, and moves the last row of labels to the top of the next page. In this instance, a blank second page is created, which you can delete by deleting the blank row.

2 Press Ctrl + F2 to display the **Print Preview**. Notice that the labels do not display in alphabetical order.

3 Click the **Mailings tab**, and then in the **Start Mail Merge group**, click the **Edit Recipient List** button to display the list of names and addresses.

4 In the **Mail Merge Recipients** dialog box, click the **Last_Name** field heading, and notice that the names are sorted alphabetically by the recipient's last name.

Mailing labels are often sorted by either last name or by ZIP Code.

5 Click the **Last_Name** field heading again, and notice that the last names are sorted in descending order. Click the **Last_Name** field one more time to return to ascending order, and then click **OK**. Press Ctrl + Home, and then compare your screen with Figure 3.40.

Figure 3.40

Labels in alphabetical order

6 From **Backstage** view, display the **Document Panel**. In the **Author** box, delete any text and then type your firstname and lastname. In the **Subject** box, type your course name and section number, and in the **Keywords** box type **newsletter mailing labels** Close ☒ the **Document Panel**.

7 Click **Save** ☐. Display **Backstage** view, and then click the **Print tab**. Examine the **Print Preview** on the right side of the window.

8 As directed by your instructor, print or submit electronically.

If you print, the labels will print on whatever paper is in the printer; unless you have preformatted labels available, the labels will print on a sheet of paper. Printing the labels on plain paper enables you to proofread the labels before you print them on more expensive label sheets.

9 **Close** the document, click **Yes** to save the data source, and then if necessary, click **Save** to save the labels.

10 In addition to your labels and address document, print or submit your **3B_Memphis_ Newsletter** document as directed. **Exit** Word.

End You have completed Project 3B

Content-Based Assessments

Summary

In this chapter, you created a research paper using the MLA style. You added a header, footnotes, citations, and a bibliography, and changed the footnote style. You created a newsletter that used multiple columns. You added a column break, a page break, and a manual line break. You added special font effects, and added a border and shading to a paragraph. Finally, you used the Mail Merge Wizard to create a set of mailing labels for the newsletter.

Key Terms

American Psychological
   Association (APA) 165

Bibliography 172

Citation 172

Clip Art 184

Column break
   indicator 184

Data source 189

Endnote 167

Fields 191

Footnote 167

Hanging indent 177

Line break indicator 187

Mail merge 189

Main document 189

Manual column break ..181

Manual line break 187

Manual page break 176

Modern Language
   Association (MLA) 165

Nameplate 182

Note 167

Page break indicator 176

Parenthetical
   reference 172

Record 191

Screenshot 186

Section 182

Section break 182

Small caps 186

Style 169

Style guide 165

Works Cited 172

Matching

Match each term in the second column with its correct definition in the first column by writing the letter of the term on the blank line in front of the correct definition.

_____ 1. A manual that contains standards for the design and writing of documents.

_____ 2. One of two commonly used style guides for formatting research papers.

_____ 3. An image of an active window on your computer that you can paste into a document.

_____ 4. In a research paper, information that expands on the topic, but that does not fit well in the document text.

_____ 5. In a research paper, a note placed at the bottom of the page.

_____ 6. In a research paper, a note placed at the end of a document or chapter.

_____ 7. A list of cited works in a report or research paper, also referred to as *Works Cited*, *Sources*, or *References*, depending upon the report style.

_____ 8. In the MLA style, a list of cited works placed at the end of a research paper or report.

_____ 9. A group of formatting commands, such as font, font size, font color, paragraph alignment, and line spacing that can be applied to a paragraph with one command.

_____ 10. A note, inserted into the text of a research paper that refers the reader to a source in the bibliography.

_____ 11. In the MLA style, a citation that refers to items on the *Works Cited* page, and which is placed in parentheses; the citation includes the last name of the author or authors, and the page number in the referenced source.

A American
  Psychological
  Association (APA)

B Bibliography

C Citation

D Endnote

E Footnote

F Hanging indent

G Manual column
  break

H Manual page break

I Note

J Page break indicator

K Parenthetical
  reference

L Screenshot

M Style

N Style guide

O Works Cited

_____ 12. The action of forcing a page to end and placing subsequent text at the top of the next page.

_____ 13. A dotted line with the text *Page Break* that indicates where a manual page break was inserted.

_____ 14. An indent style in which the first line of a paragraph extends to the left of the remaining lines, and that is commonly used for bibliographic entries.

_____ 15. An artificial end to a column to balance columns or to provide space for the insertion of other objects.

Multiple Choice

Circle the correct answer.

1. Column text that is aligned to both the left and right margins is referred to as:
   A. centered
   B. justified
   C. indented

2. The banner on the front page of a newsletter that identifies the publication is the:
   A. heading
   B. nameplate
   C. title

3. A portion of a document that can be formatted differently from the rest of the document is a:
   A. tabbed list
   B. paragraph
   C. section

4. A font effect, commonly used in titles, that changes lowercase text into uppercase letters using a reduced font size is:
   A. Small Caps
   B. Level 2 Head
   C. Bevel

5. To end a line before the normal end of the line, without creating a new paragraph, hold down the Shift key while pressing the:
   A. Enter key
   B. Ctrl key
   C. Alt key

6. The nonprinting symbol that displays where a manual line break is inserted is the:
   A. short arrow
   B. bent arrow
   C. anchor

7. In mail merge, the document that contains the text or formatting that remains constant is the:
   A. data source
   B. mailing list
   C. main document

8. In mail merge, the list of variable information, such as names and addresses, that is merged with a main document to create customized form letters or labels is the:
   A. data source
   B. mailing list
   C. main document

9. In mail merge, a row of information that contains data for one person is a:
   A. record
   B. field
   C. label

10. To perform a mail merge using Word's step-by-step guided process, use the:
    A. Mail Merge Template
    B. Mail Merge Management Source
    C. Mail Merge Wizard

Content-Based Assessments

Apply **3A** skills from these Objectives:

1. Create a Research Paper
2. Insert Footnotes in a Research Paper
3. Create Citations and a Bibliography in a Research Paper

Skills Review | Project **3C** Recycling Report

In the following Skills Review, you will format and edit a research paper for Memphis Primary Materials. The research topic is recycling in the natural environment. Your completed document will look similar to Figure 3.41.

Project Files

For Project 3C, you will need the following file:

w03C_Recycling_Report

You will save your document as:

Lastname_Firstname_3C_Recycling_Report

Project Results

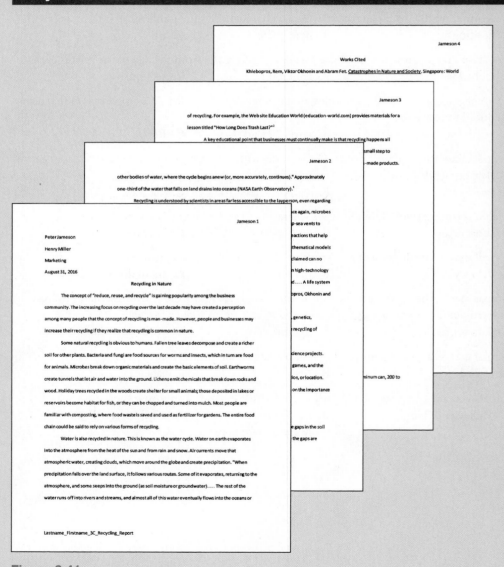

Figure 3.41

(Project 3C Recycling Report continues on the next page)

Content-Based Assessments

Skills Review | Project **3C** Recycling Report (continued)

1 **Start** Word. From your student files, locate and open the document **w03C_Recycling_Report**. Display the formatting marks and rulers. **Save** the file in your **Word Chapter 3** folder as **Lastname_Firstname_3C_Recycling_Report**

a. Press Ctrl + A. On the **Home tab**, in the **Paragraph group**, click the **Line spacing** button, and then change the line spacing to **2.0**. On the **Page Layout tab**, in the **Paragraph group**, change the **Spacing After** to **0 pt**.

b. Press Ctrl + Home, press Enter to create a blank line at the top of the document, and then click to position the insertion point in the blank line. Type **Peter Jameson** and then press Enter. Type **Henry Miller** and then press Enter. Type **Marketing** and then press Enter. Type **August 31, 2016** and then press Enter.

c. Type **Recycling in Nature** and then right-click anywhere in the title you just typed. From the Mini toolbar, **Center** the title.

d. Near the top of **Page 1**, locate the paragraph beginning *The concept of*, and then click to position the insertion point at the beginning of the paragraph. Scroll to the end of the document, hold down Shift, and then click to the right of the last paragraph mark to select all of the text from the insertion point to the end of the document. On the horizontal ruler, drag the **First Line Indent** button to **0.5"**.

e. On **Page 1**, point to the top margin area and right-click. Click **Edit Header**. In the header area, type **Jameson** and then press Spacebar.

f. On the **Design tab**, in the **Header & Footer group**, click the **Page Number** button, and then point to **Current Position**. In the displayed gallery, under **Simple**, click **Plain Number**. On the **Home tab**, in the **Paragraph group**, click the **Align Text Right** button.

g. Click the **Design tab**, and then in the **Navigation group**, click the **Go to Footer** button. In the **Insert group**, click the **Quick Parts** button, and then click **Field**. In the **Field** dialog box, under **Field names**, locate and click **FileName**, and then click **OK**.

h. Double-click anywhere outside the footer area. **Save** your document.

2 Scroll to view the top of **Page 2**, locate the paragraph that ends *drains into oceans*, and then click to position the insertion point to the right of the period following *oceans*. On the **References tab**, in the **Footnotes group**, click the **Insert Footnote** button.

a. Type **Groundwater is found in two layers of the soil, the "zone of aeration," where gaps in the soil are filled with both air and water, and, further down, the "zone of saturation," where the gaps are completely filled with water.**

b. In the lower half of **Page 2**, locate the paragraph that begins *School students*. Click to position the insertion point at the end of the paragraph and insert a footnote.

c. As the footnote text, type **A wool sock will last one year in a landfill; a soup can, 80 to 100 years; an aluminum can, 200 to 500 years; and plastic rings from a six-pack of cans, 450 years. Save** your document.

d. At the bottom of **Page 2**, right-click anywhere in either footnote. From the shortcut menu, click **Style**. In the **Style** dialog box, click the **Modify** button. In the **Modify Style** dialog box, locate the small Formatting toolbar in the center of the dialog box, click the **Font Size button arrow**, and then click **11**.

e. In the lower left corner of the dialog box, click the **Format** button, and then click **Paragraph**. In the **Paragraph** dialog box, under **Indentation**, click the **Special arrow**, and then click **First line**. Under **Spacing**, click the **Line spacing button arrow**, and then click **Double**.

f. Click **OK** to close the **Paragraph** dialog box, click **OK** to close the **Modify Style** dialog box, and then click **Apply** to apply the new style. Notice that the second footnote moves to **Page 3**. **Save** your document.

3 Scroll to view the top of **Page 2**, and then locate the footnote marker at the end of the second line of text. Click to position the insertion point to the left of the period at the end of the paragraph.

a. On the **References tab**, in the **Citations & Bibliography group**, click the **Style button arrow**, and then click **MLA** to insert a reference using MLA style. Click the **Insert Citation** button, and then click **Add New Source**. Click the **Type of Source arrow**,

(Project 3C Recycling Report continues on the next page)

and then click **Web site**. Select the **Corporate Author** check box, and then add the following information (type the URL on one line):

Corporate Author:	**NASA Earth Observatory**
Name of Web Page:	**The Water Cycle**
Year:	**2009**
Month:	**March**
Day:	**3**
Year Accessed:	**2016**
Month Accessed:	**May**
Day Accessed:	**24**
URL:	**http://earthobservatory.nasa.gov/ Features/Water/water_2.php**

b. Click **OK** to insert the citation. In the next paragraph, which begins *Recycling is understood,* in the fifth line, click to position the insertion point to the right of the quotation mark. In the **Citations & Bibliography group**, click the **Insert Citation** button, and then click **Add New Source**. Click the **Type of Source arrow**, click **Journal Article**, and then add the following information (type the Title on one line):

Author:	**Pennisi, Elizabeth**
Title:	**Shale-Eating Microbes Recycle Global Carbon**
Journal Name:	**Science**
Year:	**2001**
Pages:	**1043**

c. Click **OK**. In the text, click to select the citation, click the **Citation Options arrow**, and then click **Edit Citation**. In the **Edit Citation** dialog box, under **Add**, in the **Pages** box, type **1043** and then click **OK**. Add a period to the right of the citation and delete the period to the left of the quotation mark.

d. In the same paragraph, position the insertion point at the end of the paragraph. In the **Citations & Bibliography group**, click the **Insert Citation** button, and then click **Add New Source**. Click the **Type of**

Source arrow, click **Book**, and then add the following information (type the Author information on one line):

Author:	**Khlebopros, Rem; Okhonin, Viktor; Fet, Abram**
Title:	**Catastrophes in Nature and Society**
Year:	**2007**
City:	**Singapore**
Publisher:	**World Scientific Publishing Company**

e. Click **OK**. Click to select the citation, click the **Citation Options arrow**, and then click **Edit Citation**. In the **Edit Citation** dialog box, under **Add**, in the **Pages** box, type **111** Click **OK**. Add a period to the right of the citation and delete the period to the left of the quotation mark.

f. Press Ctrl + End to move the insertion point to the end of the document. Press Ctrl + Enter to insert a manual page break. On the ruler, drag the **First Line Indent** button to the left to **0 inches on the horizontal ruler**.

g. Type **Works Cited** and then press Enter. On the **References tab**, in the **Citations & Bibliography group**, be sure **MLA** displays in the **Style** box. In the **Citations & Bibliography group**, click the **Bibliography** button, and then click **Insert Bibliography**.

h. In the bibliography, move the pointer to the left of the first entry—beginning *Khlebopros*—to display the ⟋ pointer. Drag down to select all three references. On the **Home tab**, in the **Paragraph group**, set the **Line spacing** to **2.0**. On the **Page Layout tab**, set the **Spacing After** to **0 pt**.

i. Right-click the *Works Cited* title, and then from the Mini toolbar, click the **Center** button. **Save** your document.

4 From **Backstage** view, display the **Document Panel**, type your name and course information, and then add the keywords **recycling, nature, research paper** In the upper left corner of the panel, click the **Document Properties** button, and then click **Advanced Properties**.

(Project 3C Recycling Report continues on the next page)

Content-Based Assessments

Skills Review | Project **3C** Recycling Report (continued)

a. In the **Properties** dialog box, click the **Summary tab**. In the **Properties** dialog box, fill in the following information:

Title:	**Recycling in Nature**
Manager:	**Henry Miller**
Company:	**Memphis Primary Materials**
Comments:	**Draft of a new white paper research report on recycling**

b. At the bottom of the **Properties** dialog box, click **OK**. **Close** the **Document Panel**. **Save** your document. View the Print Preview, and then print or submit electronically as directed by your instructor. **Exit** Word.

End You have completed Project 3C ———————

Skills Review | Project **3D** Company Newsletter

In the following Skills Review, you will format a newsletter for Memphis Primary Materials, and then create a set of mailing labels for the newsletter. Your completed documents will look similar to Figure 3.42.

Project Files

For Project 3D, you will need the following files:

New blank Word document
w03D_Company_Newsletter
w03D_Addresses

You will save your documents as:

Lastname_Firstname_3D_Company_Newsletter
Lastname_Firstname_3D_Addresses
Lastname_Firstname_3D_Labels

Project Results

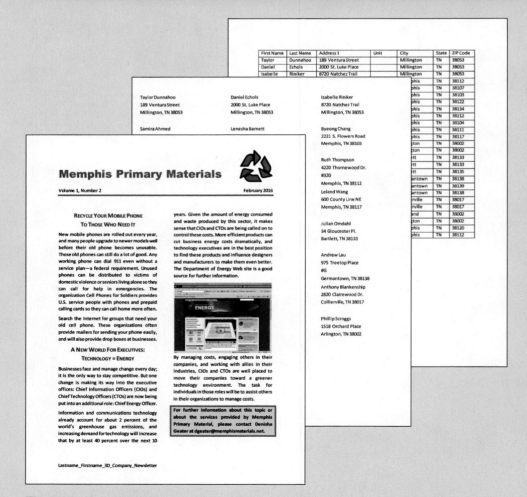

Figure 3.42

(Project 3D Company Newsletter continues on the next page)

Skills Review | Project **3D** Company Newsletter (continued)

1 **Start** Word. From your student files, open the document **w03D_Company_Newsletter**. **Save** the file in your **Word Chapter 3** folder as **Lastname_Firstname_3D_Company_Newsletter** and then add the file name to the footer.

a. Select the first paragraph of text—*Memphis Primary Materials*. From the Mini toolbar, change the **Font** to **Arial Black** and the **Font Size** to **24**. Select the title you just formatted. Click the **Font Color button arrow**, and then under **Theme Colors**, in the seventh column, click the fifth color—**Olive Green, Accent 3, Darker 25%**.

b. Select the second paragraph. On the **Home tab**, in the **Paragraph group**, click the **Borders button arrow**, and then click **Borders and Shading**. In the **Borders and Shading** dialog box, click the **Color arrow**, and then under **Theme Colors**, in the seventh column, click the fifth color—**Olive Green, Accent 3, Darker 25%**. Click the **Width arrow**, and then click **3 pt**. In the **Preview** area, click the *bottom* border of the Preview and then click **OK**.

c. Below the nameplate, locate the paragraph that begins *Recycle Your Mobile*, and then select all of the text from that point to the end of the document. On the **Page Layout tab**, in the **Page Setup group**, click the **Columns** button, and then click **Two**.

d. With the text still selected, in the **Paragraph group**, set **Spacing After** to **6 pt**. On the **Home tab**, in the **Paragraph group**, click the **Justify** button. Click anywhere in the document to deselect the text, and then **Save** the newsletter.

e. Press [Ctrl] + [Home]. On the **Insert tab**, in the **Illustrations group**, click the **Clip Art** button. In the **Clip Art** task pane, click in the **Search for** box, and then type **conservation**

f. In the **Clip Art** task pane, click the **Results should be arrow**, and be sure that only the **Illustrations** check box is selected. Be sure the **Include Office.com content** check box is selected, and then click **Go**. Locate the image of three green arrows, as shown in Figure 3.42, and then click on the image.

g. On the **Format tab**, in the **Size group**, click in the **Shape Height** box, type **1** and then press [Enter]. In the **Arrange group**, click the **Wrap Text** button, and then click **Square**. **Close** the Clip Art task pane, and then drag the image to the location shown in Figure 3.42.

h. In the second column, position the insertion point at the beginning of the paragraph that begins *By managing costs*. Open your Web browser. In the address bar, type **www.energy.gov** and then press [Enter]. Maximize the browser window. Use the taskbar to return to your Word document.

i. On the **Insert tab**, in the **Illustrations group**, click the **Screenshot** button. In the gallery, click the DOE screenshot to insert it. **Close** your Web browser, and then **Save** your document.

2 At the top of the first column, select the paragraph that begins *Recycle Your Mobile*. Be sure to include the paragraph mark. Right-click the selected text, and then click **Font**. In the **Font** dialog box, click the **Font color arrow**, and then under **Theme Colors**, in the seventh column, click the last color—**Olive Green, Accent 3, Darker 50%**. Under **Font style**, click **Bold**. Under **Size**, click **14**. Under **Effects**, select the **Small caps** check box.

a. In the **Font** dialog box, click **OK**. Right-click the selected text, and then click the **Center** button. In the title you just formatted, click to position the insertion point to the right of *Phone*, and then press [Del] to remove the space. Hold down [Shift], and then press [Enter] to insert a manual line break.

b. Select and right-click the title you just formatted, and then on the Mini toolbar, click the **Format Painter** button. Near the middle of the first column, select the paragraph that begins *A New World* to apply the same formatting.

c. At the bottom of the second column, in the paragraph that begins *For further*, select the entire paragraph. On the Mini toolbar, apply **Bold**.

d. With the text still selected, on the **Home tab**, in the **Paragraph group**, click the **Borders button arrow**, and then click **Borders and Shading**. In the **Borders and Shading** dialog box, be sure the **Borders tab** is selected. Under **Setting**, click **Box**. Click the **Width arrow**, and then click **3 pt**. If necessary, click the **Color arrow**, and then in the seventh column, click the fifth color—**Olive Green, Accent 3, Darker 25%**.

e. At the top of the **Borders and Shading** dialog box, click the **Shading tab**. Click the **Fill arrow**, and then in the seventh column, click the second color—**Olive Green, Accent 3, Lighter 80%**. At the bottom of the **Borders and Shading** dialog box, click **OK**. Click anywhere in the document to deselect the text.

(Project 3D Company Newsletter continues on the next page)

Content-Based Assessments

f. Near the bottom of the first column, in the paragraph that begins *Information and communications*, click to position the insertion point at the beginning of the sixth line. On the **Page Layout tab**, in the **Page Setup group**, click the **Breaks** button. Under **Page Breaks**, click **Column**.

g. From **Backstage** view, display the **Document Panel**, type your name and course information. Add the keywords **newsletter, energy** and then **Close** the **Document Panel**. **Save** the document, view the Print Preview, and then **Exit** Word. Hold this file until you complete this project.

3 **Start** Word and display a new blank document. Display formatting marks and rulers. **Save** the document in your **Word Chapter 3** folder as **Lastname_Firstname_ 3D_Labels Open** the file **w03D_Addresses Save** the address file in your **Word Chapter 3** folder as **Lastname_ Firstname_3D_Addresses** and then add the file name to the footer.

a. Click to position the insertion point in the last cell in the table, and then press Tab to create a new row. Enter the following new record:

First Name	Eldon
Last Name	Aarons
Address 1	5354 Thornewood Dr.
Unit	#2B
City	Memphis
State	TN
ZIP Code	38112

b. **Save**, and then **Close** the table of addresses; be sure your blank **Lastname_Firstname_3D_Labels** document displays. Click the **Mailings tab**. In the **Start Mail Merge group**, click the **Start Mail Merge** button, and then click **Step by Step Mail Merge Wizard**. Under **Select document type**, click the **Labels** option button.

c. At the bottom of the task pane, click **Next: Starting document**. Under **Select starting document**, be sure **Change document layout** is selected, and then under **Change document layout**, click **Label options**.

d. In the **Label Options** dialog box, under **Printer information**, click the **Tray arrow**, and then click **Default tray (Automatically Select)**.

e. Under **Label information**, click the **Label vendors arrow**, and then click **Avery US Letter**. Under **Product number**, scroll about halfway down the list, and then click **5160**. At the bottom of the **Label Options** dialog box, click **OK**. At the bottom of the task pane, click **Next: Select recipients**.

f. Under **Select recipients**, be sure the **Use an existing list** option button is selected. Under **Use an existing list**, click **Browse**. Navigate to your **Word Chapter 3** folder, select your **Lastname_Firstname_3D_ Addresses** file, and then click **Open**. At the bottom of the **Mail Merge Recipients** dialog box, click **OK**, and then in the **Mail Merge** task pane, click **Next: Arrange your labels**.

g. Under **Arrange your labels**, click **Address block**. If necessary, in the **Insert Address Block** dialog box, under **Insert recipient's name in this format**, select the **Joshua Randall Jr.** format.

h. Click **Match Fields**. Click the **Address 2 arrow**, and then click **Unit**. Click **OK** two times.

i. In the task pane, under **Replicate labels**, click **Update all labels**. Click **Next: Preview your labels**. Press Ctrl + A to select all of the label text, and then on the **Page Layout tab**, click in the **Spacing Before** box, type **4** and press Enter to ensure that the four-line addresses will fit on the labels. **Save** your labels, and then **Close** the **Mail Merge** task pane.

4 Add the file name to the footer, and then close the footer area. Click in the bottom empty row of the table, click the **Layout tab**, in the **Rows & Columns group**, click **Delete**, and then click **Delete Rows**. From **Backstage** view, display the **Document Panel**, type your name and course information, and then add the keywords **newsletter mailing labels Close** the **Document Panel**.

a. Print or submit electronically your 3D_Company_ Newsletter, 3D_Addresses, and 3D_Labels documents.

b. **Close** the document, click **Save** to save the labels, and then **Exit** Word.

End **You have completed Project 3D**

Content-Based Assessments

Apply 3A skills from these Objectives:

1. Create a Research Paper
2. Insert Footnotes in a Research Paper
3. Create Citations and a Bibliography in a Research Paper

Mastering Word | Project **3E** Hazards

In the following Mastering Word project, you will edit and format a research paper for Memphis Primary Materials, the topic of which is hazardous materials in electronic waste. Your completed document will look similar to Figure 3.43.

Project Files

For Project 3E, you will need the following file:

> w03E_Hazards

You will save your document as:

> Lastname_Firstname_3E_Hazards

Project Results

Figure 3.43

(Project 3E Hazards continues on the next page)

1 **Start** Word. From your student files open the document **w03E_Hazards**. **Save** the document in your **Word Chapter 3** folder as **Lastname_Firstname_3E_Hazards** Display the header area, type **Whitlock** and then press ⎵Spacebar. Display the **Page Number gallery**, and then in the **Current Position**, add the **Plain Number** style. Apply **Align Text Right** formatting to the header. Add the file name to the footer.

2 Return to the beginning of the document, press ⎆Enter to insert a blank line, click in the blank line, type **June Whitlock** and then press ⎆Enter. Type **Henry Miller** and press ⎆Enter. Type **Marketing** and press ⎆Enter. Type **July 5, 2016**

3 Select all of the text in the document. Change the **Line Spacing** to **2.0**, and change the **Spacing After** to **0 pt**. Deselect the text, right-click anywhere in the title *Hazardous Materials Found in E-Waste*, and then **Center** the title.

Starting with the paragraph that begins *Most people*, select the text from that point to the end of the document, and then set the **First Line Indent** to **0.5"**.

4 Near the middle of **Page 1**, in the paragraph that begins *One material*, in the second line, click to position the insertion point to the right of the period following *lead*, and then add the following footnote:

> **In 2009 the U.S. government required that all television signals be transmitted in digital format, which resulted in dramatically increased numbers of discarded television sets.**

On **Page 2**, in the paragraph that begins *Cadmium is another*, in the second line, click to position the insertion point to the right of the period following *devices*, and then add the following footnote:

> **Newer lithium batteries are not considered hazardous waste if they are fully discharged prior to disposal.**

5 Right-click anywhere in the footnote, modify the **Style** to set the **Font Size** to **11**, and then change the **Format** of paragraphs to add a **First line** indent and use double-spacing.

Near the bottom of **Page 1**, locate the paragraph that begins *Toxic effects*, and then click position the insertion

point to the left of the period at the end of the paragraph, which displays at the top of **Page 2**. In the **MLA** format, add the following **Journal Article** citation (type the Title on one line):

Author:	**Marshall, Eliot**
Title:	**EPA May Allow More Lead in Gasoline**
Journal Name:	**Science**
Year:	**1982**
Pages:	**1375–1377**

6 Near the top of **Page 2**, locate the paragraph that begins *Cadmium*, and then click to position the insertion point to the left of the period at the end of the paragraph. Add the following **Book** citation, using a **Corporate Author** (type the Title on one line):

Corporate Author:	**American Cancer Society**
Title:	**Cancer Source Book for Nurses, Eighth Edition**
Year:	**2004**
City:	**Sudbury, MA**
Publisher:	**Jones and Bartlett Publishers, Inc.**

Select the *Marshall* citation and add the page number **1375** At the end of the next paragraph, select the *American Cancer Society* citation and add the page number **291**

7 Move to the end of the document, and then insert a manual page break to create a new page. Change the **First Line Indent** to **0"**. Add a **Works Cited** title, and then **Insert Bibliography**. Select the two references, apply **Double** line spacing, and then remove spacing after the paragraphs. **Center** the *Works Cited* title.

Display the **Document Panel** and add your name and course information and the keywords **hazardous materials Save** your document. Display the Print Preview, make any necessary adjustments, and then print or submit electronically as directed. **Exit** Word.

 You have completed Project 3E ————————

Content-Based Assessments

Apply **3B** skills from these Objectives:

- **4** Format a Multiple-Column Newsletter
- **5** Use Special Character and Paragraph Formatting
- **6** Create Mailing Labels Using Mail Merge

Mastering Word | Project **3F** Spring Newsletter

In the following Mastering Word project, you will format a newsletter for Memphis Primary Materials, and then create a set of mailing labels for the newsletter. Your completed documents will look similar to Figure 3.44.

Project Files

For Project 3F, you will need the following files:

New blank Word document
w03F_Spring_Newsletter
w03F_Addresses

You will save your documents as:

Lastname_Firstname_3F_Spring_Newsletter
Lastname_Firstname_3F_Labels

Project Results

Figure 3.44

(Project 3F Spring Newsletter continues on the next page)

1 **Start** Word. Open **w03F_Spring_Newsletter**, and then save it in your **Word Chapter 3** folder as **Lastname_Firstname_3F_Spring_Newsletter** Add the file name to the footer. Display the rulers and formatting marks.

Select the first line of text—*Memphis Primary Materials*. Change the **Font** to **Arial Black**, the **Font Size** to **24**, and the **Font Color** to **Orange, Accent 6, Darker 25%**.

Select the second line of text—the date and volume. Change the **Font Color** to **Orange, Accent 6, Darker 25%**. Display the **Borders and Shading** dialog box, and then add an **Orange, Accent 6, Darker 25%, 3 pt** line below the selected text.

2 Click at the beginning of the newsletter title. Display the **Clip Art** task pane, search for **recycle earth** and then insert the image of the orange and tan recycle arrows. Change the **Height** to **1** and then apply **Square** text wrapping. Close the **Clip Art** task pane. Drag the image to the location shown in Figure 3.44.

Starting with the paragraph that begins *CARE enough*, select all of the text from that point to the end of the document. Change the **Spacing After** to **6 pt**, format the text in two columns, and apply the **Justify** alignment.

3 At the top of the first column, select the paragraph *CARE Enough to Recycle*. From the **Font** dialog box, change the **Font Size** to **20**, apply **Bold**, add the **Small caps** effect, and change the **Font color** to **Orange, Accent 6, Darker 25%**. **Center** the paragraph. Near the bottom of the same column, apply the same formatting to the paragraph that begins *Hazards of Old*. Add a manual line break between *Old* and *Home*.

Move to the blank line at the bottom of the second column. Open your Web browser and open the **www.epa.gov/ozone/partnerships/rad/** Web site. Maximize the browser window and return to your Word document. Insert a **Screenshot** of the EPA Web page. **Close** your Web browser.

4 Select the two lines of text above the inserted screenshot. **Center** the text and apply **Bold**. Add a **Shadow** border, change the **Color** to **Tan, Background 2, Darker 25%**, the **Width** to **1 1/2 pt**, and then on the **Shading tab** of the dialog box, apply a **Fill** of **Tan, Background 2** shading—in the third column, the first color.

Display the **Document Panel** and add your name, course information, and the **Keywords Spring newsletter** Display the **Print Preview**, return to your document and make any necessary corrections, and then **Save** and **Close** the document. Hold this document until you complete the project.

5 Display a **New** blank document. **Save** the document in your **Word Chapter 3** folder as **Lastname_Firstname_3F_Labels** On the **Mailings tab**, start the **Step by Step Mail Merge Wizard.**

In **Step 1**, select **Labels** as the document type. In **Step 2**, set **Label options** to use the **Auto default** tray (yours may vary) and **Avery US Letter 5160**.

In **Step 3**, use an existing list, browse to select **w03F_Addresses**. In **Step 4**, add an **Address block** to the labels, use the *Joshua Randall Jr.* format, and then **Match Fields** by matching *Address 2* to *Unit*.

Update all labels and **Preview**. Select all of the label text, and then on the **Page Layout tab**, click in the **Spacing Before** box, type **4** and press Enter to ensure that the four-line addresses will fit on the labels. On the **Layout tab**, in the **Table group**, if necessary click **View Gridlines** to check the alignment of the labels.

Complete the merge, and then **Close** the **Mail Merge** task pane. Delete the last two empty rows of the table, and then add the file name to the footer.

6 Display the **Document Panel**, and then add your name and course information and the keywords **mailing labels** Display the **Print Preview**, return to your document and make any necessary corrections, and then **Save**. Print or submit electronically your two files that are the results of this project—3F_Spring_Newsletter and 3F_Labels. **Exit** Word.

End **You have completed Project 3F**

Content-Based Assessments

Apply 3A and 3B skills from these Objectives:

1. Create a Research Paper
2. Insert Footnotes in a Research Paper
3. Create Citations and a Bibliography in a Research Paper
4. Format a Multiple-Column Newsletter
5. Use Special Character and Paragraph Formatting
6. Create Mailing Labels Using Mail Merge

Mastering Word | Project **3G** Economics

In the following Mastering Word project, you will edit and format a newsletter and a research paper for Memphis Primary Materials on the topic of environmental economics. Your completed documents will look similar to Figure 3.45.

Project Files

For Project 3G, you will need the following files:

New blank Word document
w03G_Economics
w03G_Addresses
w03G_April_Newsletter

You will save your documents as:

Lastname_Firstname_3G_Economics
Lastname_Firstname_3G_April_Newsletter
Lastname_Firstname_3G_Labels

Project Results

Figure 3.45

(Project 3G Economics continues on the next page)

Content-Based Assessments

Mastering Word | Project 3G Economics (continued)

1 **Start** Word. Open the document **w03G_April_ Newsletter**, and then save the document in your **Word Chapter 3** folder as **Lastname_Firstname_3G_April_ Newsletter** Add the file name to the footer. Starting with the paragraph that begins *Research on Environmental Economics*, select all of the text from that point to the end of the document—the document text extends to two pages. Set the **Spacing After** to **6 pt**, format the selected text as two columns, and set the alignment to **Justify**.

2 Near the bottom of the first column, in the paragraph that begins *Maine has already*, click to position the insertion point to the left of the sixth line, which begins *pollutants would*. Insert a column break. At the top of the first column, select the paragraph *Research on Environmental Economics*.

Display the **Font** dialog box, set the **Font Size** to **14**, apply **Bold**, set the **Font color** to **Dark Blue, Text 2**, and then add the **Small caps** effect. **Center** the paragraph. Use the Format Painter to copy the formatting and then apply the same formatting to the paragraph *The Hard Costs of Pollution* located near the bottom of the first column and to *Environmental Economics Conference* in the second column.

3 At the bottom of the second column, select the last two paragraphs of text. From the **Borders and Shading** dialog box, apply a **1 1/2 pt**, **Shadow** border using the **Dark Blue, Text 2** color, and then on the **Shading tab**, apply a **Fill** of **Dark Blue, Text 2, Lighter 80%**.

In the second column, click to position the insertion point at the beginning of the paragraph that begins *Memphis Primary Materials is a cosponsor*. Display the **Clip Art** task pane. Search for **conference** and limit your search to **Illustrations**. **Insert** the image shown in Figure 3.45, apply **Top and Bottom** text wrapping, decrease the **Height** of the image to **1"**, and position the image as shown. **Close** the Clip Art task pane.

Display the **Document Panel** and add your name and course information and the **Keywords April newsletter Save** and then **Close** the document. Hold this file until you complete this project.

4 From your student files, open the document **w03G_Economics**, and then save it in your **Word Chapter 3** folder as **Lastname_Firstname_3G_Economics** Display the header area, type **Jaworski** and then press Spacebar. In the **Header & Footer group**, add a **Plain Number** from the

Current Position gallery. Apply **Align Text Right** formatting to the header. Move to the footer area and add the file name to the footer.

Select all of the text in the document. Change the **Line Spacing** to **2.0**, and change the **Spacing After** to **0**. Near the top of the document, **Center** the title *Environmental Economics and Business*. Beginning with the text below the centered title, select the text from that point to the end of the document, and then set a **First Line Indent** at **0.5"**.

5 At the bottom of **Page 1**, in the paragraph that begins *Environmental economics also*, in the second line, click to position the insertion point to the right of the comma following *Protocol*, and then insert the following footnote:

> **The Kyoto Protocol is an international agreement under the UN Framework Convention on Climate Change that went into effect in 2005.**

In the next paragraph, which begins *In the United States*, in the second line, position the insertion point to the right of the period following *Economics*, and then insert the following footnote:

> **The NCEE offers a centralized source of technical expertise to the EPA, as well as other federal agencies, Congress, universities, and other organizations.**

Right-click in the footnote, and then modify the style to set the **Font Size** to **11** and the format of the paragraph to include a **First line** indent and double-spacing. **Save** your document.

6 Near the bottom of **Page 1**, in the paragraph that begins *Environmental economists*, position the insertion point to the left of the period at the end of the paragraph. Using **MLA** format, add the following **Article in a Periodical** citation (type the Title on one line):

Author:	Abboud, Leila
Title:	Economist Strikes Gold in Climate-Change Fight
Periodical Title:	The Wall Street Journal
Year:	2008
Month:	March
Day:	13

(Project 3G Economics continues on the next page)

Select the *Abboud* citation and add the page number **A1** Near the middle of **Page 2**, in the paragraph that begins *In the United States*, click to position the insertion point to the left of the period at the end of the paragraph. Add the following **Book** citation in **MLA** format (type the Title on one line):

Author:	Tietenberg, Tom; Folmer, Henk, Editors
Title:	The International Yearbook of Environmental Resource Economics, 2006/2007
Year:	2006
City:	Northampton, MA
Publisher:	Edward Elgar Publishers

7 Select the *Tietenberg* citation and add the page number **1** Insert a manual page break at the end of the document. On the new **Page 3**, on the ruler, set the **First Line Indent** to **0″**. Type **Works Cited** and then press Enter.

On the **References tab**, in the **Citations & Bibliography group**, be sure *MLA* displays in the **Style** box. Insert the bibliography. Select the inserted references, set the **Line Spacing** to **2.0**, and then set **Spacing After** to **0 pt**. Center the *Works Cited* title.

Display the **Document Panel** and add your name and course information and the **Keywords environmental economics** Display the **Print Preview** to check your document, make any necessary adjustments, **Save**, and then **Close** the document. Hold this file until you complete this project.

8 Display a **New** blank document. **Save** the document in your **Word Chapter 3** folder as **Lastname_Firstname_ 3G_Labels** On the **Mailings tab**, start the **Step by Step Mail Merge Wizard**. In **Step 1**, select **Labels** as the document type. In **Step 2**, set **Label options** to use the **Auto default** tray (yours may vary) and **Avery US Letter 5160**. If you cannot see the gridlines, on the **Layout tab**, in the **Table group**, click **View Gridlines**. In **Step 3**, use an existing list, browse to select **w03G_Addresses**, and then click **OK**.

In **Step 4**, add an **Address block** to the labels, use the *Joshua Randall Jr.* format, and then **Match Fields** by matching *Address 2* to *Unit*. **Update all labels** and then **Preview**. Select all of the label text, and then on the **Page Layout tab**, click in the **Spacing Before** box, type **4** and press Enter. Complete the merge, and then **Close** the **Mail Merge** task pane. Delete the last two empty rows of the table, and then add the file name to the footer, which adds an additional page.

Display the **Document Panel**, and then add your name, course information, and the keywords **mailing labels** Click **Save**. Print or submit electronically your three files that are the results of this project—3G_Economics, 3G_April_Newsletter, and 3G_Labels. **Exit** Word.

End **You have completed Project 3G** ——————————

Content-Based Assessments

GO! Fix It | Project 3H Metals Report

Project Files

For Project 3H, you will need the following file:

w03H_Metals_Report

You will save your document as:

Lastname_Firstname_3H_Metals_Report

From the student files that accompany this textbook, locate and open the file w03H_Metals_Report, and then save the file in your Word Chapter 3 folder as **Lastname_Firstname_3H_Metals_Report**

This document contains errors that you must find and correct. Read and examine the document, and then edit to correct any errors that you find and to improve the overall document format. Types of errors could include, but are not restricted to:

- Formatting does not match MLA style guidelines that you practiced in the chapter
- Incorrect header format
- Incorrect spacing between paragraphs
- Incorrect paragraph indents
- Incorrect line spacing
- Incorrect footnote format
- Incorrectly formatted reference page

Things you should know to complete this project:

- Displaying formatting marks will assist in locating spacing errors.
- There are no errors in the parenthetical references in the document.
- There are no errors in the information in the footnotes or bibliographical references.

Save your document and add the file name to the footer. In the Document Panel, add your name, course information, and the keywords **valuable metals, recycling** Save your document and submit as directed.

End You have completed Project 3H ———————————————

Apply a combination of the **3A** and **3B** skills.

GO! Make It | Project 3I Green Newsletter

Project Files

For Project 3I, you will need the following files:

New blank Word document   w03I_Kids
w03I_Competition

You will save your document as:

Lastname_Firstname_3I_Green_Newsletter

Start with a new Word document, and then save the file in your chapter folder as **Lastname_Firstname_3I_Green_Newsletter** Create the document shown in Figure 3.46. Create a nameplate, and then insert the files w03I_Competition and w03I_Kids. The title is Arial Black, 24 pt, Dark Blue, Text 2. Other titles and borders are Dark Blue, Text 2. The two titles in the columns are Calibri, 16 pt. The clip art image can be found by using the search term **recycle** and the screenshot can be found at the Web address in the last line of the newsletter.

Add the file name to the footer; in the Document Panel, add your name and course information and the Keywords **green, campuses, kids** Save your document and submit as directed.

Project Results

Memphis Primary Materials

Volume 1, Number 4   April 2016

THE COMPETITIVE SPIRIT OF GREEN

One way to increase people's willingness to reuse and recycle is to invoke their spirit of competition—and prizes do not hurt either. College campuses are proving this by participating in the America's Greenest Campus competition.

America's Greenest Campus is a nationwide contest, with the goal of reducing the carbon footprint of entire campus populations across the country.

Partnering with Smart Power and the U.S. Department of Energy, the winning campus will receive a donation of $10,000. As of February 2009, the University of Maryland has reduced its CO2 emissions by 2% and George Mason University by 3%.

Students, faculty, and staff are encouraged to recycle, turn off lights, reduce heating and air conditioning, and engage in many other small and large changes that can help the environment. Treehugger.com calls the contest, "the NCAA of sustainability."

Another college competition for environmentalism is RecycleMania. Designed to encourage colleges and universities to reduce waste, the competition collects reports on recycling and trash over a 10-week period. This competition thinks of colleges and universities as small cities that consume large amounts of resources and generate a lot of solid waste. Participating campuses are ranked by categories such as "least amount of waste per capita." Weekly results are distributed to the participants so they can benchmark against their competition and step up their efforts.

With growing awareness of the need to reduce, reuse, and recycle among students, expect some competition if you are part of a campus community!

CLEANUP IS FOR KIDS

Cleaning up the planet isn't just for college students. Younger students often have a desire to get involved with environmental activities, and there is no shortage of resources.

Start at the website of the Environmental Protection Agency. They provide resources like Cleanup for Kids, a Web site of the National Oceanic and Atmospheric Administration (NOAA), which makes the hazards of oil spills real through science demonstrations. The brochure, *Environmental Protection Begins With You*, outlines examples of community volunteer projects in which students can participate.

Learn more at the EPA website:
http://www.epa.gov/highschool/waste.htm

Lastname_Firstname_3I_Green_Newsletter

Figure 3.46

Content-Based Assessments

GO! Solve It | Project 3J Municipal Newsletter

Project Files

For Project 3J, you will need the following file:

New blank Word document

You will save your document as:

Lastname_Firstname_3J_Municipal_Newsletter

Memphis Primary Materials writes an informational newsletter for customers. Create a new document and save it in your Word Chapter 3 folder as **Lastname_Firstname_3J_Municipal_Newsletter** Use the following information to create a newsletter that includes a nameplate, multiple columns, at least two articles with article titles formatted so that they stand out, at least one clip art image, one screenshot, and one paragraph that includes a border and shading.

This issue (Volume 1, Number 6—June 2016) will focus on municipal solid waste—the waste generated by householders and small businesses. This category of waste does not include hazardous, industrial, or construction waste. The articles you write can be on any topic regarding municipal waste, and might include an introduction to the topic and a discussion of recycling in the U.S. or in the Memphis community. You will need to research this topic on the Web. A good place to start is www.epa.gov, which has many articles on solid municipal waste, and also provides links to further articles on the topic. You might also consider doing a Web search for the term **municipal solid waste recycling**

Add the file name to the footer. To the Document Panel, add your name, your course name and section number, and the keywords **municipal solid waste recycling**

Performance Element	Performance Level		
	Exemplary: You consistently applied the relevant skills	**Proficient:** You sometimes, but not always, applied the relevant skills	**Developing:** You rarely or never applied the relevant skills
Create and format nameplate	The nameplate includes both the company name and the date and volume information, and is formatted attractively.	One or more of the nameplate elements are done correctly, but other items are either omitted or not formatted properly.	The newsletter does not include a nameplate.
Insert at least two articles in multiple-column format	The newsletter contains at least two articles, displayed in multiple columns that are well written and are free of grammar and spelling errors.	The newsletter contains only one article, or the text is not divided into two columns, or there are spelling and grammar errors in the text.	The newsletter contains only one article, the article is not divided into multiple columns, and there are spelling and grammar errors.
Insert and format at least one clip art image	An appropriate clip art image is included. The image is sized and positioned appropriately.	A clip art image is inserted, but is either inappropriate, or is formatted or positioned poorly.	No clip art image is included.
Border and shading added to a paragraph	One or more paragraphs display an attractive border with shading that enables the reader to read the text.	A border or shading is displayed, but not both; or, the shading is too dark to enable the reader to easily read the text.	No border or shading is added to a paragraph.
Insert a screenshot	A screenshot is inserted in one of the columns; the screenshot is related to the content of the article.	A screenshot is inserted in the document, but does not relate to the content of the article.	No screenshot is inserted.

End You have completed Project 3J

Content-Based Assessments

Apply a combination of the 3A and 3B skills.

GO! Solve It | Project 3K Paper Report

Project Files

For Project 3K, you will need the following file:

New blank Word document

You will save your document as:

Lastname_Firstname_3K_Paper_Report

Create a new file and save it as **Lastname_Firstname_3K_Paper_Report** Use the following information to create a report written in the MLA format. The report should include at least two footnotes, at least two citations, and should include a *Works Cited* page.

Memphis Primary Materials writes and distributes informational reports on topics of interest to the people of Memphis. This report will be written by Sarah Stanger for the head of Marketing, Henry Miller. Information reports are provided as a public service of the company, and are distributed free of charge.

The topic of the report is recycling and reuse of paper and paper products. The report should contain an introduction, and then details about how much paper is used, what it is used for, the increase of paper recycling over time, and how paper products can be recycled or reused. A good place to start is www.epa.gov, which has many articles on paper use and recycling, and also provides links to further articles on the topic. You might also consider doing a Web search for the terms **paper recycling**

Add the file name to the footer, and add your name, your course name and section number, and the keywords **paper products, recycling** to the Document Panel.

	Performance Level		
	Exemplary: You consistently applied the relevant skills	**Proficient:** You sometimes, but not always, applied the relevant skills	**Developing:** You rarely or never applied the relevant skills
Format the header and heading	The last name and page number are right-aligned in the header, and the report has a four-line heading and a centered title.	The header and heading are included, but are not formatted according to MLA style guidelines.	The header or heading is missing or incomplete.
Format the body of the report	The report is double-spaced, with no space after paragraphs. The first lines of paragraphs are indented 0.5".	Some, but not all, of the report formatting is correct.	The majority of the formatting does not follow MLA guidelines.
Footnotes are included and formatted correctly	Two or more footnotes are included, and the footnote text is 11 pt, double-spaced, and the first line of each footnote is indented.	The correct number of footnotes is included, but the footnotes are not formatted properly.	No footnotes are included.
Citations and bibliography are included and formatted according to MLA guidelines	At least two citations are included in parenthetical references, with page numbers where appropriate, and the sources are included in a properly formatted Works Cited page.	Only one citation is included, or the citations and sources are not formatted correctly.	No citations or Works Cited page are included.

Performance Element is labeled along the left side spanning the rows.

End You have completed Project 3K

Outcomes-Based Assessments

Rubric

The following outcomes-based assessments are *open-ended assessments*. That is, there is no specific correct result; your result will depend on your approach to the information provided. Make *Professional Quality* your goal. Use the following scoring rubric to guide you in *how* to approach the problem, and then to evaluate *how well* your approach solves the problem.

The *criteria*—Software Mastery, Content, Format and Layout, and Process—represent the knowledge and skills you have gained that you can apply to solving the problem. The *levels of performance*—Professional Quality, Approaching Professional Quality, or Needs Quality Improvements—help you and your instructor evaluate your result.

	Your completed project is of Professional Quality if you:	Your completed project is Approaching Professional Quality if you:	Your completed project Needs Quality Improvements if you:
1-Software Mastery	Choose and apply the most appropriate skills, tools, and features and identify efficient methods to solve the problem.	Choose and apply some appropriate skills, tools, and features, but not in the most efficient manner.	Choose inappropriate skills, tools, or features, or are inefficient in solving the problem.
2-Content	Construct a solution that is clear and well organized, contains content that is accurate, appropriate to the audience and purpose, and is complete. Provide a solution that contains no errors in spelling, grammar, or style.	Construct a solution in which some components are unclear, poorly organized, inconsistent, or incomplete. Misjudge the needs of the audience. Have some errors in spelling, grammar, or style, but the errors do not detract from comprehension.	Construct a solution that is unclear, incomplete, or poorly organized; contains some inaccurate or inappropriate content; and contains many errors in spelling, grammar, or style. Do not solve the problem.
3-Format and Layout	Format and arrange all elements to communicate information and ideas, clarify function, illustrate relationships, and indicate relative importance.	Apply appropriate format and layout features to some elements, but not others. Overuse features, causing minor distraction.	Apply format and layout that does not communicate information or ideas clearly. Do not use format and layout features to clarify function, illustrate relationships, or indicate relative importance. Use available features excessively, causing distraction.
4-Process	Use an organized approach that integrates planning, development, self-assessment, revision, and reflection.	Demonstrate an organized approach in some areas, but not others; or, use an insufficient process of organization throughout.	Do not use an organized approach to solve the problem.

Outcomes-Based Assessments

Apply a combination of the 3A and 3B skills.

GO! Think | Project **3L** Jobs Newsletter

Project Files

For Project 3L, you will need the following file:

New blank Word document

You will save your document as:

Lastname_Firstname_3L_Jobs_Newsletter

The marketing manager of Memphis Primary Materials needs to create the next issue of the company's monthly newsletter (Volume 1, Number 7—July 2016), which will focus on "green jobs." Green jobs are jobs associated with environmentally friendly companies or are positions with firms that manufacture, sell, or install energy-saving or resource-saving products.

Use the following information to create a newsletter that includes a nameplate, multiple columns, at least two articles with article titles formatted so that they stand out, at least one clip art image, one screenshot, and one paragraph that includes a border and shading.

The articles you write can be on any topic regarding green jobs, and might include an introduction to the topic, information about a recent (or future) green job conference, and a discussion of green jobs in the United States. You will need to research this topic on the Web. A good place to start is www.epa.gov. You might also consider doing a Web search for the terms **green jobs** or **green jobs conference**

Add the file name to the footer. Add appropriate information to the Document Panel. Save the document as **Lastname_Firstname_3L_Jobs_Newsletter** and submit it as directed.

End You have completed Project 3L

Apply a combination of the 3A and 3B skills.

GO! Think | Project **3M** Construction Report

Project Files

For Project 3M, you will need the following file:

New blank Word document

You will save your document as:

Lastname_Firstname_3M_Construction_Report

As part of the ongoing research provided on environment topics by the staff of Memphis Primary Materials, the Marketing Director, Henry Miller, has asked a summer intern, James Bodine, to create a report on recycling and reuse in the construction and demolition of buildings.

Create a new file and save it as **Lastname_Firstname_3M_Construction_Report** Use the following information to create a report written in the MLA format. The report should include at least two footnotes, at least two citations, and should include a *Works Cited* page.

The report should contain an introduction, and then details about, for example, how much construction material can be salvaged from existing buildings, how these materials can be reused in future buildings, and how materials can be saved and recycled on new building projects. A good place to start is www.epa.gov, which has a number of articles on recycling and reuse of materials during construction and demolition. You might also consider doing a Web search for the terms **construction recycling** or **demolition recycling** or **construction and demolition**

Add the file name to the footer. Add appropriate information to the Document Panel and submit it as directed.

 End You have completed Project 3M

Outcomes-Based Assessments

Apply a combination of the 3B skills.

You and GO! | Project **3N** College Newsletter

Project Files

For Project 3N, you will need the following file:

New blank Word document

You will save your document as

Lastname_Firstname_3N_College_Newsletter

In this project, you will create a one-page newsletter. The newsletter should include at least one article describing your college and one article about an academic or athletic program at your college.

Be sure to include a nameplate, at least two articles, at least one clip art or screenshot image, and a bordered paragraph or paragraphs. Before you submit the newsletter, be sure to check it for grammar and spelling errors, and also be sure to format the newsletter in an attractive manner by using the skills you practiced in this chapter.

Save the file as **Lastname_Firstname_3N_College_Newsletter** Add the file name to the footer, and add your name, your course name and section number, and the keywords **newsletter** and **college** to the Document Panel. Save and submit your file as directed.

End **You have completed Project 3N** ——————————————————————

Business Running Case

This project relates to **Front Range Action Sports**, which is one of the country's largest retailers of sports gear and outdoor recreation merchandise. The company has large retail stores in Colorado, Washington, Oregon, California, and New Mexico, in addition to a growing online business. Major merchandise categories include fishing, camping, rock climbing, winter sports, action sports, water sports, team sports, racquet sports, fitness, golf, apparel, and footwear.

In this project, you will apply skills you practiced from the Objectives in Word Chapters 1-3. You will assist Irene Shviktar, the Vice President of Marketing, to edit and create documents for a National Sales Meeting that will precede a Winter Sports Expo sponsored by Front Range Action Sports. The first document is a cover letter from the vice president to the company president. The letter will accompany a packet of materials for the meeting and the expo, which includes a brief resume for the guest speaker, a flyer that will announce the expo, a newsletter for employees, a research paper on the history and development of skis, and a set of name tags for a group of employees attending the national sales meeting. Your completed documents will look similar to Figure 1.1.

Project Files

For Project BRC1, you will need the following files:

New blank Word document
wBRC1_Cover_Letter_Text
wBRC1_Newsletter
wBRC1_Career_Text
wBRC1_Ski_Research
wBRC1_Addresses
wBRC1_Flyer_Text
wBRC1_Downhill_Racing
wBRC1_Powder_Skiing

You will save your documents as:

Lastname_Firstname_BRC1_Cover_Letter
Lastname_Firstname_BRC1_Newsletter
Lastname_Firstname_BRC1_Resume
Lastname_Firstname_BRC1_Ski_Research
Lastname_Firstname_BRC1_Name_Tags
Lastname_Firstname_BRC1_Flyer

Project Results

Figure 1.1

Business Running Case

Front Range Action Sports

1 **Start** Word and display a new document. Display rulers and formatting marks. In the location where you are storing your projects, create a new folder named **Front Range Action Sports** or navigate to this folder if you have already created it. **Save** the new document as **Lastname_Firstname_BRC1_Cover_Letter** Add the file name to the footer. Apply the **No Spacing** style to the document, and then type the following to form a letterhead:

> **Front Range Action Sports**
>
> **1926 Quebec Street**
>
> **Denver, CO 80207**
>
> **(303) 555-0970**
>
> **www.frontrangeactionsports.com**

a. Press ⏎Enter to create a blank line below the letterhead. If the Web address changes to blue, right-click the address, and then from the shortcut menu, remove the hyperlink.

b. Select the letterhead text, but not the blank line. Change the **Font** to **Arial Rounded MT Bold**. Select the first line, and increase the **Font Size** to **28 pt** Change the **Font Size** of the remaining four lines to **12 pt**. Select all five lines of the letterhead, display the **Borders and Shading** dialog box, and then create a **6 pt**, **Black** border on the left side of the selected text.

c. Enter the following information using business letter format:

> **June 26, 2016**
>
> **Michael Dixon, President**
>
> **Front Range Action Sports**
>
> **12756 St. Aubin Drive**
>
> **Vail, CO 81658**

d. Press ⏎Enter two times. With the insertion point in the second blank line below the inside address, **Insert** the text from the file **wBRC1_Cover_Letter_Text**, and then remove the blank line at the bottom of the selected text.

e. Move to the top of the document, and then by using either the **Spelling and Grammar** dialog box, or by right-clicking selected words, correct the *three* spelling, grammar, and word usage errors. Ignore proper names. In the paragraph that begins *If you have any*, select the first sentence and move it to the end of the paragraph.

f. In the middle of the document, select the five paragraphs beginning with *A company newsletter*, and create a bulleted list. In the fourth bullet, select the text *national sales meeting*, and then on the **Home tab**, in the **Font group**, click the **Change Case** button ⟨Aa⟩, and then click **Capitalize Each Word**.

g. Display the **Document Panel**, add your name, course information, and the **Keywords expo, national sales meeting** View your document in **Print Preview**, make any necessary adjustments, **Save** and **Close** your document, and then hold this file until you complete the project.

2 From your student files, open **wBRC1_Newsletter**, and then **Save** it in your **Front Range Action Sports** folder as **Lastname_Firstname_BRC1_Newsletter** Add the file name to the footer.

a. Select the first paragraph of text—*Front Range Action Sports*. Change the **Font** to **Arial Rounded MT Bold**, the **Font Size** to **36**, and **Center** the text. Select the second paragraph of text, display the **Borders and Shading** dialog box, and then add a **Black**, **3 pt** line below the selected text.

b. Starting with the paragraph that begins *National Sales*, select all of the text from that point to the end of the document. Change the **Spacing After** to **6 pt**, format the text in two columns, and apply the **Justify** alignment.

c. At the top of the first column, select the paragraph *National Sales Meeting*. From the **Font** dialog box, change the **Font Size** to **20**, apply **Bold**, add the **Small caps** effect, and then **Center** the paragraph. Near the bottom of the same column, apply the same formatting to the paragraph *Winter Sports Expo*.

d. In the blank line above the last paragraph of the newsletter, **Insert** the picture **wBRC1_Powder_Skiing**. Set the **Width** of the picture to **3"**.

e. Display the **Document Panel**, and then add your name and course information and the **Keywords Expo newsletter** View your document in **Print Preview**, make any necessary adjustments, **Save** and **Close** your document, and then hold this file until you complete the project.

3 Display a new blank document and **Save** it in your **Front Range Action Sports** folder as **Lastname_Firstname_BRC1_Resume** Add the file name to the footer. **Insert** a **2 × 3** table.

(Business Running Case: Front Range Action Sports continues on the next page)

Business Running Case

Front Range Action Sports (continued)

a. In the first cell of the table, type on four lines:

Robert Lewis

1227 Aspen Lake Trail

Vail, CO 81657

www.boblewisskis.com

b. In the second row, in the first cell, type **CAREER HIGHLIGHTS** In the cell to the immediate right, **Insert** the text from the file **wBRC1_Career_Text**, and then press [Backspace] to remove the blank line at the bottom of the inserted text.

c. In the third row, in the first cell, type **EDUCATION** In the cell to the right, type Mr. Lewis' educational information as follows:

University of Colorado

Ph.D. in Psychology

University of Colorado

M.S. in Psychology

University of Minnesota

B.S. in Psychology

d. Insert a new row at the bottom of the table. In the first cell of the new row, type **CONSULTANT** and then in the cell to the right, type the following:

U.S. Junior Ski Team

U.S. National Ski Team

Special Olympics

e. Apply **Bold** to the headings *CAREER HIGHLIGHTS*, *EDUCATION*, and *CONSULTANT*. Drag the vertical border between the two columns to approximately **1.5 inches on the horizontal ruler**.

f. In the first row, **Merge** the two cells, and then **Center** the text. Select *Robert Lewis*, increase the font size to **24 pt**, apply **Bold**, and then add **12 pt** spacing **Before** the text. If necessary, remove the hyperlink from the Web address. Select the Web address and add **18 pt** spacing after the text.

g. Create a bulleted list for the items below *SKIING* and below *COACHING*. In the cells to the right of *EDUCATION* and *CONSULTANT*, add **12 pt** spacing **After** the last item in each cell. Add **12 pt** spacing **After** *Ph.D. in Psychology* and *M.S. in Psychology*. Apply **Bold** to the three paragraphs that begin *University*.

h. Select the table, and then remove all borders. From the **Borders and Shading** dialog box, add a **3 pt** border to the top and bottom of the table. Change the top

margin to **1.5"**. To the **Document Panel**, add your name, course information, and the **Keywords Robert Lewis resume** View your document in **Print Preview,** make any necessary adjustments, **Save** and then **Close** your document. Hold this file until you complete the project.

4 From your student files, open the document **wBRC1_Ski_Research**. **Save** the document in your **Front Range Action Sports** folder as **Lastname_Firstname_BRC1_Ski_Research** Display the header area, type **Johnson** and then press [Spacebar]. Display the **Page Number gallery**, and then in the **Current Position**, add the **Plain Number** style. Apply **Align Text Right** formatting to the header. Add the file name to the footer.

a. In the blank line at the beginning of the document, type **Walter Johnson** and then press [Enter]. Type **Irene Shviktar** and press [Enter]. Type **Marketing** and press [Enter]. Type **June 5, 2016**

b. Select all of the text in the document. Change the **Line Spacing** to **2.0**, and then change the **Spacing After** to **0 pt**. Click anywhere in the title that begins *The Evolution* and then **Center** the title.

c. Beginning with the paragraph that begins *The use of skis*, select the text from that point to the end of the document. Indent the first line of each selected paragraph to **0.5"**.

d. Near the top of **Page 1**, in the paragraph that begins *The use of skis*, in the third line, position the insertion point to the right of the period following *wood*, and then insert the following footnote:

The oldest known ski and pole is more than 4,000 years old, and is on display in the National Ski Hall of Fame and Museum in Ishpeming, Michigan.

e. Select the footnote text, change the **Font Size** to **11 pt**, add a **First Line Indent** of **0.5"**, and set **Line spacing** to **2.0"**.

f. In the paragraph that begins *The use of skis*, position the insertion point to the left of the period at the end of the paragraph. Using the **MLA** format, insert the following **Book** citation:

Author: **Huntford, Roland**

Title: **Two Planks and a Passion: The Dramatic History of Skiing**

Year: **2008**

City: **New York**

Publisher: **Continuum Press**

(Business Running Case: Front Range Action Sports continues on the next page)

Front Range Action Sports (continued)

g. In the text, select the *Huntford* citation and insert the page numbers **4-6** Position the insertion point to the left of the period at the end of the document. Add the following **Web site** citation:

Author:	**Lund, Morten; Masia, Seth**
Name of Web Page:	**A Short History of Skis**
Year Accessed:	**2016**
Month Accessed:	**May**
Day Accessed:	**25**
URL:	**www.skiinghistory.org**

h. At the end of the document, insert a manual page break to create a new page. Change the **First Line Indent** to **0"**. Add a **Works Cited** title, display the **Bibliography** gallery, and then at the bottom of the gallery, click **Insert Bibliography**. Select the two references, remove the space after the paragraphs, and change the line spacing to **2.0**. **Center** the *Works Cited* title.

i. Press Ctrl + A to move to the top of the document, and then on the **Review tab**, in the **Proofing group**, click **Spelling & Grammar**. Ignore proper names, change *polyethelene* to *polyethylene*, and correct the subject-verb agreement between *have* and *has* in the last paragraph. Display the **Document Panel** and add your name and course information and the **Keywords ski history, ski research** View your document in **Print Preview** and make any necessary adjustments. **Save** and **Close** your document, and hold this file until you complete the project.

5 Display a **New** blank document. Start the **Step by Step Mail Merge Wizard** and select **Labels** as the document type. In **Step 2**, set **Label options** to use the **Auto default** tray (yours may vary) and **Avery US Letter 74541 Clip Style Name Badges**. In **Step 3**, **Use an existing list**, browse to select **wBRC1_Addresses**, click **Open**, and then click **OK**. This is a Name Badge label, and the steps differ slightly from the steps for creating mailing labels.

a. In **Step 4**, on the Ribbon, in the **Write & Insert Fields group**, click the **Insert Merge Field button arrow**, click **First_Name** field, press Spacebar, and then repeat for the **Last_Name** field. Press Enter six times.

b. Type **Front Range Action Sports** and press Enter. Type **Employee** Select the first line of the label—

<<First_Name>> <<Last_Name>>. Change the **Font Size** to **24**, apply **Bold**, and then **Center** the text. Select the last two lines of text, change the **Font Size** to **18**, apply **Bold**, and then **Center** the text. In the **Mail Merge** task pane, click **Update all labels**, and then move to step 5—**Preview your labels**.

c. **Complete the merge**. On the **Mailings tab**, in the **Finish group**, click the **Finish & Merge** button, and then click **Edit Individual Documents**. Merge **All** of the records. **Save** the resulting document in your **Front Range Action Sports** folder as **Lastname_Firstname_BRC1_Name_Tags** and then if necessary, close the Mail Merge task pane. Add the file name to the footer. Preview the labels in **Print Preview** and make any necessary adjustments.

d. Display the **Document Panel**, and then add your name and course information and the **Keywords name tags, expo Save** and close your label document. **Close** the original document without saving. Hold this file until you complete the project.

6 From your student files, open **wBRC1_Flyer_Text**, and then **Save** it in your **Front Range Action Sports** folder as **Lastname_Firstname_BRC1_Flyer** Add the file name to the footer.

a. Select the title *Winter Sports Expo*, and apply a **Gradient Fill - Blue, Accent 1 Text Effect**—in the third row, the fourth effect. Increase the **Font Size** to **56** point, and then **Center** the title. Select the two paragraphs below the title that begin *Friday* and *Saturday*, and then change the **Spacing After** to **0**. Select the three paragraphs below the title—the three days and times—and then **Center** and apply **Bold**.

b. With the three paragraphs still selected, display the **Borders and Shading** dialog box. Apply a **Box** border using theme color **Blue, Accent 1** and a **3 pt** border, and add **Shading** using theme color **Blue, Accent 1, Lighter 80%**. Apply a **Page Border** using the **Box** setting, and the theme color **Blue, Accent 1** with a **Weight** of **6 pt**.

c. Format the seven sport topics—beginning with *Downhill skiing*—as a bulleted list, and then click anywhere to deselect the bulleted list. **Insert** the picture **wBRC1_Downhill_Racing**. Change the **Width** of the picture to **3.5"**, and then set **Wrap Text** to **Square**. Move the picture so that the right edge

(Business Running Case: Front Range Action Sports continues on the next page)

Business Running Case

Front Range Action Sports (continued)

aligns with the right margin, and the top edge aligns with the top edge of the text that begins *Workshops and how-to*. Apply a **Picture Effect** using the **Soft Edge** of **10 point**.

d. Move to the end of the document and press Enter two times. Display the **Choose a SmartArt Graphic** dialog box, select **Process**, and then choose the first style—**Basic Process**. Click the border of the SmartArt

Width of the SmartArt graphic to **6.5"** and the **Height** to **1"**; or, drag the SmartArt graphic sizing handles to change the width to **6.5"** and the height to **1"**.

In the three boxes, add the following text in this order: **Exhibits** and **Speakers** and **Workshops** On the **Design tab**, apply the **3-D Polished** style. Click anywhere outside of the SmartArt to deselect it. Display your document in **Print Preview** and make any necessary adjustments.

e. Display the **Document Panel** and add your name and course information and the **Keywords expo, flyer Save** and **Close** the document. Submit the six files that you created in this project—the cover letter, newsletter, resume, research paper, name tag labels, and flyer—as directed by your instructor. **Exit** Word.

End **You have completed Business Running Case 1** ——————————————

Glossary

Address bar The bar at the top of a folder window with which you can navigate to a different folder or library, or go back to a previous one.

Alignment The placement of paragraph text relative to the left and right margins.

All Programs An area of the Start menu that displays all the available programs on your computer system.

American Psychological Association (APA) One of two commonly used style guides for formatting research papers.

Anchor The symbol that indicates to which paragraph an object is attached.

Application Another term for a program.

Artistic effects Formats applied to images that make pictures resemble sketches or paintings.

AutoCorrect A feature that corrects common spelling errors as you type, for example, changing *teh* to *the*.

AutoPlay A Windows feature that displays when you insert a CD, a DVD, or other removable device, and which lets you choose which program to use to start different kinds of media, such as music CDs, or CDs and DVDs containing photos.

Back and Forward buttons Buttons at the top of a folder window that work in conjunction with the address bar to change folders by going backward or forward one folder at a time.

Backstage tabs The area along the left side of Backstage view with tabs to display various pages of commands.

Backstage view A centralized space for file management tasks; for example, opening, saving, printing, publishing, or sharing a file. A navigation pane displays along the left side with tabs that group file-related tasks together.

Bar tab stop A vertical bar that displays at a tab stop.

Bibliography A list of cited works in a report or research paper also referred to as *Works Cited*, *Sources*, or *References*, depending upon the report style.

Body The text of a letter.

Bulleted list A list of items with each item introduced by a symbol such as a small circle or check mark, and which is useful when the items in the list can be displayed in any order.

Bullets Text symbols such as small circles or check marks that precede each item in a bulleted list.

Cell The intersection of a column and a row.

Center alignment An arrangement of text in which the text is centered between the left and right margins.

Center alignment The alignment of text or objects that is centered horizontally between the left and right margin.

Center tab stop A tab stop in which the text centers around the tab stop location.

Citation A note inserted into the text of a research paper that refers the reader to a source in the bibliography.

Click The action of pressing the left button on your mouse pointing device one time.

Clip art Predefined graphics included with Microsoft Office or downloaded from the Web.

Column break indicator A single dotted line with the text *Column Break* that indicates where a manual column break was inserted.

Command An instruction to a computer program that causes an action to be carried out.

Common dialog boxes The set of dialog boxes that includes Open, Save, and Save As, which are provided by the Windows programming interface, and which display and operate in all of the Office programs in the same manner.

Complimentary closing A parting farewell in a business letter.

Compressed file A file that has been reduced in size and thus takes up less storage space and can be transferred to other computers quickly.

Content control In a template, an area indicated by placeholder text that can be used to add text, pictures, dates, or lists.

Context sensitive command A command associated with activities in which you are engaged.

Contextual tabs Tabs that are added to the Ribbon automatically when a specific object, such as a picture, is selected, and that contain commands relevant to the selected object.

Copy A command that duplicates a selection and places it on the Clipboard.

Cut A command that removes a selection and places it on the Clipboard.

Data source (Word) A list of variable information, such as names and addresses, that is merged with a main document to create customized form letters or labels.

Date line The first line in a business letter that contains the current date and that is positioned just below the letterhead if a letterhead is used.

Decimal tab stop A tab stop in which the text aligns with the decimal point at the tab stop location.

Default The term that refers to the current selection or setting that is automatically used by a computer program unless you specify otherwise.

Deselect The action of canceling the selection of an object or block of text by clicking outside of the selection.

Desktop In Windows, the opening screen that simulates your work area.

Details pane The area at the bottom of a folder window that displays the most common file properties.

Dialog box A small window that contains options for completing a task.

Dialog Box Launcher A small icon that displays to the right of some group names on the Ribbon, and which opens a related dialog box or task pane providing additional options and commands related to that group.

Document properties Details about a file that describe or identify it, including the title, author name, subject, and keywords that identify the document's topic or contents; also known as *metadata*.

Dot leader A series of dots preceding a tab that guides the eye across the line.

Double-click The action of clicking the left mouse button two times in rapid succession.

Drag The action of holding down the left mouse button while moving your mouse.

Drag and drop The action of moving a selection by dragging it to a new location.

Drawing objects Graphic objects, such as shapes, diagrams, lines, or circles.

Edit The actions of making changes to text or graphics in an Office file.

Ellipsis A set of three dots indicating incompleteness; when following a command name, indicates that a dialog box will display.

Enclosures Additional documents included with a business letter.

Endnote In a research paper, a note placed at the end of a document or chapter.

Enhanced ScreenTip A ScreenTip that displays more descriptive text than a normal ScreenTip.

Extract To decompress, or pull out, files from a compressed form.

Field (Word) A placeholder that displays preset content, such as the current date, the file name, a page number, or other stored information.

Fields In a mail merge, the column headings in the data source.

File A collection of information stored on a computer under a single name, for example a Word document or a PowerPoint presentation.

File list In a folder window, the area on the right that displays the contents of the current folder or library.

Fill The inside color of an object.

Floating object A graphic that can be moved independently of the surrounding text characters.

Folder A container in which you store files.

Folder window In Windows, a window that displays the contents of the current folder, library, or device, and contains helpful parts so that you can navigate.

Font A set of characters with the same design and shape.

Font styles Formatting emphasis such as bold, italic, and underline.

Footer A reserved area for text or graphics that displays at the bottom of each page in a document.

Footnote In a research paper, a note placed at the bottom of the page.

Format Painter An Office feature that copies formatting from one selection of text to another.

Formatting The process of establishing the overall appearance of text, graphics, and pages in an Office file—for example, in a Word document.

Formatting marks Characters that display on the screen, but do not print, indicating where the Enter key, the Spacebar, and the Tab key were pressed; also called *nonprinting characters*.

Gallery An Office feature that displays a list of potential results instead of just the command name.

Graphics Pictures, clip art images, charts, or drawing objects.

Groups On the Office Ribbon, the sets of related commands that you might need for a specific type of task.

Hanging indent An indent style in which the first line of a paragraph extends to the left of the remaining lines, and that is commonly used for bibliographic entries.

Header A reserved area for text or graphics that displays at the top of each page in a document.

HTML See Hypertext Markup Language (HTML).

Hypertext Markup Language (HTML) The language used to format documents that can be opened using any Web browser.

Icons Pictures that represent a program, a file, a folder, or some other object.

Info tab The tab in Backstage view that displays information about the current file.

Inline object An object or graphic inserted in a document that acts like a character in a sentence.

Insertion point A blinking vertical line that indicates where text or graphics will be inserted.

Inside address The name and address of the person receiving the letter; positioned below the date line.

Justified alignment An arrangement of text in which the text aligns evenly on both the left and right margins.

Keyboard shortcut A combination of two or more keyboard keys, used to perform a task that would otherwise require a mouse.

KeyTips The letter that displays on a command in the Ribbon and that indicates the key you can press to activate the command when keyboard control of the Ribbon is activated.

Label control A control on a form or report that contains descriptive information, typically a field name.

Landscape orientation A page orientation in which the paper is wider than it is tall.

Leader characters Characters that form a solid, dotted, or dashed line that fills the space preceding a tab stop.

Left alignment An arrangement of text in which the text aligns at the left margin, leaving the right margin uneven.

Left tab stop A tab stop in which the text is left aligned at the tab stop and extends to the right.

Letterhead The personal or company information that displays at the top of a letter.

Library In Windows, a collection of items, such as files and folders, assembled from various locations that might be on your computer, an external hard drive, removable media, or someone else's computer.

Line break indicator A small nonprinting bent arrow that displays where a manual line break was inserted.

Line spacing The distance between lines of text in a paragraph.

Live Preview A technology that shows the result of applying an editing or formatting change as you point to possible results—*before* you actually apply it.

Location Any disk drive, folder, or other place in which you can store files and folders.

Mail merge A Microsoft Word feature that joins a main document and a data source to create customized letters or labels.

Main document In a mail merge, the document that contains the text or formatting that remains constant.

Manual column break An artificial end to a column to balance columns or to provide space for the insertion of other objects.

Manual line break The action of ending a line, before the normal end of the line, without creating a new paragraph.

Manual page break The action of forcing a page to end and placing subsequent text at the top of the next page.

Margins The space between the text and the top, bottom, left, and right edges of the paper.

Metadata Details about a file that describe or identify it, including the title, author name, subject, and keywords that identify the document's topic or contents; also known as *document properties*.

Microsoft Access A database program, with which you can collect, track, and report data.

Microsoft Communicator An Office program that brings together multiple modes of communication, including instant messaging, video conferencing, telephony, application sharing, and file transfer.

Microsoft Excel A spreadsheet program, with which you calculate and analyze numbers and create charts.

Microsoft InfoPath An Office program that enables you to create forms and gather data.

Microsoft Office 2010 A Microsoft suite of products that includes programs, servers, and services for individuals, small organizations, and large enterprises to perform specific tasks.

Microsoft OneNote An Office program with which you can manage notes that you make at meetings or in classes.

Microsoft Outlook An Office program with which you can manage e-mail and organizational activities.

Microsoft PowerPoint A presentation program, with which you can communicate information with high-impact graphics.

Microsoft Publisher An Office program with which you can create desktop publishing documents such as brochures.

Microsoft SharePoint Workspace An Office program that enables you to share information with others in a team environment.

Microsoft Word A word processing program, also referred to as an authoring program, with which you create and share documents by using its writing tools.

Mini toolbar A small toolbar containing frequently used formatting commands that displays as a result of selecting text or objects.

Modern Language Association (MLA) One of two commonly used style guides for formatting research papers.

Nameplate The banner on the front page of a newsletter that identifies the publication; also referred to as a *banner*, *flag*, or *masthead*.

Navigate (Excel) The process of moving within a worksheet or workbook.

Navigation pane (Windows) In a folder window, the area on the left in which you can navigate to, open, and display favorites, libraries, folders, saved searches, and an expandable list of drives.

New from existing The Word command that opens an existing document as a new unnamed document, so that you can use it as a starting point for a new document.

No Spacing style The Word style that inserts *no* extra space following a paragraph and uses single spacing.

Nonprinting characters Characters that display on the screen, but do not print, indicating where the Enter key, the Spacebar, and the Tab key were pressed; also called *formatting marks*.

Normal template The template that serves as a basis for all new Word documents.

Note In a research paper, information that expands on the topic, but that does not fit well in the document text.

Nudge The action of moving an object on the page in small precise increments.

Numbered list A list of items in which each item is introduced by a consecutive number to indicate definite steps, a sequence of actions, or chronological order.

Office Clipboard A temporary storage area that holds text or graphics that you select and then cut or copy.

Open dialog box A dialog box from which you can navigate to, and then open on your screen, an existing file that was created in that same program.

Option button A round button that allows you to make one choice among two or more options.

Options dialog box A dialog box within each Office application where you can select program settings and other options and preferences.

Page break indicator A dotted line with the text *Page Break* that indicates where a manual page break was inserted.

Paragraph symbol The symbol ¶ that represents a paragraph.

Parenthetical citation In the MLA style, a citation that refers to items on the *Works Cited* page, and which is placed in parentheses; the citation includes the last name of the author or authors, and the page number in the referenced source.

Paste The action of placing text or objects that have been copied or moved from one location to another location.

Paste Options Icons that provide a Live Preview of the various options for changing the format of a pasted item with a single click.

PDF (Portable Document Format) file A file format that creates an image that preserves the look of your file, but that cannot be easily changed; a popular format for sending documents electronically, because the document will display on most computers.

Picture styles Frames, shapes, shadows, borders, and other special effects that can be added to an image to create an overall visual style for the image.

Placeholder text Text in a content control that indicates the type of information to be entered in a specific location.

Point The action of moving your mouse pointer over something on your screen.

Pointer Any symbol that displays on your screen in response to moving your mouse.

Points A measurement of the size of a font; there are 72 points in an inch, with 10-12 points being the most commonly used font size.

Portrait orientation A page orientation in which the paper is taller than it is wide.

Preview pane button In a folder window, the button on the toolbar with which you can display a preview of the contents of a file without opening it in a program.

Print Preview A view of a document as it will appear when you print it.

Program A set of instructions that a computer uses to perform a specific task, such as word processing, accounting, or data management; also called an *application*.

Program-level control buttons In an Office program, the buttons on the right edge of the title bar that minimize, restore, or close the program.

Protected view A security feature in Office 2010 that protects your computer from malicious files by opening them in a restricted environment until you enable them; you might encounter this feature if you open a file from an e-mail or download files from the Internet.

Pt. The abbreviation for *point*; for example when referring to a font size.

Quick Access Toolbar In an Office program, the small row of buttons in the upper left corner of the screen from which you can perform frequently used commands.

Quick Commands The commands Save, Save As, Open, and Close that display at the top of the navigation pane in Backstage view.

Read-Only A property assigned to a file that prevents the file from being modified or deleted; it indicates that you cannot save any changes to the displayed document unless you first save it with a new name.

Record All of the categories of data pertaining to one person, place, thing, event, or idea, and which is formatted as a row in a database table.

Ribbon The user interface in Office 2010 that groups the commands for performing related tasks on tabs across the upper portion of the program window.

Ribbon tabs The tabs on the Office Ribbon that display the names of the task-oriented groups of commands.

Right alignment An arrangement of text in which the text aligns at the right margin, leaving the left margin uneven.

Right tab stop A tab stop in which the text is right aligned at the tab stop and extends to the left.

Right-click The action of clicking the right mouse button one time.

Salutation The greeting line of a business letter.

Sans serif A font design with no lines or extensions on the ends of characters.

Screenshot An image of an active window on your computer that you can paste into a document.

ScreenTip A small box that that displays useful information when you perform various mouse actions such as pointing to screen elements or dragging.

Scroll bar A vertical or horizontal bar in a window or a pane to assist in bringing an area into view, and which contains a scroll box and scroll arrows.

Scroll box The box in the vertical and horizontal scroll bars that can be dragged to reposition the contents of a window or pane on the screen.

Search box In a folder window, the box in which you can type a word or a phrase to look for an item in the current folder or library.

Section A portion of a document that can be formatted differently from the rest of the document.

Section break A double dotted line that indicates the end of one section and the beginning of another section.

Select To highlight, by dragging with your mouse, areas of text or data or graphics, so that the selection can be edited, formatted, copied, or moved.

Serif font A font design that includes small line extensions on the ends of the letters to guide the eye in reading from left to right.

Shapes Lines, arrows, stars, banners, ovals, rectangles, and other basic shapes with which you can illustrate an idea, a process, or a workflow.

Shortcut menu A menu that displays commands and options relevant to the selected text or object.

Single File Web Page A document saved using HTML and that opens using a Web browser.

Small caps A font effect, usually used in titles, that changes lowercase text into capital (uppercase) letters using a reduced font size.

SmartArt A designer-quality visual representation of your information that you can create by choosing from among many different layouts to effectively communicate your message or ideas.

Spin box A small box with an upward- and downward-pointing arrow that lets you move rapidly through a set of values by clicking.

Split button A button divided into two parts and in which clicking the main part of the button performs a command and clicking the arrow opens a menu with choices.

Start button The button on the Windows taskbar that displays the Start menu.

Start menu The Windows menu that provides a list of choices and is the main gateway to your computer's programs, folders, and settings.

Status bar The area along the lower edge of an Office program window that displays file information on the left and buttons to control how the window looks on the right.

Style A group of formatting commands, such as font, font size, font color, paragraph alignment, and line spacing that can be applied to a paragraph with one command.

Style guide A manual that contains standards for the design and writing of documents.

Subfolder A folder within a folder.

Subject line The optional line following the inside address in a business letter that states the purpose of the letter.

Subpoints Secondary-level information in a SmartArt graphic.

Synonyms Words with the same or similar meaning.

Tab stop Specific locations on a line of text, marked on the Word ruler, to which you can move the insertion point by pressing the Tab key, and which is used to align and indent text.

Table (Word) An arrangement of information organized into rows and columns.

Tabs On the Office Ribbon, the name of each activity area in the Office Ribbon.

Tags Custom file properties that you create to help find and organize your own files.

Task pane A window within a Microsoft Office application in which you can enter options for completing a command.

Template An existing document that you use as a starting point for a new document; it opens a copy of itself, unnamed, and then you use the structure—and possibly some content, such as headings—as the starting point for the new document.

Text box A movable resizable container for text or graphics.

Text control A content control that accepts only a text entry.

Text effects Decorative formats, such as shadowed or mirrored text, text glow, 3-D effects, and colors that make text stand out.

Text wrapping The manner in which text displays around an object.

Theme A predesigned set of colors, fonts, lines, and fill effects that look good together and that can be applied to your entire document or to specific items.

Thesaurus A research tool that provides a list of synonyms.

Title bar The bar at the top edge of the program window that indicates the name of the current file and the program name.

Toggle button A button that can be turned on by clicking it once, and then turned off by clicking it again.

Toolbar In a folder window, a row of buttons with which you can perform common tasks, such as changing the view of your files and folders or burning files to a CD.

Top-level points The main text points in a SmartArt graphic.

Triple-click The action of clicking the left mouse button three times in rapid succession.

Trusted Documents A security feature in Office 2010 that remembers which files you have already enabled; you might encounter this feature if you open a file from an e-mail or download files from the Internet.

USB flash drive A small data storage device that plugs into a computer USB port.

Views button In a folder window, a toolbar button with which you can choose how to view the contents of the current location.

Window A rectangular area on a computer screen in which programs and content appear, and which can be moved, resized, minimized, or closed.

Windows Explorer The program that displays the files and folders on your computer, and which is at work anytime you are viewing the contents of files and folders in a window.

Windows taskbar The area along the lower edge of the Windows desktop that contains the Start button and an area to display buttons for open programs.

Wordwrap The feature that moves text from the right edge of a paragraph to the beginning of the next line as necessary to fit within the margins.

Works Cited In the MLA style, a list of cited works placed at the end of a research paper or report.

Writer's identification The name and title of the author of a letter, placed near the bottom of the letter under the complimentary closing—also referred to as the *writer's signature block*.

Writer's signature block The name and title of the author of a letter, placed near the bottom of the letter, under the complimentary closing—also referred to as the *writer's identification*.

Zoom The action of increasing or decreasing the viewing area on the screen.

Index

A

Access 2010, 7
Address bar, 5
addresses
 labels, 191, 195
 mail merges, 190
alignment, 34, 68–69
 pictures, 56–57
 tab alignment options, 78
All Programs menu, 7
anchors, 56
applications
 definition, 6
 viewing options, 25–26
Apply to box, 188
artistic effects (pictures), 57
assessments
 content-based assessments, 84–101, 140–159, 196–215
 outcomes-based assessments, 102–104, 160–162, 216–218
AutoCorrect, recording entries, 123–124
AutoCorrect Options button, 75
automatic numbered lists, activating, 75
AutoPlay, definition, 3
Avery 5160 address label, 191

B

Back button, 5
Backstage tabs, 14
Backstage view, 14, 64
Bar tab alignment option, 78
bibliographies
 definition, 172
 page breaks, 175–176
block style cover letters, 124–126
body (cover letters), 123
borders
 adding, 57–58
 adding to paragraphs, 188–189
 tables, 116–118
 text, 188
Borders and Shading dialog box, 188
bulleted lists
 creating, 73–74
 customizing bullets, 77
 definition, 73
 spacing between bulleted points, 74
 tables, creating, 110–111
bullets
 customizing documents, 77
 definition, 73
 SmartArt, 83
 subpoints, 81
Business Communication texts, creating cover letters, 124–126
business letters
 creating letterheads, 120–121
 recording AutoCorrect entries, 123–124
Business Running Cases, 219–223
buttons. *See* individual names of buttons
By Series option (chart animation sequence), 775

C

cells (tables), merging, 113–114
center alignment, 34, 68–69
Center tab alignment option, 78
citations
 adding to research papers, 172–175
 corporate authors, 173
 definition, 172
 Web sites, 174
clip art. *See also* graphics; pictures, 184–185
Clipboard group, commands, 39
closing programs, 13–18
column break indicators, 184
column breaks
 inserting into newsletters, 183–184
 manual column breaks, 181
columns
 newsletters
 changing text into two columns, 181–182
 inserting breaks, 183–184
 justifying text, 183
 multiple columns, 182–183
 tables, changing width, 111–112
commands
 Clipboard group, 39
 context-sensitive, 11
 Copy, 39
 Cut, 39–40
 definition, 5, 26
 KeyTips, 31–32
 Mini toolbar, 36
 New from existing, 121–122
 Paste, 39
 performing from dialog boxes, 11–13
 performing from Ribbon, 26–31
 Quick, 14
 Quick Access Toolbar, 27
 Save, 15
 Spelling and Grammar, 131
complimentary closings (cover letters), 123
compressed files, 44–45
 definition, 44
 extracting, 45
content-based assessments, 84–101, 140–159, 196–215
context-sensitive commands, 11
contextual tabs, 30
control buttons, 8
Copy command, 39
copying, 38
corner sizing handles, 54
corporate authors, citations, 173
cover letters
 creating, 124–126
 creating letterheads, 120–121

cover letters (*Continued*)
    finding/replacing text, 126–128
    recording AutoCorrect entries, 123–124
customizing. *See also* **formatting**
    bullets, 77
Cut command, 39–40
cutting, 38

D

data sources, definition, 189
date lines
    definition, 123
    position, 124
Decimal tab alignment option, 78
defaults, 9, 51
deselecting, definition, 29
Design tab, Table Tools, 107
desktop, definition, 3
Details pane, 5
Dialog Box Launcher, 39
dialog boxes
    Borders and Shading, 188
    definition, 11
    Find and Replace, 127
    Font, 187
    More Commands, 28
    Object, displaying, 52
    Options, 25
    performing commands, 11–13
    Save As, 15
    Source Manager, 175
    Spelling and Grammar, 131
    Style, 170
displaying Object dialog box, 52
documents
    borders, 57–58
    bulleted lists
        creating, 73–74
        customizing bullets, 77
        definition, 73
        spacing between bulleted points, 74
    citations, 172–175
        corporate authors, 173
        Web sites, 174
    clip art, 184–185
    columns
        changing text to two columns, 181–182
        inserting breaks, 183–184
        justifying text, 183
    cover letters
        creating, 124–126
        finding/replacing text, 126–128
        letterheads, 120–121
        recording AutoCorrect entries, 123–124
    creating, 51–53
        from existing documents, 121–123
        from templates, 134–139
    default settings, 51
    fonts, 51, 186–187
    footers
        adding file names to, 62–64
        fields, 62
        file names, 167
    footnotes, 167–172
    formatting, multiple columns, 182–183

hanging indents, 177
headings, 166
letterheads, creating, 120–121
line spacing, 70–71
lines, 51
mail merges, 189–194
    previewing, 194–195
    printing, 194–195
main, definition, 189
margins, 51, 67–68
nameplates, 182
navigating with keyboard shortcuts, 38
numbered lists
    creating, 74–76
    definition, 73
page breaks, 175–176
page numbers
    formatting, 165–167
    suppressing, 167
paragraphs
    adding shading, 188–189
    adding spacing after, 71–73
    alignment, 68–69
    anchors, 56
    borders, 188–189
    line break indicators, 187
    No Spacing style, 120
    spacing, 51, 169
pictures
    artistic effects, 57
    inserting, 54–55
    moving, 56–57
    sizing, 54–55
    sizing handles, 54
    styles, 57
    wrapping text around, 55–56
previewing, 62–65
printing, 41–43, 62–65
proofreading, 130–134
    grammar errors, 131–133
    spelling errors, 131–133
    Thesaurus, 133–134
properties, 14
    adding, 18–20
    management, 177–179
reference pages, creating, 176–177
screenshots, 186
section breaks, 182
sections, 182
sentence spacing, 51
shapes
    formatting, 60–62
    inserting, 58–59
    moving, 60–62
    sizing, 60–62
SmartArt
    bullets, 83
    definition, 80
    inserting, 80–81
    modifying, 81–83
statistics, 178
tab stops
    dot leaders, 80
    leader characters, 80
    modifying, 79–80
    setting, 78–79

tables
    adding rows, 112–113
    adding text, 108–110
    borders, 116–118
    changing column widths, 111–112
    creating, 107
    creating bulleted lists, 110–111
    fields, 191
    formatting, 111–118, 130
    formatting text, 114–116
    inserting, 130
    merging cells, 113–114
    records, 191
text
    alignment, 68–69
    borders, 188
    finding, 126–128
    formatting, 53–54, 165–167
    indenting, 71–73, 167
    inserting, 51–53
    line spacing, 70–71
    moving, 128–129
    replacing, 126–128
    replacing placeholder text, 135–137
    selecting, 128–129
    wordwrap, 51
text boxes
    formatting, 60–62
    inserting, 58–59
    moving, 60–62
    sizing, 60–62
docx extension, 123
dot leaders, 80
dotx extension, 123
double spacing, 70–71
double-clicking
    definition, 5
    Format Painter, 37
drag and dropping
    moving text, 128–129
    selecting text, 128–129
dragging, 10
drawing objects, 53

E

editing text, 9–11
effects
    artistic effects, 57
    text effects, 53–54
ellipses, definition, 11
enabling
    content, 24
    toggle buttons, 36
endnotes, definition, 167
enhanced ScreenTips, 28
Excel 2010, 7
extracting compressed files, 45

F

field list, definition, 487
fields
    footers, 62
    tables, 191
File list, 5

File name box, 17
File tab, 8
files
    compressing, 44–45
    definition, 3
    extracting compressed files, 45
    finding, 3–6
    management, Backstage view, 14
    names, adding to footers, 62–64, 167
    opening, 22–25
    printing, 18–20
    properties, Read-Only, 23
    saving, 13–18
        with new names, 22–25
        as templates, 123
    storing, 14
fills, 12
Find and Replace dialog box, 127
finding
    files, 3–6
    folders, 3–6
    templates, 134–135
    text, 126–128
First Line Indent tab alignment option, 78
flash drives, USB, 6
floating objects, 55
folder window, 4–5
Folder window toolbar, 5
folders
    creating, 13–18
    definition, 3
    finding, 3–6
Font Color button, 36
Font dialog box, 187
font size setting, 51
fonts, 35, 51
    font styles, 36
    points (pt), 35
    sans serif, 35
    serif, 35
    small caps, 186–187
    styles, 36
footers, 33
    adding file names to, 62–64
    fields, 62
    file names, 167
footnotes
    definition, 167
    research papers, 167–169
        modifying, 169–172
Format Painter, 37
formatting, 32–34
    documents, multiple columns, 182–183
    page numbers, 165–167
    resumes, 138–139
    shapes, 60–62
    tables, 111–118, 130
    text, 34–38, 53–54
        Format Painter, 37
        research papers, 165–167
    text boxes, 60–62
    text in tables, 114–116
formatting marks
    definition, 25, 51
    Show/Hide button, 27
Forward button, 5

G

galleries
    definition, 12
    Paste Options, 40
grammar errors, proofreading documents, 131–133
grammar rules, 130–134
graphics. *See also* clip art; pictures, 53
    size, 55
    SmartArt
        bullets, 83
        definition, 80
        inserting into documents, 80–81
        modifying, 81–83
    spin boxes, 55
groups
    Clipboard, commands, 39
    definition, 26
    Dialog Box Launcher, 39
    names, 8
    size, 30

H

Hanging Indent tab alignment option, 78
hanging indents, 177
headers, 33
headings, research papers, 166
Help, 43–44
HTML (Hypertext Markup Language), 139

I

icons, definition, 5
indentation
    hanging indents, 177
    page breaks, 176
    text, 71–73, 167
Info tab, 14
InfoPath, 7
inline objects, 54
inserting
    clip art into newsletters, 184–185
    column breaks into newsletters, 183–184
    file names into footers, 62–64
    footnotes into research papers, 167–169
    page breaks into documents, 175–176
    pictures into documents, 54–55
    rows into tables (Word), 112–113
    screenshots into newsletters, 186
    shapes into documents, 58–59
    SmartArt graphics into documents, 80–81
    tables into documents, 130
    text, 9–11
        into documents, 51–53
        into tables, 108–110
    text boxes into documents, 58–59
insertion point, 9
inside addresses
    definition, 123
    spacing, 124

J

justification (text alignment), 68
justification (text alignment) in newsletters, 183

K

keyboard keys
    controlling Ribbon, 31–32
    nudging, 57
keyboard shortcuts, 10, 38
KeyTips, 31–32

L

labels, mail merges, 191, 195
landscape orientation, 33
Layout tab, Table Tools, 107
leader characters, 80
left alignment, 68
Left Indent tab alignment option, 78
Left tab alignment option, 78
letterheads, creating, 120–121
libraries, definition, 4
line break indicators, 187
line spacing, 51, 70–71, 120
lists. *See* bulleted lists; numbered lists
Live Preview
    definition, 31
    Paste Options gallery, 40
locations, 13

M

Mail Merge Wizard, 192–194
    opening, 189–192
mail merges (documents), 189–192
    labels, 191, 195
main document, definition, 189
manual column breaks, 181
manual line breaks, 187
manual page breaks, 175–176
    definition, 176
    indentation, 176
margins, 51, 67–68
    alignment, 34
    center alignment, 34
    rulers, 27
Match case check box, 128
menus
    shortcut menus, 11
    Start, All Programs, 7
merging table cells, 113–114
metadata, 14
Microsoft InfoPath, 7
Microsoft Office 2010, 6
    Help, 43–44
    starting programs, 6–8
Microsoft Office Access 2010, 7
Microsoft Office Clipboard, 38–41
Microsoft Office Excel 2010, 7
Microsoft Office Outlook 2010, 7
Microsoft Office PowerPoint 2010, 7
Microsoft Office Word 2010, 7
    Business Running Cases, 219–223
    content-based assessments, 84–101, 140–159, 196–215
    outcomes-based assessments, 102–104, 160–162, 216–218
Microsoft OneNote, 7
Microsoft Publisher 2010, 7
Microsoft SharePoint Workspace, 7

Mini toolbar, 10, 36
minimizing Ribbon, 31–32
misspelled words, recording AutoCorrect entries, 123–124
MLA style
    citations, 172–175
    footnotes, 169–172
    formatting page numbers, 165–167
    formatting text, 165–167
    indenting text, 167
    parenthetical references, 174
    reference pages, 176–177
More Commands dialog box, 28
mouse pointer, 9
moving
    in documents, keyboard shortcuts, 38
    pictures in documents, 56–57
    shapes, 60–62
    text, 128–129
    text boxes, 60–62
multiple 1.5 spacing, 70–71
multiple columns, newsletters, 181–182, 182–183

N

nameplates (newsletters), 182
names
    groups, 8
    saving files, 22–25
navigation
    definition, 3
    documents, keyboard shortcuts, 38
Navigation pane, 5
New from existing command, 121–122
newsletters
    clip art, 184–185
    columns
        changing text to two columns, 181–182
        inserting breaks, 183–184
        justifying text, 183
    columns, inserting breaks, 183–184
    formatting multiple columns, 182–183
    nameplates, 182
    paragraphs
        adding shading, 188–189
        borders, 188–189
    screenshots, 186
    section breaks, 182
    sections, 182
    small caps, 186–187
No Spacing style, 120
nonprinting characters, definition, 25, 51
Normal template, 120
notes
    definition, 167
    symbols, 169
nudging, 57
numbered lists
    automatic, activating, 75
    creating, 74–76
    definition, 73

O

Object button arrow, 52
Object dialog box, displaying, 52

objects
    drawing, 53
    floating, 55
    inline, 54
Office Clipboard, 38–41
OneNote, 7
opening
    files, 22–25
    Mail Merge Wizard, 189–192
    templates, 134–135
option buttons, 12
Options dialog box, 25
outcomes-based assessments, 102–104, 140–159, 216–218
Outlook 2010, 7

P

page breaks, 175–176
    indentation, 176
    indicators, definition, 176
page numbers
    formatting, 165–167
    notes, 169
    suppressing, 167
paragraph symbol, 28
paragraphs
    adding shading, 188–189
    adding spacing after, 71–73
    alignment, 34, 68–69
    anchors, 56
    borders, 188–189
    indenting text, 167
    line break indicators, 187
    line spacing, 70–71
    No Spacing style, 120
    spacing, 51, 169
parenthetical references, 172, 174
Paste button, 40
Paste button arrow, 40
Paste command, 39
Paste Options gallery, 40
pasting, 38
performing
    commands from dialog boxes, 11–13
    commands from Ribbon, 26–31
pictures. *See also* clip art; graphics
    artistic effects, 57
    inserting, 54–55
    moving, 56–57
    sizing, 54–55
    sizing handles, 54
    styles, 57
    wrapping text around, 55–56
placeholder text
    definition, 136
    templates, replacing, 135–137
pointer (mouse), 9
points (pt), 35
portrait orientation, 33
PowerPoint 2010, 7
PowerPoint Slide pane, 8
Preview pane button, 5
previewing
    documents, 62–65
    mail merge documents, 194–195

Print Preview, 41–43
    previewing documents, 62–65
Print tab (Backstage view), 64
printing
    documents, 41–43, 62–65
    files, 18–20
    mail merge documents, 194–195
programs
    closing, 13–18
    control buttons, 8
    definition, 6
    starting, 6–8
proofreading documents, 130–134
    grammar errors, 131–133
    spelling errors, 131–133
    Thesaurus, 133–134
properties, 14
    management, 177–179
    Read-Only, 23
Protected View, 24
Publisher, 7
punctuation, 130–134

Q

Quick Access Toolbar, 8, 27
Quick commands, 14

R

Read-Only property, 23
recording AutoCorrect entries, 123–124
records (tables), 191
reference pages, creating, 176–177
removing template controls, 138–139
replacing text, 126–128
reports, footnotes, 167–169
research papers
    citations, 172–175
        corporate authors, 173
        Web sites, 174
    creating
        formatting page numbers, 165–167
        formatting text, 165–167
    footnotes, 167–169
        modifying, 169–172
    headings, 166
    page breaks, 175–176
    reference pages, creating, 176–177
Reset Slide Background feature, 747
resumes
    adding text to tables, 108–110
    changing column widths, 111–112
    creating
        removing template controls, 138–139
        replacing placeholder text, 135–137
        templates, 134–135
    creating bulleted lists in tables, 110–111
    creating tables, 107
    formatting, 138–139
    formatting text in table cells, 114–116
    merging table cells, 113–114
    saving as Web pages, 139
    table borders, 116–118

Ribbon, 8
    controlling with keyboard, 31–32
    definition, 26
    groups. See groups
    minimizing, 31–32
    performing commands from, 26–31
    tabs, 8
right alignment, 68
Right tab alignment option, 78
right-clicking, definition, 11
rotate handles, 54
rows, adding to tables, 112–113
rulers, 27

S

salutations (cover letters), definition, 123, 125
sans serif font, 35
Save As dialog box, 15
Save command, 15
saving
    files, 13–18
        with new names, 22–25
        as templates, 123
    resumes as Web pages, 139
screenshots, newsletters, 186
ScreenTips
    definition, 12
    enhanced, 28
scroll bars, 16
scroll box, 16
Search box, 5
    finding/replacing text in documents, 127
section breaks, 182
sections, newsletters, 182
security
    Protected View, 24
    Trusted Documents, 24
selecting
    definition, 10
    text, 128–129
sentences, spacing, 51
serif font, 35
shading, adding to paragraphs, 188–189
shapes
    definition, 58
    formatting, 60–62
    inserting, 58–59
    moving, 60–62
    sizing, 60–62
SharePoint Workspace, 7
shortcut menus, 11
Show/Hide button, 27
Single File Web Page, 139
single spacing, 70–71
sizing
    graphics, spin boxes, 55
    groups, 30
    pictures, 54–55
    shapes, 60–62
    text boxes, 60–62
sizing handles, 54
small caps
    definition, 186
    newsletters, 186–187

SmartArt graphics
bullets, 83
inserting into documents, 80–81
modifying, 81–83
Source Manager dialog box, 175
spacing
adding after paragraphs, 71–73
bulleted points, 74
date line, 124
inside addresses, 124
lines, 51, 70–71
No Spacing style, 120
paragraphs, 51, 169
salutations, 125
sentences (documents), 51
spelling
checking documents, 131–133
recording AutoCorrect entries, 123–124
Spelling and Grammar command, 131
Spelling and Grammar dialog box, 131
spin boxes, graphics, 55
split button, 5
square text wrapping, 56
Start button, 4
Start menu, 4
All Programs, 7
starting programs, 6–8
statistics (document), 178
status bars, 8
storing, files, 14
Style dialog box, 170
styles, pictures, 57
subfolders, definition, 3
subpoints, 81
suppressing page numbers, 167
symbols
bullets
customizing, 77
definition, 73
notes, 169
synonyms, Thesaurus, 133–134

T

tab stops
dot leaders, 80
leader characters, 80
modifying, 79–80
setting, 78–79
Table Tools, 107
tables
adding rows, 112–113
adding text, 108–110
borders, 116–118
changing column widths, 111–112
creating, 107
creating bulleted lists, 110–111
fields, 191
formatting, 111–118, 130
formatting text, 114–116
inserting, 130
merging cells, 113–114
records, 191
tabs
Backstage, 14
contextual, 30

definition, 26
Design, 107
File, 8
Info, 14
Layout, 107
Ribbon, 8
task panes, definition, 28
taskbar (Windows), 4
templates
creating documents, 120–123, 134–139
finding, 134–135
Normal template, 120
opening, 134–135
placeholder text, replacing, 135–137
removing controls, 138–139
saving files as, 123
text
alignment, 68–69
borders, 188
editing, 9–11
finding, 126–128
font styles, 36
fonts, 35
formatting, 34–38, 53–54, 165–167
indenting, 71–73, 167
inserting, 9–11, 51–53
line spacing, 70–71
moving, 128–129
newsletters, justifying text in
columns, 183
replacing, 126–128
replacing placeholder text, 135–137
selecting, 128–129
tables, adding text to, 108–110
wordwrap, 51
wrapping around pictures, 55–56
text boxes
definition, 58
formatting, 60–62
inserting, 58–59
moving, 60–62
sizing, 60–62
text effects, 53–54
themes, 35
Thesaurus, 133–134
title bar, 8
toggle button, 36
toolbars
Folder window, 5
Mini, 10, 36
Quick Access Toolbar, 8, 27
top-level points, definition, 81
triple-clicking, definition, 36
turning on toggle buttons, 36

U–V

USB flash drives, 6

View setting, 51
viewing
application options, 25–26
pages, 32–34
Views button, 5
views, Backstage, 64

W–Z

Web pages, saving resumes as, 139
Web sites, citations, 174
width, table columns, 111–112
windows
  definition, 3
  folder, 4–5
Windows desktop, definition, 3
Windows Explorer, definition, 3
Windows taskbar, 4
wizards, Mail Merge Wizard, 189–194
Word 2010, 7
  Business Running Cases, 219–223

content-based assessments, 84–101, 140–159,
  196–215
outcomes-based assessments, 102–104, 160–162,
  216–218
wordwrap, definition, 51
Works Cited
  creating, 176–177
  definition, 172
wrapping text around pictures, 55–56
writer's identification (cover letters), definition, 123
writer's signature block (cover letters), definition, 123

zooming, definition, 33